MENTAL HEALTH AND WELL-BEING INTERVENTIONS IN SPORT

Now in its second edition, this book provides a focused, comprehensive overview of up-to-date mental health research, models, and approaches in sport, with expertise from global experts in the field.

Mental health remains a widely growing area in the field of sport psychology, which requires expert guidance and care in promoting effective well-being for athletes, coaches and sport officials. Fully updated throughout, *Mental Health and Well-being Interventions in Sport* is an indispensable guide for researchers, practitioners and students wanting to understand and implement sport-based intervention processes. This important book adopts an evidenced based approach, discussing the context of the intervention, its design and implementation, and its evaluation and legacy. Exploring areas such as injury, rehabilitation, depression, eating disorders, verbal and physical abuse, and athletic burnout, this insightful volume dissects emerging research into straightforward accessible chapters. Offering a cutting-edge overview of the key issues involved in this burgeoning area, as well as example cases of how sport has been used in extreme environments such as prisons as a method to improve mental health, the book will benefit practitioners, policy makers and researchers.

Written for newcomers and established practitioners across a variety of sports setting and contexts, the authors highlight the need for "another call to action" to support the mental health and wellbeing of all involved in sport. Presenting current research, theory and practice in the field, the text is an essential read for researchers, practitioners, and coaches to better understand sport-based intervention processes.

Gavin Breslin is Senior Lecturer in Psychology at Queen's University Belfast, UK.

Gerard Leavey is Director of the Bamford Centre for Mental Health and Well-being at Ulster University, UK.

Routledge Psychological Interventions

Mental Health and Well-being Interventions in Sport
Research, Theory and Practice *(Second Edition)*
Ed. by Gavin Breslin and Gerard Leavey

Organizational Interventions for Health and Well-being
A Handbook for Evidence-Based Practice
Ed. by Karina Nielsen and Andrew Noblet

For more information about this series, please visit: www.routledge.com/Routledge-Psychological-Interventions/book-series/RPI

MENTAL HEALTH AND WELL-BEING INTERVENTIONS IN SPORT

Research, Theory and Practice

Second Edition

Edited by Gavin Breslin and Gerard Leavey

Routledge
Taylor & Francis Group
LONDON AND NEW YORK

Cover Image: © Getty Images

Second edition published 2024
by Routledge
4 Park Square, Milton Park, Abingdon, Oxon, OX14 4RN

and by Routledge
605 Third Avenue, New York, NY 10158

Routledge is an imprint of the Taylor & Francis Group, an informa business

First edition published by Routledge 2019

British Library Cataloguing-in-Publication Data
A catalogue record for this book is available from the British Library

ISBN: 978-1-032-27183-5 (hbk)
ISBN: 978-1-032-27110-1 (pbk)
ISBN: 978-1-003-29169-5 (ebk)

DOI: 10.4324/9781003291695

Typeset in Galliard
by Newgen Publishing UK

I dedicate this book to Emmylou, Aoife, Erin and my parents. I also dedicate this book to the Well-being Committee and coach volunteers at St Patrick's Gaelic Athletic Club, Lisburn who support the well-being of all our club members
Gavin Breslin

To my son Reuben, who turns up every week, rain or shine, without complaint. To his coaches, Dee and Stevie, who give everything, always
Gerard Leavey

CONTENTS

CONTRIBUTORS

Emily Arnold, PhD candidate, Global Alliance for Mental Health and Sport, University of Wollongong. Emily is a PhD candidate in the School of Psychology at the University of Wollongong designing and evaluating a mental health literacy programme specific to female athletes.

Jamie B. Barker, PhD, CPsychol, HCPC Reg, CSci. Jamie is a Senior lecturer in Sport and Exercise Psychology at Loughborough University, UK. Jamie conducts internationally recognised research in the area of applied psychology and has an extensive range of applied practice with many groups in high performance environments (e.g., elite sport, business, military, health).

Jürgen Beckmann is Professor of Sport Psychology, Emeritus of Excellence at the School of Medicine and Health of Technical University of Munich, Germany. He is currently a member of the Psycho-Cardiological Consultation Group at the German Heart Centre Munich. He is also Honorary Professor in the School of Human Movement and Nutrition Sciences at the University of Queensland, Australia.

Gavin Breslin, PhD, C.Psychol, SFHEA, is Senior Lecturer in Psychology at Queen's University Belfast since 2023. He is a former Professor of Psychology, Research Director and Head of Department at Ulster University. Gavin's research and teaching interests explore the psychology of performance, mental health and wellbeing. He is a British Psychological Society (BPS) Chartered Sport and Exercise Psychologist, a registered practitioner of the Health Care Professions Council (HCPC), and a Senior Fellow of the Higher Education Academy. Gavin has led on policy development and has consulted with national and international athletes and teams in sport psychology. His research was instrumental in establishing the national Action Plan for Well-being in Sport, in Northern Ireland (2019–2025) and developing an international consensus statement on mental health and wellbeing in sport.

Noel Brick is Lecturer and researcher in Sport and Exercise Psychology at Ulster University, Ireland. Noel's research primarily focuses on experiences of abuse and mental health in sports officials, and on attentional focus and cognitive strategies in endurance performance.

Kristin Brooks, Stand Tall Consulting, United States of America. Kristin Brooks is the Executive Director of Stand Tall Consulting. She has a MS.Ed. in Elementary Education and Leadership, and recipient of Florida's prestigious Golden Apple Teacher Award; she is a certified provider of The Optimum Performance Program in Sports (TOPPS).

Brendan Coyle is Lecturer in Criminology and Course Director of Criminology and Criminal Justice at Ulster University, Belfast. With specialisms in young adult development, maturation and desistance, his research addresses the interface between individuals' constructions of maturity, criminal justice policies and practices, and processes of desistance from crime.

Brad Donohue, PhD is Distinguished Professor and Director of The Optimum Performance Program in Sports at the University of Nevada, Las Vegas. He is a licensed clinical psychologist with interest in optimization science.

Hannah Hammond, MSc, PhD Forensic Psychology from the School of Law at Royal Holloway, University of London. Hannah researches the relationship between motivation, physical activity and wellbeing in prisons.

Tandy Jane Haughey is Senior Lecturer in Sports Coaching and researcher in athlete mental health and well-being at Ulster University Belfast.

Jon Jones is Senior Programme Manager for The People's Place at Everton in the Community, the official charity of Everton Football Club. He is responsible for managing various health and wellbeing programmes, and former project manager of Tackling the Blues.

Ailish King graduated with a BSc in Psychology at the University of Leeds in 2014, and an MSc in Sport and Exercise Psychology at Loughborough University in 2019. Ailish worked in a custodial setting within the field of forensic and as a Research Associate at the University of Birmingham where she undertook projects commissioned by the World Anti-Doping Agency and the International Olympic Committee. Ailish works as a National Trainer for UK Anti-Doping and carries out consultancy work with athletes and teams.

Gerard Leavey is Professor of Mental Health and Director of the Bamford Centre for Mental Health and Well-being at Ulster University. His work ranges from epidemiological studies on ethnic elders and refugee children to qualitative investigations of community level agencies such as sport, schools and faith-based organisations and their role in the recognition and management of mental illness. Current research includes social exclusion and building a coalition to tackle mental health and inequalities. Some studies are exploring mental health in young people, trust and help-seeking, mental health promotion evaluations in sport, and service use in the context of suicide in Northern Ireland.

Caitlin Liddelow, PhD, Global Alliance for Mental Health and Sport, University of Wollongong. Caitlin is a Postdoctoral Research Associate in the School of Psychology at the University of Wollongong. Her research interests are in mental health and sport, particularly among women and new mothers, as well as health behaviour change more broadly.

Sarah K. Liddle, PhD, Monash University. Sarah is Research Fellow in the Turner Institute for Brain and Mental Health at Monash University. Her research interests are in mental health during adolescence, with a particular interest in young men and sport.

Angelina Lim, PhD candidate, Global Alliance for Mental Health and Sport, University of Wollongong. Angelina is a PhD candidate in the School of Psychology at the University of Wollongong studying the implementation process of sport-based mental health programmes.

Thomas McCabe is Consultant Psychiatrist in Glasgow. He has developed a specialist interest in sports and exercise psychiatry, cumulating in editing one of the leading publications on the topic – 'Case Studies in Sports Psychiatry.' Dr McCabe has published in leading international journals on various aspects of mental health and elite sport – including in cricket, football, rugby and weight-lifting. He is an author on the landmark FIELD study, as well as being the educational lead for the Royal College of Psychiatry Sport and Exercise Specialist Interest Group and a clinical lecturer at the University of Glasgow. Dr McCabe is a keen Parkrunner. He has previously worked for Glasgow Rangers FC, Crusaders FC, Glasgow Hawks Rugby Football Club and developed mental health resources for the International Cricket Board.

Rosie Meek is Professor of Psychology and chartered psychologist and prison scholar, experienced in both quantitative and qualitative research approaches. She joined Royal Holloway University of London in 2013 as Head of Department, and during her extended tenure as a senior leader she established and led the interdisciplinary School of Law. She co-directs the Crime & Punishment Research Cluster, and has led on prison based research for government policy.

Mikel Mellick is Principal Lecturer in mental health at Cardiff Metropolitan University, Wales. Mikel is a former elite referee with Rugby Australia, a former national referee manager at England Rugby, and is a Practitioner Psychologist. Mikel supports athletes during periods of psychological trauma using existential and positive psychology interventions.

Aston Monro is Research Assistant in Sport, Mental Health and Education in the Faculty of Education at Edge Hill University, UK. He co-leads the evaluation of the Tackling the Blues programme, and his research interests focus on the links between sport, physical activity and mental health in education and other community settings.

Conor Murray is Lecturer in Criminology at Ulster University (UU). Conor has a distinct focus on widening access to higher education and he is the co-founder and Course Director of the Stay Onside: Applied Football Studies Personal and Professional Development Course delivered to prisoners in HMP Maghaberry. The course is delivered as an academically accredited sport-based intervention, which he co-delivers with the Irish Football Association.

Insa Nixdorf is Professor of Psychology at the International University of Applied Sciences, Germany.

Raphael Nixdorf is Research associate and the Chair of Sport Psychology, Department of Sport and Health Sciences, Technical University of Munich.

Helen O'Keeffe is Associate Dean in the Faculty of Education at Edge Hill University, UK. Her research interests focus on mental health, the arts and education, and she has also undertaken research on the involvement of imprisoned fathers in children's education. She is co-lead of the Tackling the Blues programme.

Matthew J. Schweickle, PhD, Global Alliance for Mental Health and Sport, University of Wollongong. Matthew is Career Development Fellow in the School of Psychology at the University of Wollongong. His research interests are in mental health, psychological safety, and optimal performance states in sport.

Stephen Shannon, BSc, PhD, is Lecturer in Sport and Exercise Psychology, and a researcher in mental health and wellbeing. He is a Senior Fellow of the Higher Education Academy. Stephen is a member of the Sport and Exercise Science Research Institute and the Bamford Centre for Mental Health and Well-Being at Ulster University.

Andy Smith is Professor of Sport and Physical Activity in the Department of Sport and Physical Activity at Edge Hill University, UK. His research interests focus on the relationship between sport, physical activity and mental health in community and professional sport, and in education. He is co-lead of the Tackling the Blues programme.

Christian Swann, PhD, Southern Cross University. Christian is Lead: Physical Activity, Sport and Exercise Research Theme and Deputy Director: Manna Institute at Southern Cross University. His research interests are in goal setting, optimal performance states, and mental health in sport and physical activity settings.

Martin J. Turner, PhD, CPsychol, HCPC Reg, CSci, Martin is Reader in Sport and Exercise Psychology at Manchester Metropolitan University, UK. He is a researcher, chartered consultant psychologist (BPS, HCPC Reg., CSci) and book author. He is most known for his work examining the use of Rational Emotive Behaviour Therapy (REBT) within performance settings. Martin works within elite sport (Lead Psychologist for FA England Futsal), and private and public sector organisations.

Stewart A. Vella, PhD, Global Alliance for Mental Health and Sport, University of Wollongong. Stewart is currently Associate Professor in the School of Psychology, and Director of the Global Alliance for Mental Health and Sport at the University of Wollongong. His research interests are in mental health promotion through recreational sports.

Tom Webb is Senior Lecturer and researcher in sport management at the University of Portsmouth, UK. Tom's research focuses on sports officials from multi-disciplinary perspectives including abuse towards sports officials, mental health and wellbeing, recruitment and retention of sports officials around the world and the barriers that women sports officials can face.

Rachel Wilcock is Research Assistant in Sport, Mental Health and Education in the Faculty of Education at Edge Hill University, UK. She co-leads the evaluation of the Tackling the Blues programme, and her research interests focus on the links between sport, physical activity and mental health in education and other community settings.

Andrew G. Wood, PhD, BSc, MSc, MBPsS, FHEA, Andrew is Lecturer in Sport and Exercise Psychology at Manchester Metropolitan University.

David Woods, PhD, MSc, BSc in Psychology, David is Lecturer in Sport and Exercise Psychology at Ulster University, Belfast. David's research explores the use of sport and exercise-based interventions to benefit the mental wellbeing of people in prison.

1

GETTING STARTED

An overview

Gavin Breslin and Gerard Leavey

Welcome to the 2nd edition of Mental Health and Well-being Intervention in Sport: Research Theory and Practice. In this edition, our international authors have contributed their expertise to provide the most up to date research on sport based mental health interventions. In the 2nd edition we provide up-to-date knowledge about intervention methodology, design and content. We have extended the number of chapters to include mental health programmes delivered to sports officials, and interventions provided by sport psychiatrists. This new edition also engages with sport-based interventions developed to enhance prisoner rehabilitation. For those new to this fascinating area of research and practice we hope you enjoy reading our book, and share with us, our aspirations to promote the science behind intervention design in supporting the mental health of all those involved in sport.

Introduction

Mental health has been defined as "a state of well-being in which every individual realises his or her own potential, can cope with the normal stresses of life, can work productively and fruitfully, and is able to make a contribution to her or his community" (World Health Organization, 2014). A sport-sensitive definition of mental health to which athletes may relate, was developed as part of an international consensus statement on mental health awareness. In the revised definition we expanded the WHO's definition; that is, mental health is not merely the absence of illness, but a state of well-being in which those involved in competitive sport realise their purpose and potential, can cope with competitive sport demands and normal life stressors, can work productively and fruitfully, can act autonomously according to their personal values, are

DOI: 10.4324/9781003291695-1

able to make a contribution to their community and feel they can seek support when required (Breslin et al. 2019).

Psychiatric disorders, account for most of the global disease burden, and are enormously costly to the individual and society. The true prevalence of psychiatric disorders in athletes is undetermined, particularly in youth athletes (Donohue, Gavrilova, & Strong, 2020). While, adult athletes appear to experience rates of depression, anxiety, eating and substance use disorders similar to the general population (Rice et al., 2016), symptom severity rates vary greatly across studies due to differences in population characteristics, study year, measurement and methodology (Donohue, Breslin & Murphy, 2021). For instance, rates of symptoms associated with mood disorders have ranged from 4% (Schaal et al., 2011) to 68% (Hammond et al., 2013). Thus, well-designed epidemiological studies of athletes' mental health are warranted as well as robust intervention studies on how to enhance athlete mental health and wellbeing.

The salutogenic aspects of sport participation are well-established (Biddle et al., 2021). However, paradoxically perhaps, recent evidence suggests that various dimensions of competitive sport may undermine mental health and that athletes are exposed to specific stressors that hinder optimal mental health (Henriksen et al., 2019). These stressors are: pressure to achieve success; long periods of separation from family; negative psychological sequelae following injury; alcohol and substance misuse; fear of failure and social opprobrium; relationship difficulties and interpersonal conflict, and financial problems. To date, there is a paucity of published interventions that offer guidance on how to improve the mental health of sports participants. The chapters within this book describe programmes that are intended to inform the reader of how to use research, theory and integrate into practice from international experts in the field of sport psychology.

Going back to the ancient Greeks and Romans, Western societies have adopted a view of athletes as paragons of health and attendant virtues of discipline, morality, strength and beauty. Often lionised within cinema, the creative arts and literature, a more realistic or balanced portrayal of athletes and athleticism tends to be eschewed (Golden, 1998; Kyle, 2007). Traditionally, athletes have been poorly supported to manage their mental health needs and, moreover, mental health promotion within sports settings are considered as superfluous and irrelevant. Instead, like the ancient Greek gymnasia, sport club culture celebrates mental toughness and disapproval of weakness disclosure. Consequently, emotional and psychiatric problems can remain hidden, with the stigma of mental illness preventing athletes from seeking timely and appropriate help. Furthermore, sports coaches – those who instruct athletes on technique, lifestyle and key decisions for success, can also experience stress and require support for managing their mental health. Our discussions with athletes and coaches suggests that all too often they strive to exude a steely projection of confidence and composure, while inwardly feeling fragile and vulnerable within a culture that demands peak performance, and only rewards winning. Unfortunately, athletes and coaches alike are often trapped in a culture of denial in which the mental health costs are high and for some catastrophic.

There has been a recent surge of interest in supporting the mental health and well-being of those involved in sport and their supporters (e.g., athletes, coaches, officials, parents, fans and the local community) (Breslin et al., 2022; Vella et al., 2021). Commendably, several psychological approaches and theoretical frameworks have been applied in attempts to tackle mental health and well-being of athletes, but theory, policy and practice in this field although developed since our first edition of the book in 2019, is still embryonic. Such approaches include, i) increasing knowledge about mental health to aid prevention, reduce stigma and promote help seeking, ii) the development of cognitive-behavioural techniques to enhance coping (i.e., mindfulness, resilience, rational emotive behaviour therapy), iii) the expansion of support provision through a better understanding of whole systems approaches and iv) the use of sport organisations and clubs to engage groups (i.e., men, those from low income areas) to promote psychosocial well-being.

What is this book about?

The development of mental health and well-being interventions in sport settings remain relatively underdeveloped and often poorly theorised (Breslin, Shannon, Cummings, & Leavey, 2022). This book is about applying psychology to the development of interventions to enhance mental health and well-being of those involved in participating in competitive sport (athletes, coaches, match officials). Our focus is on the design process and the content of the interventions, with an emphasis on methodological advances and what has been shown to improve awareness of mental health and well-being. Our principal goal is to help researchers and practitioners to understand better, the sport setting-based intervention processes through presenting current research, theory and practice, applicable in an interesting variety of sports settings and contexts. In doing so, the authors encourage a transition from theory to the practical aspects of conducting and evaluating mental health and well-being interventions in and through sport. We also build on the first edition of the book by providing more up to date references to relevant literature, information on intervention design, and outcomes.

Ultimately, we intend that this book will stimulate interventions in the area of sport so that athletes, coaches, officials and parents of youth athletes will be better supported. More specifically, the authors of each chapter have highlighted the foundations of sport for mental health and well-being interventions. Drawing from their own activities and experience, the authors provide guidance on how to plan, design and select an appropriate programme content, and then how to implement and evaluate such interventions. The chapters of this book should be helpful to those who are new to the subject, and established practitioners. Two sub-sections will include: i) mental health awareness programmes for athletes, coaches, match officials (referees) and parents and ii) engaging the wider community in mental health awareness through sport.

Section 1: Development of mental health awareness programmes for athletes, coaches, match officials and parents

In Chapter 2, *Donohue and Brooks* present The Optimum Performance Programme in Sport (TOPPS) and review of the evidence for its effectiveness across various case studies and groups of college and adolescent athletes. Based on Family Centred Therapy (FCT), the authors use a unique adaptation of FCT to sport culture. They sought to examine improvements in sport performance, relationships and mental health among a vulnerable population but do so in a non-stigmatising manner and context. The authors provide descriptions of the content of their evidenced based programme and provide recommendations for enhancing college athlete mental health and grapple with the challenges of engaging athletes in positive mental health through on-campus services. Donohue describes how he has created an Optimization Center at the University of Nevada, Las Vegas in the United States, with plans in place for the centre to expand to Europe.

In Chapter 3, *Insa Nixdorf, Beckmann and Raphael Nixdorf* based in Germany summarise recent studies among athletes experiencing depression, burnout and chronic stress. They provide a description of how group coaching of junior elite athletes of the Bavarian Swim Association can help prevent the emergence of psychological problems, in particular burnout and depression as consequences of extensive stress. Interventions including mindfulness, cognitive-behavioural therapy and imagery were applied. The Transactional Model of Stress was utilised in their intervention and once adapted can be successfully applied within sport environments to address the needs of junior elite swimmers.

In Chapter 4, *Turner, Wood, Barker* and King based in England, (they) build on their ongoing work and the abundance of research on Rational Emotive Behaviour Therapy (REBT) to promote psychological well-being with a 42-year-old Paralympic athlete. At its core, REBT is based upon the premise that "people are not disturbed by things, but by the view which they take of them" (Epictetus, 1948, 55–135 AD, in Dryden & Still, 2018). REBT offers a valuable way to help athletes to reinterpret their beliefs. Using the ABC (DE) framework, the intervention consisted of five one-to-one sessions and homework tasks each lasting 45-minutes each. The intervention evaluation and the accompanying insightful reflections are discussed in terms of intervention effects, professional competence, the blurred boundaries between therapy and mental skills training, consultant's experience and practical guidelines for practitioners. Looking ahead, we are recommended to explore how irrational and/or rational beliefs are socialised in the pursuit of psychological health and performance.

In Chapter 5 *Breslin, Haughey, and Shannon* provide a description of their State of Mind Ireland mental health awareness and self-management programme that includes daily mindfulness activities for university student athletes in Ireland. This multi-component programme delivered in partnership with students, staff and student support services was a response to the paucity of evidence-based programmes designed to enhance mental health awareness of student athletes. Knowledge of mental health and intentions to offer support to peers increased for the intervention group. The programme, with some modification, was integrated into non-sport university courses to promote mental health awareness. The authors emphasise theory-driven hypothesis testing, and present evidence for improvements in wellbeing through perceptions of competence, mindfulness practice and stress. Chapter 6, *Vella, Liddle, Schweickle, Swann, Lim, Arnold and Liddelow*, present Ahead of the Game (AOTG), a multi-component mental health awareness and prevention programme delivered through community sports clubs in Australia. In recent years, the programme has been scaled-up and delivered in various countries. The programme includes interventions for adolescents targeting mental health literacy and resilience, a parent mental health literacy intervention, and an intervention for coaches aimed at helping to facilitate self-determined motivation. Using a Community Based Participatory Research (CBPR) framework, AOTG was tested in community level sporting clubs. The authors provide insight into the development and delivery of the programme. Of particular interest are the online modules for adolescents and the references to evidence for the AOTG programme. The depth of evaluation during each phase of the programme delivery (from pilot through to international scale up) will provide those developing such programmes, valuable practical information. The authors also consider the challenges with international programme scale-up and delivery, and describe lessons learned in the process, concluding with the suggestion that systems-based approaches may be beneficial.

Chapter 7, *McCabe*, a Consultant Sport Psychiatrist in Scotland presents a case study of a male rugby league player who experienced a head injury. McCabe applies the Biopsychosocial Model to highlight the importance of holistic care when considering therapeutic interventions during the diagnosis of mental illness. He critically considers first line options and practical considerations of medication use for athletes. The practical obstacles that are encountered are described, as are the optimised and joined up care that is required in professional and amateur sport.

Chapter 8, *Brick, Breslin, Mellick and Webb* introduce mental illness prevalence and drop-out rates (leaving the sport because of verbal or physical abuse) of sports officials. They highlight that there is a dearth of mental health research with sport officials despite the verbal and sometimes physical abuse and pressure placed on them by coaches, players, and fans. In this chapter you will be more aware of the stressors on officials and be able to critically evaluate the value of using psychological theory-based interventions to support sports officials' mental health. The Trauma Informed Practice Developmental Model is applied to an intervention for football referees, consideration is given to the norms that surround how match officials are negatively treated, when this can lead to mental health concerns.

Section 2: Engaging the wider community in mental health awareness through sport

In Section 2, we focus on how sport has been used to promote mental health awareness programmes in the community, and in somewhat more challenging contexts and environments. The four chapters offer a thorough presentation of theory, research and practice intended for use among researchers in the design of community-based projects that promote mental health. In Chapter 9 *Smith, Wilcock, Monro, O'Keeffe and Jones,* discuss the key theoretical assumptions and design principles which were used to inform the development of Tackling the Blues, a sport and education-based mental health awareness programme delivered by the official charity of Everton, the English Premier League Football Club. Tackling the Blues is delivered in schools and community settings by staff and student mentors trained in accredited mental health awareness courses. The authors reflect upon the effectiveness of the programme in its use for training undergraduate student peer mentors in programme delivery and the co-production of knowledge suitable for delivery in schools and hard-to-reach groups, mainly men in working-class communities. Particularly interesting and somewhat surprising, the programme reveals that once engaged, the appeal of the brand of a professional football club became progressively less important than other mental health features of the programme design. The authors describe how they conducted a realist evaluation of the programme and offer insights into various challenges to engaging youth and assessing programme outcomes.

Hammond and Meek in Chapter 10 present the Cell Workout programme to engage prisoners in looking after their mental health. The authors highlight how prisons frequently fail to adopt a proactive approach to improving mental health and well-being through physical activity. Given the restrictive physical space associated with a cell in prison, the authors show individuals can overcome such barriers to remain active for mental health. A reflection is provided on the process of using both physiological and psychological outcome measures within a prison environment. The authors describe the core components of Self Determination Theory's basic psychological needs within the intervention (Autonomy, Competence, Relatedness). Furthermore, the recent policy work conducted by Meek in England is described and a case is presented for how the introduction and maintenance of exercise in prisons can have positive effects on inmate mental health and well-being.

The theme of mental health and prisons is continued in Chapter 11 by *Woods and Breslin* in which they describe the Active Choices in Rugby and State of Mind Programme for males prisoners. Prisons are often viewed, with much supporting evidence, as forbidden places in which attempts to undertake research have failed as often as prison breakouts! However, introducing sport and encouraging exercise in prisons may offer a partial solution to the very high levels of mental illness and suicide. In this chapter, the authors examine the particular myths and difficulties of undertaking research in prison environments. For those about to embark on mental health in sport prison research, this chapter has considerable insights developed within a closed and bewildering environment structured within its opaque culture and rationale. The authors discuss the development of the programme, the importance of incorporating a psychological theory of behaviour change, the need to engage prisoners and the crucial, but often overlooked, role and identity maintenance of the researcher during the project.

In Chapter 12, *Murray, Breslin and Coyle* describe the Stay Onside: Applied Football Studies university accredited sport-based intervention delivered in a prison in Northern Ireland. The programme was devised by the Irish Football Association in partnership with academic researchers with the aim to improve the well-being of prisoners through classroom-based learning, and football (soccer) pitch-based physical activity. The authors discuss how they deliver the theoretical and applied content and evaluate the programme using qualitative and quantitative research methods. The challenges faced in using technology in teaching in prison, assessment, availability of reading materials, having access to teaching and practical space, as well as the restrictions on timing are discussed. This chapter will be particularly interesting to those considering sport-based prison research for accredited courses with multiple partners/ stakeholders.

Finally, in Chapter 13, a critical reflection and the way forward for mental health in sport are presented. Specific focus will be on intervention evaluation, depth of practitioner reflections, intervention effects, professional competence, professional boundaries, and practical guidelines for practitioners. We explore the benefits that the recent introduction of consensus statements and position statements have had to increasing awareness of mental health issues in sport. Furthermore, the increase in the number of systematic reviews of mental health awareness programmes delivered in sport across many countries since the publication of our first edition of the book is promising for the future. Collectively, we hope you enjoy reading this textbook that emphasises the benefits of considering research, theory and practice in promoting mental health in sport. We also wish that as well as developing an appreciation for the significant progress made by the authors in bringing about positive changes to many people's lives, you take this information and apply it in your own practice, and that you to will reflect on your practice for the improvement of mental health in sport.

References

Biddle, S., Mutrie, N., Gorely, T., & Faulkner, G. (2021). *Psychology of Physical Activity: Determinants, Well-Being and Interventions* (4th ed.). Routledge. https://doi.org/10.4324/9781003127420

Breslin, G., Smith, A., Donohue, B., Donnelly, P., Shannon, S., Haughey, T. J., ... & Leavey, G. (2019). International consensus statement on the psychosocial and policy-related approaches to mental health awareness programmes in sport. *BMJ Open Sport & Exercise Medicine*, *5*(1), e000585.

Breslin, G., Shannon, S., Cummings, M., & Leavey, G. (2022). An updated systematic review of interventions to increase awareness of mental health and well-being in athletes, coaches, officials and parents. *Systematic Reviews*, *11*(1), 1–29.

Donohue, B., Breslin, G., & Murphy, S. (2021). 'Mental health', in Edson Filho, and Itay Basevitch (eds), *Sport, Exercise and Performance Psychology: Research Directions to Advance the Field*. New York, 2021; online edn, Oxford Academic, 21 Oct. 2021. https://doi.org/10.1093/oso/9780197512494.003.0013 accessed 28 Aug. 2023.

Donohue, B., Gavrilova, E., Strong, M., & Allen, D. N. (2020). A sport-specific optimization approach to mental wellness for youth in low-income neighborhoods. *European Physical Education Review*, *26*(3), 695–712. https://doi.org/10.1177/1356336X20905324

Dryden, W., & Still, A. (2018). *The historical and philosophical context of rational psychotherapy: The legacy of Epictetus*. Routledge.

Golden, M. (1998). *Sport and Society in Ancient Greece*. Cambridge: Cambridge University Press.

Hammond, T, Gialloreto, C., Kubas, H., and Davis, H. (2013). The prevalence of failure-based depression among elite athletes. *Clin. J. Sport. Med.* 23, 273–277. doi: 10.1097/JSM.0b013e318287b870

Henriksen K, Schinke R, Moesch K, et al. (2019). Consensus statement on improving the mental health of high performance athletes. *International Journal of Sport and Exercise Psychology*, *14*, 1–8.

Kyle, D. G. (2007). *Sport and Spectacle in the Ancient World*. Malden, MA and Oxford: Wiley-Blackwell.

Rice, S. M., Purcell, R., De Silva, S., Mawren, D., McGorry, P. D., & Parker, A. G. (2016). The mental health of elite athletes: A narrative systematic review. *Sports medicine*, *46*, 1333–1353.

Schaal, K., Tafflet, M., Nassif, H., Thibault, V., Pichard, C., Alcotte, M., ... & Toussaint, J. F. (2011). Psychological balance in high level athletes: gender-based differences and sport-specific patterns. *PloS one*, *6*(5), e19007.
Vella, S. A., Schweickle, M. J., Sutcliffe, J. T., & Swann, C. (2021). A systematic review and meta-synthesis of mental health position statements in sport: Scope, quality and future directions. *Psychology of Sport and Exercise*, *55*, 101946.
World Health Organization. (2014). *Mental Health: A State of Well-Being*. Geneva: World Health Organization.

SECTION 1

Development of mental health awareness programmes for athletes, coaches, match officials and parents

2

THE OPTIMUM PERFORMANCE PROGRAM IN SPORTS (TOPPS)

Brad Donohue and Kristin Brooks

Learning objectives

After reading this chapter you should be able to:

1 Understand Optimum Performance Theory
2 Be familiar with scientific support for The Optimum Performance Program in Sports (TOPPS).
3 Appreciate methods of engaging athletes into TOPPS.
4 Understand sport-specific psychometrically validated assessment and intervention components in TOPPS.

Introduction to the theme

This chapter provides a framework from which to understand The Optimum Performance Program for Sports (TOPPS), including its scientific support, tenets underlying optimization theory, and phases of service implementation specific to athletes' mental health and sport performance (i.e., engagement, assessment, intervention). The chapter concludes with a brief report of its future development.

Consistent with recommendations of Donohue et al. (2022), TOPPS addresses the full continuum of mental health care within the context of sport performance optimization (Donohue & Perry, 2022). Components of TOPPS are based on Family Behaviour Therapy (FBT; Azrin et al., 1994), a cognitive behavioural intervention for children, youth, and adults that has been shown to significantly reduce substance use and psychiatric symptomology while improving relationships and everyday functionality in non-athlete populations.

DOI: 10.4324/9781003291695-3

The number and duration of TOPPS performance meetings vary somewhat depending on the goals desired by athletes, but usually includes 8 to 12 meetings at 60 minutes duration. Components of TOPPS are most often implemented in performance meetings with individual athletes and their invited teammates, peers, family and/or coaches. Athletes' supportive others are included to facilitate athletes' goal achievement through their modeling of skill sets and provision of valuable information. Indeed, studies indicate mental health outcomes greatly improve for athletes in TOPPS when various types and combinations of supportive others are strategically involved (Gavrilova et al., 2022). However, sport performance-oriented workshops are also implemented in groups or teams of athletes to facilitate recruitment, teach basic optimization skills, and establish optimization culture within sport organizations. All program components are standardized in step by step manuals, and training videos and messaging platforms are available to facilitate program implementation and integrity assessment.

The TOPPS protocols were adapted from FBT to explicitly address performance within the culture of sport. The nomenclature of TOPPS, and its orientation to goal achievement, is focused on optimization, which is unique to most traditional psychologically-based programmes that are focused on the reduction of pathology and assume or require the presence of pathology at the start of programming. Thus, TOPPS is applicable to athletes desiring optimization in sports or life in general, regardless of the presence of common mental health disorders. Indeed, the focus of TOPPS on performance optimization reduces perceptions of stigma that are often associated with attempts to pursue mental healthcare in traditional therapeutic milieus.

Describe the client or group being targeted

Clinical evaluations of TOPPS have involved adolescent and emerging adult athletes with, and without, mental health disorders (e.g., Attention Deficit Hyperactivity Disorder, Oppositional Defiant Disorder, mood, anxiety, eating and substance use disorders). Evaluations have also included self-identified males and females playing various sports at various competitive levels. Between 2012 and 2022, the components of TOPPS were developed in a series of controlled and uncontrolled clinical evaluations involving young adult athletes at the University of Nevada, Las Vegas (UNLV) and adolescent athletes participating in high schools in Las Vegas. The first study was supported by the National Institutes of Health (NIH; NIDA1R01DA031828R01) in the United States. The study was important because it was the first NIH grant aimed at empirically developing a sport-specific mental health treatment, including 1) interviews to improve engagement (Donohue et al., 2004; Donohue et al., 2021; Donohue, et al., 2016), 2) screens to identify athletes who are likely to benefit from intervention (Donohue et al., 2019; Donohue, et al., 2021;

Hussey et al., 2019), 3) intervention implementation and integrity guides (e.g., Donohue, et al., 2018; Donohue & Perry, 2022), and 4) intervention. The initial intervention evaluation involved a comparison between collegiate athletes who were randomly assigned to campus counseling or TOPPS; athletes in TOPPS improved their relationships with coaches, teammates and family, decreased substance use and psychiatric symptoms, and factors interfering with sport performance, and these results were sustained up to 4-months follow-up; Donohue, Gavrilova et al., 2018). In this study, as the severity of mental health symptomology increased during baseline, improvements for participants in TOPPS were enhanced relative to those assigned to campus counseling. Similar positive outcomes for TOPPS have been found in other evaluations involving collegiate student athletes (Chow et al., 2015; Donohue et al., 2015; Galante et al., 2019; Gavrilovaet al., 2017; Pitts et al., 2015), and adolescent athletes (Donohue, Phrathep et al., 2021; Phrathep, Donohue, & Allen, 2022; Phrathep, Donohue, Krauset al., 2021; Phrathep, Donohue, Renn, Mercer et al. 2022; Phrathep, Donohue, Renn, Mercer, & Allen, 2023).

Initial needs assessment

A variety of methods are used in the initial needs assessment prior to TOPPS implementation. First, athletes are invited to visit and tour the TOPPS facilities on campus to determine their interest in pursuing goal-oriented mental wellness and sport performance meetings with their supportive others (Donohue et al., 2019; Donohue, Gavrilova, Danlag et al., 2021; Donohue, O'Dowd et al., 2016). Strategies to engage athletes into these tours include sport performance workshops, course credit from class instructors, playing competitive and fun games outside on campus, and structured interviews that are focused on sport culture, brainstorming goals and reviewing personal ambitions. For instance, semi-structured interviews that are performed with athletes to assess their perceptions of their sport culture have resulted in greater participation in assessment and intervention services (Donohue, Gavrilova et al., 2021). Along this vein, athletes are interviewed about their experiences with sport culture using a 12-minute validated semi-structured interview (i.e., extent to which they believe sport culture is a big part of their life, important to them, want to address sport culture in performance meetings, rude or offensive remarks or problems experienced due to sport culture).

After the engagement meeting, athletes complete a pre-intervention assessment to guide performance programming, facilitate dynamic goals, and determine functional and mental health factors that have been shown to interfere with performance in sports and life outside of sports. The specific battery of assessment tools varies based on athletes' presenting goals, and qualifications of providers. However, the Student Athlete Relationship Inventories for Coaches, Teammates and Family (Donohue, Miller et al.,

2007) is a recommended sport-specific measure because TOPPS includes the athletes' supportive others. This instrument has demonstrated reliability and validity in the assessment of relationship issues that are specific to sport participation, including predictive validity specific to identifying athletes with significant mental health symptomology (Hussey et al., 2019).

The Sport Interference Checklist (SIC; Donohue, Silver et al., 2007) is another hallmark sport-specific measure that has demonstrated psychometric support, and scores on the SIC have been found to predict psychiatric conditions (Donohue et al., 2019; Donohue et al., 2020). As summarized in Donohue and Perry (2022), the SIC measures various factors that have been determined to interfere with sport performance in both training (Problems in Sport Training Scale, PSTS; 26 items) and competition (Problems in Sport Competition Scale, PSCS; 26 items). Athletes report how frequently each item interferes with their performance in training and competition using a 7-point Likert scale. Responses to all items are summed to obtain total scores for PSTS and PSCS, with higher scores indicating more severe interferences in training and competition. A third inventory assesses the extent to which athletes desire sport psychology consultation for each of the aforementioned items (Desire for Sport Psychology Scale, DSPS, Yes = 1; No = 0). Scores are summed to obtain a total score with higher scores indicating greater desire to see a professional.

Collegiate athletes who report a PSTS cutoff score above 70 or PSCS cutoff score above 65 are High Risk for psychiatric symptomology. In student circus artists, a SIC Training score of 64 may warrant follow-up screening for Fatigue; a score of 68 for Anxiety; a score of 69 for Depression, Social Isolation, or Sleep Disturbance; a score of 71 for low Informational Support; and a score of 72 for low Satisfaction with Social Roles and Responsibilities. In a professional artist sample, a SIC Training score of 60 may warrant follow-up screening for Sleep Disturbance, a score of 61 for Fatigue, a score of 62 for Anxiety, and a score of 67 for Depression. A SIC Competition score of 55 may warrant follow-up screening for Fatigue, a score of 56 for Anxiety, and a score of 61 for Depression. Scoring procedures are reviewed in Donohue and Perry (2022), the SIC is available in Figure 2.1 below.

Specific performance scenarios are assessed using the Performance Timeline Worksheet (see Figure 2.2). In this procedure a recent performance situation, event or competition that is desired for optimization is solicited (e.g., high bars in gymnastics, free throw in basketball). The optimizer (traditionally referred to as the mental health professional) specifies that each time period during, before and after the performance scenario influences performance outcomes, and that some time periods have a greater influence than others. Optimizers are certified to provide TOPPS with integrity using structured training procedures that are consistent with evidence-based practice (see Donohue & Perry, 2022). Athletes are prompted to identify the specific time

Directions: *Below is a list of things that sometimes occur during training or during competition. Please circle the* ***number*** *that represents how often each of these things interfere with your performance* ***during training****, and separately, your performance* ***during competition****. Then circle either "yes" or "no" to indicate if you* ***would*** *see a sport psychologist if this happened to you, and if a good sport psychologist were available to you.*
Please use the following scale for the following i tems:

1 = Never, 2 = Very Seldom, 3= Seldom, 4 = Sometimes, 5 = Often, 6 = Very Often, 7 = Always

		How often does this interfere with your performance during ***training?***	*How often does this interfere with your performance during* ***competition?***	*Would you go to a sport psychologist for this, if possible?*
1	Negative thoughts about personal performance	1 2 3 4 5 6 7	1 2 3 4 5 6 7	❑ Yes ❑ No
2	Being too critical of myself	1 2 3 4 5 6 7	1 2 3 4 5 6 7	❑ Yes ❑ No
3	Being too critical of teammates	1 2 3 4 5 6 7	1 2 3 4 5 6 7	❑ Yes ❑ No
4	Distracted (or upset) by people who observe me	1 2 3 4 5 6 7	1 2 3 4 5 6 7	❑ Yes ❑ No
5	Difficulty concentrating or maintaining focus on the task at hand	1 2 3 4 5 6 7	1 2 3 4 5 6 7	❑ Yes ❑ No
6	Difficulty thinking positively once negative thoughts have occurred	1 2 3 4 5 6 7	1 2 3 4 5 6 7	❑ Yes ❑ No
7	Difficulty relaxing	1 2 3 4 5 6 7	1 2 3 4 5 6 7	❑ Yes ❑ No
8	Overconcerned or worry too much about what others think about my performance	1 2 3 4 5 6 7	1 2 3 4 5 6 7	❑ Yes ❑ No
9	Overly optimistic (cocky) thoughts	1 2 3 4 5 6 7	1 2 3 4 5 6 7	❑ Yes ❑ No
10	Feeling stressed out	1 2 3 4 5 6 7	1 2 3 4 5 6 7	❑ Yes ❑ No
11	Hard to recover mentally once errors are made	1 2 3 4 5 6 7	1 2 3 4 5 6 7	❑ Yes ❑ No

FIGURE 2.1 Sport Interference Checklist (SIC).

Directions: *Below is a list of things that sometimes occur* ***during training*** *or* ***during competition****. Please circle the number that represents how often each of these things interfere with your performance during training, and separately, your performance during competition. Then circle either "yes" or "no" to indicate if you would see a sport psychologist if this happened to you, and if a good sport psychologist were available to you.*
Please use the following scale for the following i tems:

1 = Never, 2 = Very Seldom, 3= Seldom, 4 = Sometimes, 5 = Often, 6 = Very Often, 7 = Always

		How often does this interfere with your performance during ***training?***	*How often does this interfere with your performance during* ***competition?***	*Would you go to a sport psychologist for this, if possible?*
12	Inability to motivate or push myself	1 2 3 4 5 6 7	1 2 3 4 5 6 7	❑ Yes ❑ No
13	Lack of desire and will to win	1 2 3 4 5 6 7	1 2 3 4 5 6 7	❑ Yes ❑ No
14	Others have commented that I am not motivated in my sport	1 2 3 4 5 6 7	1 2 3 4 5 6 7	❑ Yes ❑ No
15	Problems with my coach(es)	1 2 3 4 5 6 7	1 2 3 4 5 6 7	❑ Yes ❑ No
16	Problems with my teammates	1 2 3 4 5 6 7	1 2 3 4 5 6 7	❑ Yes ❑ No
17	Problems with my family	1 2 3 4 5 6 7	1 2 3 4 5 6 7	❑ Yes ❑ No
18	Problems or stress due to lack of money	1 2 3 4 5 6 7	1 2 3 4 5 6 7	❑ Yes ❑ No
19	Problems with others who are too involved in telling you what to do in your sport	1 2 3 4 5 6 7	1 2 3 4 5 6 7	❑ Yes ❑ No
20	Being home sick or lacking close social supports	1 2 3 4 5 6 7	1 2 3 4 5 6 7	❑ Yes ❑ No
21	Fear of getting injured or sick	1 2 3 4 5 6 7	1 2 3 4 5 6 7	❑ Yes ❑ No
22	Difficulties dealing with physical pain	1 2 3 4 5 6 7	1 2 3 4 5 6 7	❑ Yes ❑ No

FIGURE 2.1 (Continued)

period that most impacts their performance for the provided scenario, and for this time (e.g., seconds before the situation) the athlete is instructed to rank the impact of each of the factors listed below the respective time period. The athlete is then asked to describe how the top ranked factors (e.g., thoughts) influenced optimal performance in a recent situation during the respective time period. After descriptive praise, the athlete, supportive other(s) and optimizer brainstorm how the respective factor could be optimized in the future. Optimizers and supportive others are encouraged to model skills and facilitate real-time feedback for future performance.

Framework and intervention for delivery

After assessment, athletes are oriented to TOPPS. Confidentiality is discussed along with structure of meetings, and preliminary dynamic goals are generated to assist optimum performance in the 5 domains of: relationships, sport/physical health, school/work, creative activities, mental strength and stability/mental wellness. The Theory of Performance Optimization is reviewed.

According to Performance Optimization Theory (Donohue et al., 2018; Phrathep & Donohue, 2021), mental health and performance optimization occur when thoughts, behaviours, and feelings are determined to be optimal, and each reciprocally interact to manage stressors (see Figure 2.3). This adaptation to the CBT Triangle is a good fit with athletes, and helps them to destigmatize programming in regards to the pursuit of mental healthcare. Athletes appreciate the line pointing from left to right, which shows the theoretical continuum of cognitive and behavioural skills ranging from nonoptimal to optimal. Athletes are instructed that behavioural and cognitive skills are theoretically somewhere on this continuum, with some skills being developed more than others.

As shown in Figure 2.4, after reviewing the Optimization Theory, athletes are encouraged to appreciate how cognitive and behavioural skills and values can be optimized by comparing non-optimal and optimal thoughts and behaviours and subsequently practicing optimal thoughts and behaviours in role-plays or in talk aloud imagery. Athletes also read lists that include strategies that are consistent with optimal thoughts and behaviours and values, and subsequently provide recent personal examples in which they used these strategies themselves. They are then descriptively praised for their efforts and encouraged or challenged to optimize these strategies for use in future situations. Optimized strategies are recorded in their Dynamic Goals recording form.

Optimize it! List

2 Examples of strategies consistent with optimum thinking

1. Think objectively (just the facts).
2. Think flexibly (imagine multiple possibilities).

Days Before Situations, Events, Competitions	*Minutes Before Situations, Events, Competitions*	*Seconds Before Situations, Events, Competitions*	*During Situations, Events, Competitions*	*Seconds After Situations, Events, Competitions*	*Minutes After Situations, Events, Competitions*	*Days After Situations, Events, Competitions*
PERFORMANCE FACTORS						
• Body/physical	• Body/physical	• Body/physical	• Body/physical	• Body/physical	• Body/physical	• Body/physical
• Eating/drinking	• Eating/drinking	• Eating/drinking	• Eating/drinking	• Eating/drinking	• Eating/drinking	• Eating/drinking
• Routines	• Routines	• Routines	• Routines	• Routines	• Routines	• Routines
• Interactions with others	• Interactions with others	• Interactions with others	• Interactions with others	• Interactions with others	• Interactions with others	• Interactions with others
• Thoughts	• Thoughts	• Thoughts	• Thoughts	• Thoughts	• Thoughts	• Thoughts
• Interpretation of perceptions (hear, see, smell, taste, feel)	• Interpretation of perceptions (hear, see, smell, taste, feel)	• Interpretation of perceptions (hear, see, smell, taste, feel)	• Interpretation of perceptions (hear, see, smell, taste, feel)	• Interpretation of perceptions (hear, see, smell, taste, feel)	• Interpretation of perceptions (hear, see, smell, taste, feel)	• Interpretation of perceptions (hear, see, smell, taste, feel)

• Emotions	• Emotions	• Emotions	• Emotions	• Emotions	• Emotions	• Emotions
• Energy & motivation	• Energy & motivation	• Energy & motivation	• Energy & motivation	• Energy & motivation	• Energy & motivation	• Energy & motivation
• Training & Strategy	• Training & Strategy	• Training & Strategy	• Training & Strategy	• Training & Strategy	• Training & Strategy	• Training & Strategy
• Skills	• Skills	• Skills	• Skills	• Skills	• Skills	• Skills
• Other:	• Other:	• Other:	• Other:	• Other:	• Other:	• Other:

FIGURE 2.2 Performance factors before, during, and after competition.

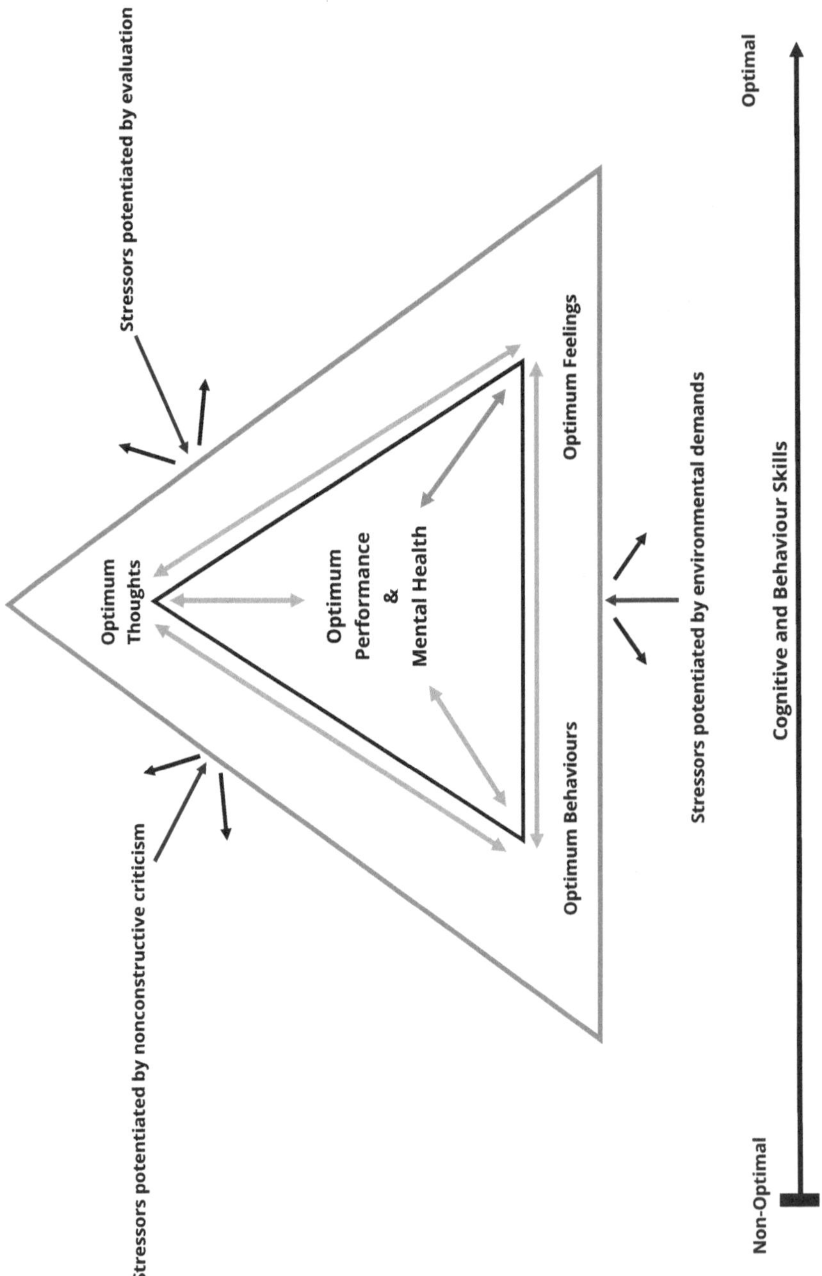

FIGURE 2.3 The TOPPS Model.

2 Examples of Non-Optimal Thoughts	*2 Examples of Optimal Thoughts*
1. Outcome-oriented thinking (e.g., I will score 30 points)	1. Process-oriented, neutral thinking (e.g., set, focus, shoot)
2. Pressure words (e.g., I have to, I need to)	2. Choice statements (e.g., I'd like to, I want to)

FIGURE 2.4 Optimize it! List.

2 Examples of strategies consistent with optimum behaviour

1. Schedule, prepare, attend events on time or early.
2. Solicit feedback regarding optimization.

2 examples of optimal values

1. Accepting & open-minded
2. Respectful

Performance Agendas, Optimal Performance Preparation, and Reviews Before and After Meetings. Prior to the start of each performance meeting a structured agenda is reviewed. Each planned performance intervention is reviewed with suggested implementation times. Athletes are given opportunities to alter meeting agendas, and to determine how their supportive others will be strategically involved in their meetings. Evidence-supported mental preparation strategies (Donohue et al., 2001; Donohue, Miller, et al., 2006; Miller and Donohue, 2003), are used to facilitate an exercise in which athletes report, in the first person, an optimum performance situation that occurred during the past week (e.g., competing in the final round of a boxing match), as if it is occurring currently. In these situations, athletes sequentially report aloud themselves performing optimal thoughts and actions (e.g., "I'm throwing my left jab. Moving to the rightside of my opponent. I'm focused on his shoulders..."). Throughout these reviews, athletes are challenged to optimize their thoughts and actions. Optimization nomenclature is generated during the scenarios, including prompts for athletes to describe their positive qualities, say words that are motivating, report optimum performance of skills, provide instructions, and use relaxation-oriented self-statements. During the exercise athletes are instructed to pair what they are sensing with positive feelings ("You feel the tightness of your gloves and it lets you know how hard your punches feel") and perceive environmental stimuli as positive, uplifting or helpful in some way (e.g., "Instead of saying the boxing ring stinks say the smell of sweat in the ring energizes you"). Optimizers model and coach athletes to practice statements aloud in the simulated scenario to encourage appropriate timing, intensity and so on through feedback. When athletes report non-optimal statements (e.g., "I feel like I'm doing o.k. and I'm going to throw my right") optimizers immediately point out these non-optimal thoughts and prompt them to optimize these statements (e.g., "Say I'm doing incredible and I'm throwing my right with power and confidence"). In providing real-time cognitive instruction athletes are able to restructure their thought patterns into functional pathways. Along a related vein, athletes are often behaviourally slowed down due to overly restrictive or cautionary thinking patterns that are designed to be protective. For instance, an athlete may report a dangerous stimulus is not present (e.g., "I look to make sure there's no blockers. They're not there so I kick the ball."). These checks are fine when initially establishing good habits at the novice level, but they unnecessarily slow down decision-making processes at the elite level. So alternatively athletes are instructed to immediately report what they are doing in response to stimuli that are actually present (e.g., "I see an opening and I confidently kick the ball"). With the passage of time, and improved cognitive skill development, athletes are instructed to reduce detailed processes to keywords (e.g., "Opening, kick!").

At the end of each meeting optimizers prompt athletes to disclose what they enjoyed about the respective meeting and they generate potential supportive others to bring to their next meeting, including how they might be strategically involved during the meeting.

Performance Planning. Athletes and supportive others rank the performance intervention components in order of preference from a menu. The intervention components are subsequently prioritized based on these rankings (i.e., successive and cumulative implementation).

Dynamic Goals. There are 5 primary goal domains that are targeted for optimization throughout TOPPS (i.e., relationship performance, sport/physical health performance, school/work performance, creative activities performance, mental strength & stability/mental wellness performance). These goals are purposefully broad, permitting athletes to additionally develop and monitor personal goals that are specific and measurable within each domain (e.g., attending a team practice 5 minutes early). Athletes are taught to appreciate how specific goals facilitate reliability and definitive outcomes, unlike the broad-based dynamic goal domains which can be rapidly developed and flexible to accommodate discussion of optimum thoughts and actions during meetings. Within each performance meeting, athletes are prompted to articulate how they achieved optimum thoughts and actions in each of the goal domains since the last performance meeting. They are then descriptively praised for optimum behavioural and cognitive skills that are reported to be optimum, and then challenged to explain how these thoughts and actions could be further optimized in the future ("optimize it!"). Consequently, athletes realize their efforts are always reinforced to some extent, and encouragement to optimize actions and thoughts are reviewed non-judgmentally. "Talk aloud" strategies of optimal thoughts may be practiced during performance meetings while optimal actions are role-played with the optimizer in simulated role-played scenarios. As plans for goal accomplishment are determined and reviewed, supportive others are prompted to commit how goal accomplishment will be rewarded and/or supported.

Goal Inspiration and Motivational Enhancement. Athletes are prompted to comprehensively review anticipated positive consequences associated with goal achievement in great detail. Checklists are used to prompt potential positive consequences, and optimizers encourage athletes to think ambitiously. Exercises include choosing from a list which words in various categories (e.g., spiritual, aggressive) are most motivating and subsequently exchanging these words with supportive others or in imagery scenarios during agenda reviews at the start of meetings. Assignments to practice stating motivational words while alternating focus statements are made (e.g., I'm going to dominate; I will move to my right; I'm strong and steady; Donohue et al., 2001).

Positive Request and HEARD. To facilitate optimal relationships and communication between athletes and their supportive others, optimizers prompt all parties to exchange statements of appreciation, usually at the beginning of performance meetings once every other month or as needed. Athletes who experience disagreements with others, learn to assertively and respectfully initiate positive requests. Written prompts are used to teach skills impromptu or during role-plays (e.g., request a specific action, indicate why request is important). Athletes also practice the acronym HEARD to assist them in positively responding to upset in others (Hear, Empathize, Ask for solutions, Review potential solutions, Decide what to do).

Environmental Control. People, places, activities and emotions compatible and incompatible with goal attainment are generated and recorded on a weekly monitoring form. Future meetings facilitate thoughts and actions that are consistent with optimal performance that occurred, and optimizers challenge athletes to optimize their thoughts and behaviours when spending time with these stimuli in the future. Optimizers and supportive others work in tandem to assist athletes in optimizing their thoughts and actions. Scheduled pleasant activities are planned to occur with supportive others.

Self-Control. Athletes are taught to identify triggers or early antecedents to nonoptimal thoughts and actions and immediately shout aloud, Focus! They then sequentially practice a series of cognitive and behavioural skills that would likely optimize performance in that situation (i.e., motivational statement, cue-controlled relaxation and diaphragmatic breathing, brainstorming solutions, imagining successful performance of one or more of the selected options, imagining positive consequences for optimal thoughts and actions performed in the talk aloud imagery). Optimizers assist by making suggestions for optimal thoughts and actions. Athletes practice these strategies at home.

Career (Dream Job) Development and Job Getting Skills Training. Athletes are prompted to brainstorm desired career options that are consistent with their "dream job" while supportive others assist the athletes in generating positive consequences for selected jobs. Optimizers and supportive others facilitate the development of thoughts and actions that are consistent with gaining resources and skills necessary to plan to assist in achieving their dream job. This exercise assists in the review and visualisation of potential job experiences. Subsequently, athletes are taught job interviewing skills and methods of soliciting job interviews via networking and solicitation of meetings with potential employers while supportive others assist networking and interviewing skill development.

Financial Management. Athletes examine their current or anticipated income and expenses, and they review their desired financial decision making. A financial budget worksheet is used to prompt methods of earning and saving income and decreasing expenses for both the present and future.

Last Meeting Review. In the final meeting optimizers solicit positive experiences gained from optimization programming, and prompt athletes to report with their supportive others, how they accomplished optimal thoughts and actions in each of the Dynamic Goal domains (i.e., relationships, physical health/sport participation, school/work, creativity, mental strength and stability). Optimizers then solicit how these skills will be used to optimize future performance in the 5 goal domains. Athletes and their supportive others are encouraged to stop by the TOPPS performance facility to update goal progress, and solicit methods of optimizing their thoughts and actions.

Intervention evaluation and lessons learned

As indicated in the Introduction to the Theme section above, TOPPS has undergone more than a decade of scientific study. The program appears to be robust and consistently supported by evidence in achieving program engagement, improving mental health and factors that have been indicated to enhance sport performance using standardized case evaluations and randomized clinical trials. Psychometrically validated measures have been used to assess outcomes with assessors who are blind to experimental assignment in controlled trials, and intervention integrity assessment has consistently indicated high scores. However, consistent with the majority of science supported behavioural interventions for mental health, with the exception of sport performance-oriented engagement meetings, TOPPS implementation is focused on a single athlete and the athlete's supportive others. This approach is problematic when attempting to manage mental health optimization in large groups of athletes, such as sport-based little leagues, sport performance organizations and sport training centers. Therefore, our research team at the University of Nevada, Las Vegas is in the process of evaluating TOPPS services in group format to enhance its reach to more people and health economic impact. Modifications to TOPPS implementation checklists to fit group application in over 200 adolescent hockey players (mostly males between 6 and 16 years of age) and approximately 30 male and female adolescents in an elite swim club that includes Olympic medalists indicate TOPPS can be safely implemented with integrity. Future evaluations of group-based implementation of TOPPS will be focused on efficacy evaluations utilising case evaluations followed by controlled experimental methodology (i.e., multiple baseline and randomized controlled trials).

The first author has created an Optimization Center at the University of Nevada, Las Vegas in the United States. This center includes a cost-free help line (702 895 2468) for scientists, athletes and administrators of sport organizations and councils who are interested in learning more about TOPPS (www.toppscience.com/). The website currently includes videos that focus on TOPPS intervention components, electronic messaging platforms that depict applied research articles that support optimization science, methods of becoming certified in TOPPS, and available paid practicum and continuing education opportunities. A European Base is also being established at the Queen's University of Belfast. Estimated to start in 2024 it is anticipated that there will be Avatar-assisted TOPPS software available for certified instructors to teach TOPPS. It is especially hoped that this center will facilitate cooperative partnerships that are focused on the implementation of clinical trials and development of independent TOPPS training centers.

References

Azrin, N. H., McMahon, P. T., Donohue, B., Besalel, V. A., Lapinski, K. J., Kogan, E. S., ... & Galloway, E. (1994). Behavior therapy for drug abuse: A controlled treatment outcome study. *Behaviour Research and Therapy*, *32*(8), 857–866.

Chow, G., Donohue, B., Pitts, M., Schubert, K., Loughran, T., Gavrilova, Y., & Diaz, E. (2015). Results of a single case controlled study of the Optimum performance program in sports in a collegiate athlete. *Clinical Case Studies*, *14*(3) 191–209. https://doi.org/10.1177/1534650114548313

Donohue, B., Barnhart, R., Covassin, T., Carpin, K., & Corb, E. (2001). The development and initial evaluation of two promising mental preparatory methods in a sample of female cross country runners. *Journal of Sport Behavior*, *24*(1), 19–30.

Donohue, B. Chow, G., Pitts, M., Loughran, T., Schubert, K., Gavrilova, Y., Allen, D. N. (2015). Piloting a family-supported approach to concurrently optimize mental health and sport performance in Athletes. *Clinical Case Studies*, *14*(3), 159–177. https://doi.org/10.1177/1534650114548311

Donohue, B., Dickens, Y., Lancer, K., Covassin, T., Hash, A., Miller, A., & Genet, J. (2004). Improving athletes' perspectives of sport psychology consultation: A controlled evaluation of two interview methods. *Behavior Modification*, *28*(2), 182–193. https://doi.org/10.1177/0145445503259399

Donohue, B., Galante, M., Maietta., J., Lee, B., Paul, N., Perry, J. E., Corey, A., & Allen, D. N. (2019). Empirical development of a screening method to assist mental health referrals in collegiate athletes. *Journal of Clinical Sport Psychology*, *13*, 561–579.

Donohue, B., Gavrilova, E., Danlag, A., Perry, J. Phillips, C., Allen, D. A., & Benning, S. (2021). A comprehensive examination of collegiate athletes' utilization of psychological assessment and intervention services. *Psychology in the Schools*, *58*(3), 458–474. https://doi.org/10.1002/pits.22458

Donohue, B., Gavrilova, Y., Galante, M., Burnstein, B., Aubertin, P., Gavrilova, E., Funk, A., Light, A., & Benning, S.D. (2020). Empirical development of a screening method for mental, social, and physical wellness in amateur and professional circus artists. *Psychology of Aesthetics, Creativity, and the Arts*, *14*, 313–324. https://doi.org/10.1037/aca0000199

Donohue, B., Gavrilova, Y., Galante, M., Gavrilova, E., Loughrana, T., Scott, J., Chow, G., Plant, C., & Allen, D. A. (2018). Controlled evaluation of an optimization approach to mental health and sport performance. *Journal of Clinical Sport Psychology*, *12*(2), 234–267. https://doi.org/10.1123/jcsp.2017-0054

Donohue, B., Loughran, T., Pitts, M., Gavrilova, Y, Chow, G. M., Soto-Nevarez, A, & Schubert, K. (2016). Preliminary development of a brief intervention to prevent alcohol misuse and enhance sport performance in collegiate athletes. *Journal of Drug Abuse*, *2*(3), 1–9. https://doi.org/10.21767/2471-853X.100035

Donohue, B., Miller, A., Beisecker, M., Houser, D., Valdez, R., Tiller, S., & Taymar, T. (2006). Effects of brief yoga exercises and motivational preparatory interventions in distance runners: Results of a controlled trial. *British Journal of Sports Medicine*, *40*(1), 60–63. http://dx.doi.org/10.1136/bjsm.2005.020024

Donohue, B., Miller, A., Crammer, L., Cross, C., & Covassin, T. (2007). A standardized method of assessing sport specific problems in the relationships of athletes with their coaches, teammates, family, and peers. *Journal of Sport Behavior*, *30*(4), 375–397.

Donohue, B., Murphy, S., Rice, S., & Carr, C. (2022). Clinical sport psychology in practice: Sport specific roles, settings, strategies, and recommendations for its advancement. In D. Marks (Ed.), *The Routledge Handbook of Clinical Sport Psychology*, London, U.K.: Routledge Taylor & Francis.

Donohue, B. & Perry, J. (2022). *Athlete Mental Health and Performance Optimization: The Optimum Performance Program in Sports (TOPPS)*. Amsterdam. ISBN: 9780323952774

Donohue, B., Phrathep, D., Stucki, K., Kowal, I., Breslin, G., Cohen, M., White, S., Jefferson, L., White, T., Irvin, J., Reese, G., Kessler, FHP, Kieslich da Silva, A.,

Gabriel Santos da Silva, F., Fothergill, M., Robinson, G., Allen, H., Light, A., & Allen, D. A. (2021). Adapting an evidence-supported intervention to optimize mental health and sport performance for collegiate athletes to fit youth from ethnic/racial minority and low-income neighborhoods: A national institutes of health supported stage model feasibility study. *The International Journal of Psychiatry in Medicine*, *57*(3), 226–247. https://doi.org/10.1177/00912174211006547

Donohue, B., O'Dowd, A., Plant, C.P., Phillips, C., Loughran, T.A., & Gavrilova, Y. (2016). Controlled evaluation of a method to assist recruitment of participants into treatment outcome research and engage student athletes into substance abuse intervention. *Journal of Clinical Sport Psychology*, *10*, 272–288. http://dx.doi.org/10.1123/jcsp.2015-0022

Donohue, B., Silver, N. C., Dickens, Y., Covassin, T., & Lancer, K. (2007). Development and initial psychometric evaluation of the sport interference checklist. *Behavior Modification*, *31*(6), 937–957. https://doi.org/10.1177/0145445507303827

Galante, M. & Donohue, B. (2019). The optimum performance program in sports: A case of Bulimia Nervosa in a lean sport athlete. In G. Breslin & G. Leavey (Eds.), *Mental Health and Well-Being Interventions in Sport: A Case Study Analysis*. New York, NY: Routledge Taylor & Francis Group.

Gavrilova, E., Donohue, B., Kalita, J., Paul, M., Pharr, J.R., & Allen, D. (2022). Empirical justification for the involvement of athletes' supportive others when conducting sport specific mental health interventions. *Sport Social Work Journal*, *1*, 1–12.

Gavrilova, Y., Donohue, B., & Galante, M. (2017). Mental health and sport performance programming in athletes who present without pathology: A case examination supporting optimization. *Clinical Case Studies*, *16*(3), 234–253. https://doi.org/10.1177/15346501166689302

Hussey, J., Donohue, B., Barchard, K., & Allen, D. N. (2019). Family contributions to sport performance and their utility in predicting appropriate referrals to mental health optimization programmes. *European Journal of Sport Science*, *19*(7), 972–982. https://doi.org/10.1080/17461391.2019.1574906

Miller, A., & Donohue, B. (2003). The development and controlled evaluation of athletic mental preparation strategies in high school distance runners. *Journal of Applied Sport Psychology*, *15*(4), 321–334. https://doi.org/10.1080/714044200

Phrathep, D., Donohue, B., & Allen, D. (2022). Family-based optimization intervention implemented through video-conferencing to address major depressive disorder in a Latina adolescent athlete during COVID-19. *Sports Social Work Journal*, *1*(1), 13–34.

Phrathep, D., Donohue, B., Kraus, S., Paul, M., & Mercer, J. (2021). A controlled evaluation of a sport-specific performance optimization program in an athlete diagnosed with attention deficit hyperactivity disorder and oppositional defiant disorder within the context of COVID 19. *Clinical Case Studies*, *21*(3), 209–234. https://doi.org/10.1177/15346501211048508

Phrathep, D., Donohue, B., Renn, B. N., Mercer, J., & Allen, D. N. (2022). Controlled evaluation of a sport-specific performance optimization program in a biracial black and white athlete diagnosed with social anxiety disorder and agoraphobia. *Clinical Case Studies*. https://doi.org/10.1177/15346501221117827

Phrathep, D., Donohue, B., Renn, B. N., Mercer, J., & Allen, D. N. (2023). Sport and mental health performance optimization in an adolescent gymnast: A case evaluation. *Frontiers in Sports and Active Living*, 5. https://doi.org/10.3389/fspor.2023.1018861

Pitts, M., Donohue, B., Schubert, Chow, G., K. N., Lougrhan, T., Gavrilova, Y. (2015). A systematic case examination of the Optimum performance program in sports (TOPPS) in a combative sport. *Clinical Case Studies*, *14*(3), 178–190. https://doi.org/10.1177/1534650114548312

Further reading

Donohue, B. & Perry, J. (2022). *Athlete Mental Health and Performance Optimization: The Optimum Performance Program in Sports (TOPPS)*. Amsterdam. ISBN: 9780323952774

This book is a treatment manual that reviews all engagement interviews, sport-specific mental health screens/assessments and interventions specific to TOPPS.

Donohue, B., Gavrilova, E., Danlag, A., Perry, J. Phillips, C., Allen, D. A., & Benning, S. (2020). A comprehensive examination of collegiate athletes' utilization of psychological assessment and intervention services. *Psychology in the Schools*, *58*(3), 458–474. https://doi.org/10.1002/pits.22458

This is a peer reviewed journal article that describes methods of engaging athletes into TOPPS.

Donohue, B., Gavrilova, Y., Galante, M., Gavrilova, E., Loughrana, T., Scott, J., Chow, G., Plant, C., & Allen, D. A. (2018). Controlled evaluation of an optimization approach to mental health and sport performance. *Journal of Clinical Sport Psychology*, *12*(2), 234–267. https://doi.org/10.1123/jcsp.2017-0054

This is the first controlled clinical trial of TOPPS in collegiate student athletes. It introduces Optimization Theory, and reports demonstrated outcomes specific to mental health, relationships with teammates, coaches and family, and factors interfering with sport performance.

Donohue, B., Phrathep, D., Stucki, K., Kowal, I., Breslin, G., Cohen, M., White, S., Jefferson, L.,White, T., Irvin, J., Reese, G., Kessler, FHP, Kieslich da Silva, A., Gabriel Santos da Silva, F., Fothergill, M., Robinson, G., Allen, H., Light, A., & Allen, D. A. (2021). Adapting an evidence-supported intervention to optimize mental health and sport performance for collegiate athletes to fit youth from ethnic/racial minority and low-income neighborhoods: A national institutes of health supported stage model feasibility study. *The International Journal of Psychiatry in Medicine*, *57*(3), 226–247. https://doi.org/10.1177/00912174211006547

This article shows methods of initially adapting TOPPS in the treatment of collegiate athletes to fit adolescent athletes using the NIH stage model of development.

3

PREVENTION OF BURNOUT AND DEPRESSION IN JUNIOR ELITE SWIMMERS

Insa Nixdorf, Jürgen Beckmann and Raphael Nixdorf

Learning objectives

After reading this chapter you should have:

1 Learned the basic theoretical and epidemiological information on depression and burnout in elite athletes.
2 Gained important knowledge to distinguish between syndromes of depression and burnout in elite athletes.
3 Learned about the most important psychological predictors for depressive syndromes and burnout.
4 Examined prevention strategies for depression and burnout.

Introduction to the theme

Clinical disorders and mental health issues among elite athletes is a topic of increasing interest and public awareness (Schinke, Stambulova, Si, & Moore, 2017; Moesch et al., 2018; Reardon et al., 2019). Many studies among athletes illustrate the severity of psychological problems such as depression and burnout. Depression can be regarded as a multisystem disorder with affective, cognitive and physiological manifestations (Insel & Charney, 2003; Lee, Jeong, Kwak, & Park, 2010). Depressive syndromes are characterised by symptoms of depressed mood, anhedonia, fatigue, feelings of guilt and suicidal ideation (Diagnostic and Statistical Manual of Mental Disorders-5 (DSM-5), American Psychiatric Association, 2013; International Classification of Diseases-11 (ICD-11), World Health Organization, 2022). Burnout is mainly

DOI: 10.4324/9781003291695-4

described as a three-dimensional syndrome in response to occupational stress, involving emotional exhaustion, cynicism and lack of professional efficacy (Maslach & Jackson, 1981; Maslach, Schaufeli, & Leiter, 2001). In sports, the syndrome is referred to as athlete burnout with the three core dimensions a) physical and emotional exhaustion, b) sport devaluation and c) reduced sense of accomplishment (Raedeke & Smith, 2001).

Although sport participation can be a protective factor for young people (Panza et al, 2020), this effect is not apparent in higher levels of sport participation (Gorczynski, Coyle, & Gibson, 2017). In elite athletes, depending on the sample and the assessment method prevalence rates for depression appear to be at a concerning level (Gulliver, Griffiths, Mackinnon, Batterham, & Stanimirovic, 2015; Nixdorf, Frank, Hautzinger, & Beckmann, 2013; Wolanin, Hong, Marks, Panchoo, & Gross, 2016). Junior elite athletes seem to be at especially high risk (Nixdorf et al., 2013). Many correlative study designs identified sport related variables connected to elevated depression scores in elite athlete samples (e.g., injury, failure). Athletes competing in individual sports were more prone to depressive symptoms than athletes competing in team sports (Nixdorf, Frank, & Beckmann, 2016). Longitudinal data suggest coping strategies, dysfunctional attitudes and recovery as important psychological variables associated with depressive syndromes (I. Nixdorf, Beckmann, & Nixdorf, 2020). Interestingly, athlete burnout appears to be a research topic for a longer period of time when compared to other disorders. Thus, more mechanisms have been discovered regarding burnout (Eklund & DeFreese, 2015; Goodger, Gorely, Lavallee, & Harwood, 2007). Psychological factors such as personality dispositions (particularly adaptive and maladaptive perfectionism) or motivational aspects are being researched and discussed. However, recent research points out comparable psychological variables for development of burnout and depression with a primarily focus on stress (Frank, Nixdorf, & Beckmann, 2017) and important variables interacting with stress, such as coping with stress and dysfunctional attitudes (I. Nixdorf et al., 2020; Martinent et al., 2022). These findings provide useful information for prevention strategies among elite athletes (Gustafsson, DeFreese, & Madigan, 2017). Furthermore, both syndromes can be viewed from an integrated perspective (Nixdorf, Madigan, Kenttä & Hassmén, 2023) and prevention programmes can effectively address both syndromes with a specific emphasis on stress and further, shared protective factors. Based on this research applied sport psychology is now able to generate more specific prevention programmes in order to stabilise mental health and prevent burnout and depression. The following book chapter gives an insight on how fresh empirical evidence can be implemented into a screening and prevention programme for burnout and depression specific to a target group of junior elite athletes competing in an individual sport discipline.

Description of the group being targeted

The group targeted in our prevention programme were junior elite swimmers. The programme was part of an applied project called "Group coaching of selected athletes of the Bavarian Swim Association", which was founded by the German Federal Institute of Sport Science (Bundesinstitut für Sportwissenschaft; BISp). The project was conducted with junior elite swimmers in order to strengthen prospectively important factors and therefore help prevent the development of psychological problems. In this matter, the prevention programme was a transfer-project developed from a research project (2014–2016), in which the goals were to identify important predictors for burnout and depression in elite athletes. Results showed that athletes in individual sports are at higher risk for depressive syndromes (Nixdorf et al., 2016). Therefore, junior elite swimmers were assumed to gain most from a preventive intervention programme.

A total of 27 female and male swimmers (aged between 12 and 16 years) participated in the applied sport psychology programme. All swimmers were part of a regional, high level swim squad. Therefore, most athletes were members of the German D/C cadre squad for swimming. In order to maintain and develop their performance levels athletes endured an extensive training schedule and programme. Athletes trained approximately 8 to 9 times a week swimming between 30 and 40 kilometres (km) depending on the training phase during season. In total, most of the athletes completed 1500 km a year. In addition, athletic training was scheduled 3 times a week. Three different training facilities with locations across Munich in Germany were provided for each training group. Thus, changing locations on a regular basis was necessary. During season, athletes competed in 15 tournaments, approximately, mostly on weekends. In addition to the training obligations, all athletes attended school and had to study for their examinations on a regular basis. Therefore, training had to be fitted into a tight schedule with little spare time for other leisure time hobbies and interests. Participation in the present programme was voluntary, however parental informed consent was provided.

Initial needs assessment

In line with previous research, it was found that athletes in individual disciplines reported higher depression scores than athletes in team sports (see Nixdorf et al., 2016; Pluhar et al., 2019). In particular, the present cohort of elite swimmers also had relatively high levels of depressive symptoms. This finding is supported by Hammond, Gialloreto, Kubas, and Davis (2013) who report a prevalence of 68% for depression in Canadian swimmers, with a strong correlation to perceived failure.

Based on the findings reported above, there is a need for improvement of athlete's mental health. However, less apparent is the question on how to improve athlete's mental health. Therefore, information on which relevant factors intervention and prevention programmes can be based on were needed and understanding of mechanisms how depression and burnout can be developed in athletes is necessary (Frank, Nixdorf, & Beckmann, 2013). In general, both constructs (depression and burnout) can be regarded in a stress-based perspective (Frank, et al., 2017).

Depression does not involve a homogeneous disease pattern. The heterogeneity of the symptoms of depressive disorders also makes it unlikely that one factor alone is responsible for the development of depression. Therefore, adopting multifactorial explanatory concepts such as vulnerability-stress models may be warranted (e.g., Alloy et al., 2006; Haffel et al., 2005; Hyde, Mezulis, & Abramson, 2008). Here, certain vulnerabilities (genetic, social or cognitive factors) in combination with a stressor (chronic or acute) can lead to depression (Lee et al., 2010). Among athletes the relation to stress is also apparent as stressors such as training loads, pressure to perform well (Nixdorf, Frank, & Beckmann, 2015) or an important competition (Hammond et al., 2013) have been associated with depressive symptoms. Thus, vulnerability-stress models are particularly important for elite athletes (Nixdorf & Nixdorf, 2023). Frameworks to be considered regarding athlete burnout can be based on personal factors such as the ability to efficiently cope with chronic psychological stress involved in sports (Smith, 1986), based on the conditions and environmental factors leading to autonomy and identity challenges in young athletes (Coakley, 1992), or the integration of various facets is assumed for a theoretical foundation of athlete burnout (Gustafsson, Kentta, & Hassmen, 2011).

These stress-based perspectives appear valuable, as the present sample indicated high levels of various stressors by their training schedule already. Based on vulnerability-stress models, various important factors (vulnerabilities and stressors) have been associated with burnout and depression. However, little evidence has shown longitudinal evidence for factors to have a prospective impact on either construct (Eklund & DeFreese, 2015; Frank et al., 2013). The beforementioned research project addressed this question and found that dysfunctional attitudes and negative coping strategies (such as resignation) act as vulnerabilities, and chronic stress as well as a lack of recovery act as stressors predicting burnout and depression among junior elite athletes across a season (I. Nixdorf et al, 2020). Therefore, these factors appear to be important predictors and represent salient factors for prevention of mental disorders in athletes. Consequently, these factors have been the basis for the present intervention programme for junior elite swimmers. In addition, these factors served as an evaluation indicator for the assessment pre- and post-intervention.

In the present sample, the factors: coping strategies, athlete burnout, chronic stress and current state of stress and recovery were assessed. Due to the stigma and strong reservations expressed by the coaches and parents of the swimmers, an assessment of depression was resigned. Athletes' coping responses to life stressors were measured using relevant strategies from the Stressverarbeitungs-Fragebogen (SVF; Erdmann & Janke, 2008), namely resignation, flight, self-pity and positive self-instruction. The SVF focuses on dispositional coping, rather than on situational coping i.e., it indicates a temporally consistent coping style in the tested subject. The scale has good validity and reliability and was previously applied in elite athlete samples (e.g., Nixdorf et al., 2013). Chronic stress was assessed using the Screening of the Trier Inventory of Chronic Stress (TICS; Schulz, Schlotz, & Becker, 2004). The scale is designed to measure experiences of chronic stress and therefore covers the last 3 months and offers a valid and reliable scale for assessment in the general population (Schulz et al., 2004). Also, for (junior) athletes, the scale was validated and normed with adequate psychometric properties (Sallen & Hoffmann, 2012). Burnout in athletes was assessed using the German version of the Athlete Burnout Questionnaire (ABQ; Raedeke & Smith, 2001; German version Ziemainz, Abu-Omar, Raedeke, & Krause, 2004). The ABQ is a valid self-report scale designed to assess the three core dimensions of athlete burnout: physical and emotional exhaustion, sport devaluation and reduced sense of accomplishment. For covering the current state of stress and recovery the sport-specific Acute Recovery and Stress Scale (ARSS; see Kellmann und Kölling, 2019; Hitzschke et al., 2016) was used. The scale was specifically developed and validated for assessing current states of stress and recovery in athletes using 32 adjectives on a 7 point Likert rating scale.

Furthermore, these factors were supplemented by qualitative interviews on personal goals, needs and motivation for participation in the programme. Most athletes indicated a personal need to reduce the amount of stress in their lives. In this regard, reasons for stress (stressors) mentioned mostly concerned training and school schedule, which led to difficulties in attending every obligation. Especially, time to study and time for other activities (hobbies, time with friends and family) was drastically minimised. Other important needs were based on the pressure of important events or criteria the athletes were supposed to meet, such as qualification times, personal records or championships. However, perceived pressure was also mentioned regarding school and obligations besides their main sport. Reducing stress and improving ways to cope with stressors could therefore be considered as the overall topic for all interventions delivered.

Framework and intervention for delivery

The main goal of the intervention programme was to prevent burnout and depression as consequences of extensive stress. In regard to prevention, Romano and Hage (2000) define prevention as including one or more of the following: (1) stopping a problem behaviour from ever occurring; (2) delaying the onset of a problem behaviour, especially for those at risk for the problem; (3) reducing the impact of a problem behaviour; (4) strengthening knowledge, attitudes and behaviours that promote emotional and physical well-being; and (5) promoting institutional, community, and government policies that further physical, social and emotional well-being of the larger community. This conceptualisation is consistent with Caplan (1964) who identified prevention interventions as primary, secondary and tertiary prevention, and with the alternative definition by Gordon (1983) that identified prevention interventions as universal, selected and indicated for those not at risk, at risk, and those experiencing early signs of problems. Romano and Hage (2000) also mention that although dimensions 1, 2 and 3 can be conceptualised in traditional primary, secondary and tertiary terms and refer to the individual, dimensions 4 and 5 are conceptualised within a "risk-reduction" framework. Therefore, the present programme aimed at interventions according to primary and secondary prevention. The goal was to stabilise and strengthen the athletes in order to stop burnout and depression from occurring (point 1) and, according to Romano and Hage (2000), to strengthen knowledge, attitudes and behaviours that promote emotional and physical well-being (point 4).

As mentioned previously, depression and burnout can be addressed from a stress-based perspective. Thus, the present programme was based on a concept of improving athlete's abilities to cope with stressors and therefore enhance resilience in this regard. So, the main focus was centred on strengthening athlete's competences rather than on social or organisational factors. Thus, interventions were based on a cognitive-behavioural perspective of learning. In general, Ingram and Luxton (2005) point out that most psychological approaches rely on assumptions of dysfunctional learning as the genesis of vulnerability. Following this assumption, interventions from a cognitive-behavioural perspective seemed suitable and have been mainly applied in the programme.

In line with other cognitive-behavioural programmes on stress management (Kaluza, 2015), different approaches on stress were considered and implemented. Therefore, intervention can be focused on the stressor (instrumental management), on the cognitive beliefs (mental management) or the stress reaction (regenerative management). Many programmes consider all of these aspects in an integrated approach (Gunthner & Batra, 2012; Kaluza, 2015). For theoretical reasons however, the transactional model from Lazarus and Folkman (1987) is the most applied and adapted as it relates the stressor with the stress reaction based on the personal beliefs and resources. In this perspective, the transaction between people and their external environment is central. The model assumes two appraisals of a person regarding a potentially stressful situation. Primary appraisal evaluates whether a stressor is dangerous, positive or irrelevant. In a secondary appraisal, the person's resources (sufficient or insufficient) to deal with the stressor are analysed. If stress arises based on

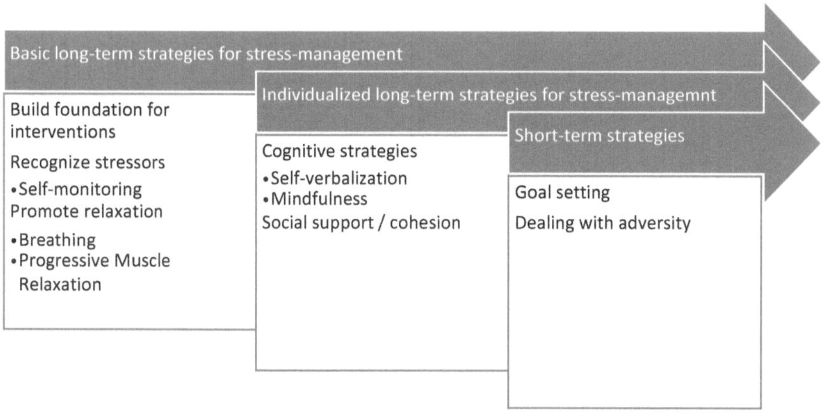

FIGURE 3.1 Overview of interventions planning.

the appraisals, coping strategies have to be applied in order to overcome the stressful situation (Lazarus, 1991, 2006).

Illustrating the implemented programme, first considerations were due to the athlete's surrounding. Time and place of the delivered interventions were carefully chosen, and evening swimming sessions were replaced with the sport psychological intervention programme. This should help minimise additional stress through the intervention meetings. In addition, as all coaches supported and scheduled the intervention dates it should help underpin the importance of the sport psychological programme for the athlete's perception.

In order to establish contact with the athletes and to introduce the prevention programme a "kick-off" meeting was arranged. The main focus was on explaining the schedule of the programme, to collect any further needs and topics of the athletes and to educate on burnout and depression in elite athletes (e.g., symptoms, aetiopathology and treatment). The intervention programme itself was divided into 3 main sections, building gradually up upon itself (see Figure 3.1).

Part 1: "Recognize stressors, promote relaxation (long-term strategies for stress management)"

In this block of interventions, core competences were trained for stress relief and the identification of personal stressors. In addition, a goal was to establish good working conditions with the groups, which should be characterised by a collegial atmosphere during group meetings and independent transfer of the contents. As concrete interventions content from the area of mindfulness was used. Thereby, the advantage was gained that both the recognition of one's own mental processes as well as the ability to relax and self-regulate (for example in the case of focusing) are simultaneously promoted. In addition, at least one classical relaxation procedure (Progressive Muscle Relaxation (PMR), breathing exercises or autogenetic training) was practiced with each group.

Example of an intervention: "Picture of my week"

Background

Often the time passes by, and we ask ourselves at the end of the week what we did for us and where we also had joy, fun and recreation. In order to plan your own everyday life a bit better and to ensure sufficient recovery, you can try the following strategy.

Execution

- Draw up a weekly schedule for the next 7 days.
- Enter your fixed dates, e.g., School, training and time to learn.
- Use a different pen (such as other colour) to recreate activities. Try to be very specific (What do you want to do, specifically with whom and how long?). Also, make sure that it is a pleasant activity for you.
- You can now mark with a "–" which activities are a burden for you during the week, and mark with a "+" which activities are recreational.
- See if you have enough rest in your week?
- Change your plan so you can plan enough restorative things during the week.

Try to follow your plan and start a new plan in 7 days. Consider your experiences from the previous week.

Goal

The goal of this strategy is to plan and schedule a week at a time, so an athlete is not overwhelmed and finds him or herself working off many obligations with time to recover (mentally and physically). The declaration of positive and negative (+ and -) to an activity helps athletes to observe their needs and to reflect on their habits. In doing so, the intervention helps identify personal stressors and resources. Its focus is therefore on instrumental stress management (Kaluza, 2015). In addition, the planning creates a basis for implementing recreation and relaxation strategies in regard to regenerative management (Kaluza, 2015).

Part 2: "Stress management techniques (long-term strategies for stress management)"

In the second block of interventions, various techniques and competences were developed, as planned, with the multitude of stressors of the swimmers.

Coping strategies such as positive self-verbalisation and the introduced content of mindfulness were applied in stressful situations of the swimmers. Also, individual exercises were conducted as a group exercise or with the involvement of the group in order to strengthen the social structure and thus the support in the training group. Here, the implementation was also closely linked to the planned content. The essential work involved the individual implementation and transfer of the exercises to the stressors and challenges of the individual athlete.

Example of an intervention: "My mental rule of three"

Background

Especially in athletes' everyday life starting early in the morning (school, training, physiotherapy, competitions), the athletes should learn to use the little time as best as possible. Often, in addition to a full calendar of appointments, it is aggravating that our thoughts are not focusing on the current activity, but we are worrying about the future or thinking about the past. This exercise helps to focus on the here and now and on the essentials: What do I need now? What is important to do now?

Execution

Take a moment, breathe three times, and answer the following three questions (in thought or written). If you digress, that is ok. Try again and think about what is important at this moment. My mental rule of three:

1 A thought about the past: (What happened? How was that?)
2 A thought about the future: (What will come? How will that be?)
3 A thought about the current situation: (What is now? What do I need now? What is important now?)

Goal

The goal of this strategy is to focus on the here and now and to reduce distracting thoughts about the past or future by deliberately being aware of these thoughts, giving them their space and time. That way distracting thoughts or worries don't have to force themselves on an athlete at any given moment and the athlete can take control of their thoughts and focus on a current task or need.

Part 3: "Success, goals, attitudes (short-term strategies for stress management)"

In the third block, the interventions focused on the setting of goals and functional attitudes. At the same time, the goal was, above all, to work out a realistic, yet motivating assessment of one's own abilities with the individual athletes. Interventions focusing on personal values and beliefs tried to promote self-esteem, self-efficacy and self-accepting attitudes. These attitudes were additionally applied in setting personal goals.

Example of an intervention: "My own perfect companion"

Background

Each one of us has people who do a good job and people who are sometimes obstructive. For instance, they put an additional pressure on us, put high demands that are too high on us, or we get the feeling that they would not believe in us. First of all, it is important that we believe in ourselves. This exercise is designed to help you support yourself, encourage yourself, motivate yourself positively and master difficult situations.

Execution

Take a moment and think about imminent difficulties. There are probably a few sentences that pop up. "This will be difficult!" or "Do not fail!". You may also remember sentences and statements from other people. Perhaps you can imagine what your father, a team colleague or your trainer would say in such a situation.

Now imagine there is a personal companion for you. A person who supports you unconditionally, who is always loyal to you and always likes you. Whatever you're doing, this companion will always stick to you and will always have your back. Now imagine what this perfect companion would say to you? What would he/she advise you, how would he/she cheer you up, and what would he/she do in your situation? Try to sketch this companion as well and as accurately as possible before your inner eye (What does he/she look like? What age is he/she? Does he/she have a comforting voice?). You can now ask him/her for advice, whenever you need him/her.

It is best to repeat this exercise a few times, so you can imagine your companion easier and quicker. You can also give him/her a name or link him/her with a symbol or small mascot (e.g., a key pendant or figure). That way he/she can always be with you in the sports bag.

Goal

The goal of this strategy is to establish a positive, supportive voice for the athletes. The imagined companion is always accessible, which can help build self-esteem and self-efficacy. This intervention can be regarded as a cognitive technique, which could be applied in cognitive-behavioural therapy and mental stress management (Kaluza, 2015; Leahy, 2017). The focus is on the athlete's attitudes and beliefs and offers a possibility to promote functional, positive beliefs and therefore reduce possible negative consequences by dysfunctional or perfectionistic attitudes (Ashby & Rice, 2002; Bianchi & Schonfeld, 2016; Madigan, Stoeber, & Passfield, 2015).

For all parts and interventions athletes were motivated to practice and try different interventions at home. In the subsequent meeting these interventions were discussed, and open questions addressed. At the end of the intervention programme an overview highlighting the most valuable intervention for each participant was reviewed.

Intervention evaluation and lessons learned through self-reflection

Overall, the programme was welcomingly appreciated by participating athletes, coaches and parents. Rating of the intervention programme by the athletes was $M = 1.35$ ($SD = 0.48$) on a scale from 1 = *very good* to 5 = *bad*. In order to evaluate the implemented interventions, central markers were tested at the beginning and the end of the programme. As mentioned above the following questionnaires were assessed: the Trierer inventory for chronic stress screening, TICS (Schulz et al., 2004), relevant scales of the stress processing questionnaire, SVF (Erdmann & Janke, 2008), and the sport-specific acute recovery and stress scale (ARSS; Hitzschke et al., 2016) and the Athlete Burnout Questionnaire, ABQ (Raedeke & Smith, 2001) in its German version (Ziemainz et al., 2004).

The results in Table 3.1 show a general positive trend. All variables improved on a descriptive level. Given the small sample size ($n = 11$), no statistical analyses were performed due to questionable generalisability of such results.

TABLE 3.1 Mean scores of assessed variables for intervention evaluation

	Pre-intervention		*Post-intervention*	
	Mean	*SD*	*Mean*	*SD*
TICS	23.55	9.50	21.00	8.53
SVF – resignation	8.90	4.30	8.36	4.37
SVF – flight	7.55	3.86	7.27	3.86
SVF – self-pity	11.00	5.00	9.82	5.00
SVF – positive self-instruction	14.18	3.54	14.64	3.83
ARSS – recovery	38.18	10.25	41.09	9.51
ARSS – stress	39.36	10.44	35.00	12.30
ABQ	19.91	7.97	19.45	8.78

In an anonymous evaluation at the end of the programme, the athletes rated the sessions overall as highly valuable (M = 1.35; 1 represents highest grade and 5 represents lowest grade). Especially the useful information and the comprehensive education (both rated with M = 1.47) were positively evaluated. The only difficulties were apparent with the application and practicability of the content, which received the lowest score, however they were still positively graded (M = 1.65).

Unfortunately, as in all longitudinal studies there was a loss of data due to incomplete data sets for a considerable number of participants. Only 11 athletes completed the online post-intervention measures. An "online" approach can appear as a convenient way of gathering information, however access to the internet for those participating was low. Therefore, paper and pencil face to face methods may have been preferable and should be considered in future studies. Aspects of anonymity and blinding should however be carefully considered in this regard (Brown & Fletcher, 2017).

From the reflection during the interventions, qualitative feedback and individual performance results, there remain some important aspects to be noted. A first important issue was to catch up with the daily stressors and hazards of the athlete's lives. This contributed to a diverse programme, topics and examples for upcoming interventions and eventually positively affected the athlete's motivation for participation in the programme due to a high level of autonomous regulation (Adie, Duda, & Ntoumanis, 2008; Ryan & Deci, 2000).

Another aspect for consideration was the timing of the sessions themselves. Although already carefully considered, the intervention sessions to some degree increased the amount of the weekly obligations and were therefore counterproductive for promotion of recovery. However, based on long-term considerations, the temporary increase might be justified. For future programmes it would be valuable to consider an even closer attunement of intervention and daily programme. In this regard, training camps might offer a perfect opportunity in order to avoid additional stress. In addition, training camps offer further possibilities to practice and apply sport psychological content in practice. Further considerations are based on the results of the participating athletes. According to Brown and Fletcher (2017) the effects of psychological interventions on sport performance are moderate in general. In the present programme the overall performance of most athletes was good and, in some cases, even exceedingly high. This could be seen as evidence that a focus on athletes' mental health and well-being does not have to be counterproductive in terms of performance enhancement. The conclusion would be rather that promotion of mental health can be a considerable aspect not just for mental health issues but also for building a basis for sport performance. Strengthening athletes' personality, developing competencies for sports and other aspects in life, therefore offers ways to build stable and resilient athletes. This would not only be morally obligatory but might as well promote sport performance.

As indicated, the initial needs assessment did not involve screening for depressive syndromes for different reasons with stigmatization amongst them. However, screening for high risk of depression is important to prevent severe depressive episodes and implement a layer of safety for the risk of suicidality. To account for economic purpose on the one hand and reliable screening on the other hand, an indirect screening was generated, based on the present findings and data. This indirect screening uses the beforementioned, relevant psychological variables (coping, dysfunctional attitudes and recovery) as indicators for possible depressive episodes. R. Nixdorf, Beckmann and Nixdorf (2020) supported the use of these variables and showed, that certain cut-off scores in the psychological variables predicted significant higher risks for depressive episodes. Using this approach, depressive syndromes can be roughly estimated, while focusing on the main purpose of assessment, which is structuring and planning of the intervention strategy. Such indirect screenings can be used in applied sport psychological coaching and training as well as in and internet-based applications, were an individual feedback and recommendations based on the assessment results is provided. Recommendations would favourably address the, in this chapter, explained variables and could use the here presented intervention strategies.

References

Adie, J. W., Duda, J. L., & Ntoumanis, N. (2008). Autonomy support, basic need satisfaction and the optimal functioning of adult male and female sport participants: A test of basic needs theory. *Motivation and Emotion*, *32*(*3*), 189–199. doi:10.1007/s11031-008-9095-z

Alloy, L. B., Abramson, L. Y., Whitehouse, W. G., Hogan, M. E., Panzarella, C., & Rose, D. T. (2006). Prospective incidence of first onsets and recurrences of depression in individuals at high and low cognitive risk for depression. *Journal of Abnormal Psychology*, *115*(*1*), 145–156. doi:10.1037/0021-843X.115.1.145

American Psychiatric Association. (2013). *Diagnostic and Statistical Manual of Mental Disorders* (5th ed.). Washington, DC: American Psychiatric Association.

Ashby, J. S., & Rice, K. G. (2002). Perfectionism, dysfunctional attitudes, and self-esteem: A structural equations analysis. *Journal of Counseling & Development*, *80*(*2*), 197–203.

Bianchi, R., & Schonfeld, I. S. (2016). Burnout is associated with a depressive cognitive style. *Personality and Individual Differences*, *100*, 1–5. doi:10.1016/j.paid.2016.01.008

Brown, D. J., & Fletcher, D. (2017). Effects of psychological and psychosocial interventions on sport performance: A meta-analysis. *Sports Medicine*, *47*(*1*), 77–99. doi:10.1007/s40279-016-0552-7

Caplan, G. (1964). *Principles of Preventive Psychiatry*. New York, NY: Basic Books.

Coakley, J. (1992). Burnout among adolescent athletes – a personal failure or social-problem. *Sociology of Sport Journal*, *9*(*3*), 271–285.

Eklund, R. C., & DeFreese, J. (2015). Athlete burnout: What we know, what we could know, and how we can find out more. *International Journal of Applied Sports Sciences*, *27*(*2*), 63–75.

Erdmann, G., & Janke, W. (2008). *Stressverarbeitungsfragebogen SVF (Handbuch): Stress, Stressverarbeitung und ihre Erfassung durch ein mehrdimensionales Testsystem*. Göttingen: Hogrefe.

Frank, R., Nixdorf, I., & Beckmann, J. (2013). Depressionen im Hochleistungssport: Prävalenzen und psychologische Einflüsse [Depression in elite athletes: Prevalence and psychological factors]. *Deutsche Zeitschrift Fur Sportmedizin*, *64*(*11*), 320–326. doi:10.5960/dzsm.2013.088

Frank, R., Nixdorf, I., & Beckmann, J. (2017). Analyzing the relationship between depression and burnout in junior elite athletes. *Journal of Clinical Sport Psychology*, *11*(*4*), 287–303. doi: 10.1123/JCSP.2017-0008

Goodger, K., Gorely, T., Lavallee, D., & Harwood, C. (2007). Burnout in sport: A systematic review. *The Sport Psychologist*, *21*, 127–151.

Gorczynski, P. F., Coyle, M., & Gibson, K. (2017). Depressive symptoms in high-performance athletes and non-athletes: Aa comparative meta-analysis. *British jJournal of sSports mMedicine*, *51(18)*, 1348–1354. https://doi.org/10.1136/bjsports-2016-096455

Gordon, R. S. (1983). An operational classification of disease prevention. *Public Health Reports*, *98*(*2*), 107.

Gulliver, A., Griffiths, K. M., Mackinnon, A., Batterham, P. J., & Stanimirovic, R. (2015). The mental health of Australian elite athletes. *Journal of Science and Medicine in Sport*, *18*(*3*), 255–261. doi:10.1016/j.jsams.2014.04.006

Gunthner, A., & Batra, A. (2012). Stressmanagemant als burn-out-prohylaxe [Prevention of burnout by stress management]. *Bundesgesundheitsblatt Gesundheitsforschung Gesundheitsschutz*, *55*(*2*), 183–189. doi:10.1007/s00103-011-1406-y

Gustafsson, H., DeFreese, J., & Madigan, D. J. (2017). Athlete burnout: Review and recommendations. *Current Opinion in Psychology*, *16*, 109–113. doi:10.1016/j.copsyc.2017.05.002

Gustafsson, H., Kentta, G., & Hassmen, P. (2011). Athlete burnout: An integrated model and future research directions. *International Review of Sport and Exercise Psychology*, *4*(*1*), 3–24. doi:10.1080/1750984x.2010.541927

Haffel, G. J., Abramson, L. Y., Voelz, Z. R., Metalsky, G. I., Halberstadt, L., Dykman, B. M., ... Alloy, L. B. (2005). Negative cognitive styles, dysfunctional attitudes, and the remitted depression paradigm: A search for the elusive cognitive vulnerability to depression factor among remitted depressives. *Emotion*, *5*(*3*), 343–348. doi:10.1037/1528-3542.5.3.343

Hammond, T., Gialloreto, C., Kubas, H., & Davis, H. (2013). The prevalence of failure-based depression among elite athletes. *Clinical Journal of Sport Medicine*, *23*(*4*), 273–277. doi:10.1097/JSM.0b013e318287b870

Hitzschke, B., Holst, T., Ferrauti, A., Meyer, T., Pfeiffer, M., & Kellmann, M. (2016). Entwicklung des Akutmaßes zur Erfassung von Erholung und Beanspruchung im Sport. *Diagnostica*, *62*(*4*), 212–226.

Hyde, J. S., Mezulis, A. H., & Abramson, L. Y. (2008). The ABCs of depression: Integrating affective, biological, and cognitive models to explain the emergence of the gender difference in depression. *Psychological Review*, *115*(*2*), 291–313. doi:10.1037/0033-295X.115.2.291

Ingram, R. E., & Luxton, D. D. (2005). Vulnerability-stress models. In B. L. Hankin & J. R. Z. Abela(Eds.), *Development of Psychopathology: A Vulnerability-Stress Perspective* (pp. 32–46). Thousand Oaks, CA: Sage Publications.

Insel, T. R., & Charney, D. S. (2003). Research on major depression: Strategies and priorities. *JAMA*, *289*(*23*), 3167–3168.

Kaluza, G. (2015). *Stressbewältigung: Trainingsmanual zur psychologischen Gesundheitsförderung*. Heidelberg: Springer-Verlag.

Kellmann, J. & Kölling, S. (2019). The acute recovery and stress scale. In M. Kellmann & S. Kölling (Eds.), *Recovery and Stress in Sport* (pp. 16–38). Abingdon: Routledge.

Lazarus, R. S. (1991). *Emotion and Adaptation*. New York, NY: Oxford University Press.

Lazarus, R. S. (2006). *Stress and Emotion: A New Synthesis*. New York, NY: Springer Publishing Company.

Lazarus, R. S., & Folkman, S. (1987). Transactional theory and research on emotions and coping. *European Journal of personality*, *1*(*3*), 141–169.

Leahy, R. L. (2017). *Cognitive Therapy Techniques: A Practitioner's Guide*. New York, NY: The Guilford Press.

Lee, S., Jeong, J., Kwak, Y., & Park, S. K. (2010). Depression research: Where are we now? *Molecular Brain*, *3*, *8*. doi:10.1186/1756-6606-3-8

Madigan, D. J., Stoeber, J., & Passfield, L. (2015). Perfectionism and burnout in junior athletes: A three-month longitudinal study. *Journal of Sport & Exercise Psychology*, *37*(*3*), 305–315. doi:10.1123/jsep.2014-0266

Martinent, G., Cece, V., & Guillet-Descas, E. (2022). The impact of stress, recovery and coping on burnout symptoms of young elite table-tennis players: A prospective multilevel study. *Frontiers in Psychology*, *13*, 1007697. https://doi.org/10.3389/fpsyg.2022.1007697

Maslach, C., & Jackson, S. E. (1981). The measurement of experienced burnout. *Journal of Organizational Behavior*, *2*(*2*), 99–113.

Maslach, C., Schaufeli, W. B., & Leiter, M. P. (2001). Job burnout. *Annual Review of Psychology*, *52*(*1*), 397–422.

Moesch, K., Kentta, G., Kleinert, J., Quignon-Fleuret, C., Cecil, S., & Bertollo, M. (2018). FEPSAC position statement: Mental health disorders in elite athletes and models of service provision. *Psychology of Sport and Exercise*, *38*, 61–71. https://doi.org/10.1016/j.psychsport.2018.05.013

Nixdorf, I. & Nixdorf, R. (2023). Depression in elite athletes. In I. Nixdorf, R. Nixdorf, J. Beckmann, S. Martin, & T. MacIntyre (Eds.), *Routledge Handbook of Mental Health in Elite Sport* (pp. 83–98). London: Routledge.

Nixdorf, I., Beckmann, J., & Nixdorf, R. (2020). Psychological predictors for depression and burnout among German junior elite athletes. *Frontiers in Psychology*, *11*, 601. https://doi.org/10.3389/fpsyg.2020.00601

Nixdorf, I., Frank, R., & Beckmann, J. (2015). An explorative study on major stressors and its connection to depression and chronic stress among German elite athletes. *Advances in Physical Education*, *5*(*4*), 255–262. doi:10.4236/ape.2015.54030

Nixdorf, I., Frank, R., & Beckmann, J. (2016). Comparison of athletes' proneness to depressive symptoms in individual and team sports: Research on psychological mediators in junior elite athletes. *Frontiers in Psychology*, *7*, *893*. doi:10.3389/fpsyg.2016.00893

Nixdorf, I., Frank, R., Hautzinger, M., & Beckmann, J. (2013). Prevalence of depressive symptoms and correlating variables among German elite athletes. *Journal of Clinical Sport Psychology*, *7*, 313–326.

Nixdorf, R., Beckmann, J., & Nixdorf, I. (2020). Risikoeinschätzung für depressive Syndrome anhand eines Screenings psychologischer Variablen [Risk assessment for depressive syndromes by screening of psychological variables]. *Zeitschrift für Sportpsychologie*, *27*(3), 95–105. https://doi.org/10.1026/1612-5010/a000305

Nixdorf, R., Madigan, D., Kenttä, G., & Hassmén, P. (2023). Depression, athlete burnout, and overtraining: A review of similarities and differences. In I. Nixdorf, R. Nixdorf, J. Beckmann, S. Martin, & T. MacIntyre (Eds.), *Routledge Handbook of Mental Health in Elite Sport* (pp. 188–200). London: Routledge.

Panza, M. J., Graupensperger, S., Agans, J. P., Doré, I., Vella, S. A., & Evans, M. B. (2020). Adolescent sport participation and symptoms of anxiety and depression: A systematic review and meta-analysis. *Journal of Sport and Exercise Psychology*, *42*(3), 201218.

Pluhar, E., McCracken, C., Griffith, K. L., Christino, M. A., Sugimoto, D., & Meehan III, W. P. (2019). Team sport athletes may be less likely to suffer anxiety or depression than individual sport athletes. *Journal of Sports Science & Medicine*, *18*(3), 490.

Raedeke, T. D., & Smith, A. L. (2001). Development and preliminary validation of an athlete burnout measure. *Journal of Sport & Exercise Psychology*, *23*(*4*), 281–306.

Reardon, C. L., Hainline, B., Aron, C. M., Baron, D., Baum, A. L., Bindra, A., Budgett, R., Campriani, N., Castaldelli-Maia, J. M., Currie, A., Derevensky, J. L., Glick, I. D., Gorczynski, P., Gouttebarge, V., Grandner, M. A., Han, D. H., McDuff, D., Mountjoy, M., Polat, A., Purcell, R., … Engebretsen, L. (2019). Mental health in elite athletes: International Olympic Committee consensus statement (2019). *British Journal of Sports Medicine*, *53*(11), 667–699. https://doi.org/10.1136/bjsports-2019-100715

Romano, J. L., & Hage, S. M. (2000). Prevention and counseling psychology revitalizing commitments for the 21st century. *The Counseling Psychologist*, *28*(*6*), 733–763.

Ryan, R. M., & Deci, E. L. (2000). Intrinsic and extrinsic motivations: Classic definitions and new directions. *Contemporary Educational Psychology*, *25*(*1*), 54–67. doi:10.1006/ceps.1999.1020

Sallen, J., & Hoffmann, K. (2012). Spezifische Normierung des Trierer Inventars zum chronischen Stress (TICS) zur diagnostischen Anwendung im Spitzensport. *Zeitschrift für Sportpsychologie*, *19*(*3*), 95–109. doi:10.1026/1612-5010/a000074

Schinke, R. J., Stambulova, N. B., Si, G., & Moore, Z. (2017). International society of sport psychology position stand: Athletes' mental health, performance, and development. *International Journal of Sport and Exercise Psychology*, *16*(6), 1–18.

Schulz, P., Schlotz, W., & Becker, P. (2004). *Trierer Inventar zum chronischen Stress.* Göttingen: Hogrefe.

Smith, R. E. (1986). Toward a cognitive-affective model of athletic burnout. *Journal of Sport Psychology*, *8*(*1*), 36–50.

Wolanin, A., Hong, E., Marks, D., Panchoo, K., & Gross, M. (2016). Prevalence of clinically elevated depressive symptoms in college athletes and differences by gender and sport. *British Journal of Sports Medicine*, *50*(*3*), 167–171. doi:10.1136/bjsports-2015-095756

World Health Organization (2022). *International Classification of Diseases – 11th Revision*. https://icd.who.int/en

Ziemainz, H., Abu-Omar, K., Raedeke, T., & Krause, K. (2004). Burnout im sport. *Leistungssport*, *34*(6), 12–17.

Further reading

Nixdorf, R., Madigan, D., Kenttä, G., & Hassmén, P. (2023). Depression, athlete burnout, and overtraining: A review of similarities and differences. In I. Nixdorf, R. Nixdorf, J. Beckmann, S. Martin, & T. MacIntyre (Eds.), *Routledge Handbook of Mental Health in Elite Sport* (pp. 188–200). Routledge.

Burnout and depression share important features and are sometimes difficult to distinguish. In elite sport, this circumstance is even exacerbated, as the overtraining syndrome adds further complexity to the overlapping syndromes. The chapter provides therefore an integrative model for understanding of the similarities and differences and draws practical recommendations based upon this model.

Schinke, R. J., Stambulova, N. B., Si, G., & Moore, Z. (2017). International society of sport psychology position stand: Athletes' mental health, performance, and development. *International Journal of Sport and Exercise Psychology*, *16*(6), 1–18.

This publication offers a good overview on mental health research in sport psychology. The authors advocate a continuum from active mental illness, to sub-syndromal illness, to normal, to good mental health and to peak performance. This approach is favourable to a dichotomous classification, but further development and elaboration on this understanding is needed.

Nixdorf, I., Beckmann, J., & Nixdorf, R. (2020). Psychological predictors for depression and burnout among German junior elite athletes. *Frontiers in Psychology*, *11*, 601. https://doi.org/10.3389/fpsyg.2020.00601

This publication describes a longitudinal study with the purpose of identifying psychological predicters for burnout and depression. It therefore offers important information for development and prevention of both syndromes.

4

"IT IS JUST A BAD DAY"

Using Rational Emotive Behaviour Therapy to bolster healthy adaptation in a Paralympic athlete

Martin J. Turner, Andrew G. Wood, Jamie B. Barker and Ailish King

Learning objectives

After reading this chapter you should be able to:

1 Understand the origins and central tenets of Rational Emotive Behaviour Therapy (REBT).
2 Understand the effects of irrational and rational beliefs on psychological health.
3 Outline the applications of REBT as an intervention to promote psychological health.
4 Glean professional practice insights into the application of REBT with athletes.

Introduction to REBT

We humans are supposed to be rational creatures, right? The nomenclature that describes our species, Homo Sapiens, would suggest that we are "wise". But as we all know, we (yes, even you) frequently think and act in ways that are unwise, and develop and perpetuate beliefs and ideas about ourselves and the world that are irrational. It is this proclivity for irrationality that is at the centre of psychopathology according to one prominent cognitive behaviour therapy (CBT), namely Rational Emotive Behaviour Therapy (REBT; Ellis, 1957; 1994). But this irrationality is codified very specifically in REBT – in REBT it is not just a lack of applied wisdom that defines irrationality – rather, there are a set of irrational beliefs that have been shown to be particularly pervasive and pernicious for human functioning (e.g., Visla et al., 2016). As

DOI: 10.4324/9781003291695-5

can be seen in Figure 4.1, there are four core irrational beliefs and four core rational beliefs – rational beliefs negate the irrational beliefs. Importantly, the differences between irrational and rational beliefs is not merely academic, it has implications for well-being and performance (Turner, 2016a).

"*There are three musts that hold us back, I must do well, you must treat me well, and the world must be easy*" (Epstein, 2001). The relevance of these "musts" for sport is quite clear, where wanting to do well, wanting people to treat you well, and wanting things to be easy are reasonable hedonistic desires. The problem comes when these desires are elevated to demands. In REBT, we work with clients to challenge and weaken these musts, alongside the other irrational beliefs if relevant, and strengthen rational beliefs. We do this with a view to helping athletes adapt to the adversity of sporting pursuit, maintaining and enhancing health and performance. In this chapter we offer insights into the application of REBT for this aforementioned purpose.

At its core, REBT is based upon the premise that "people are not disturbed by things, but by the view which they take of them" (Epictetus, 1948, 55–135 A.D.) captured within a GABCDE framework (Ellis, 1994; Turner, 2022) as seen in Figure 4.2. To explain, when encountered with an adversity (A, i.e., failure, rejection, setbacks) to ones goals (G) those who harbour irrational beliefs (iB) will experience emotional and behavioural consequences (C) that are *unhealthy* and *maladaptive* for goal attainment (Vîslă, Flückiger, Grosse Holtforth, & David, 2016; David, Szentagotai, Eva, & Macavei, 2005). Whereas those with (rB) rational beliefs, will experience emotional and behavioural consequences (C) that are *healthy* and *adaptive* (Dryden &

Core Irrational Beliefs	*Core Rational Beliefs*
Demandingness: *'I want to, and therefore I must be successful'*	**Preference:** *'I want to, but that does not mean I must be successful'*
Awfulising: *'It would be terrible if I did not win'*	**Anti-Awfulising:** *'It would be bad, but it certainly would not be terrible if I did not win'*
Self-deprecation: *'Losing makes me a complete failure'*	**Unconditional Self-acceptance:** *'If I lost it does not make me a complete failure, only that I have failed this time'*
Frustration Intolerance: *'I could not tolerate losing today'*	**Frustration Tolerance:** *'Although uncomfortable, I could tolerate losing, and it is worth it to do so'*

FIGURE 4.1 Defining characteristics of irrational and rational beliefs.

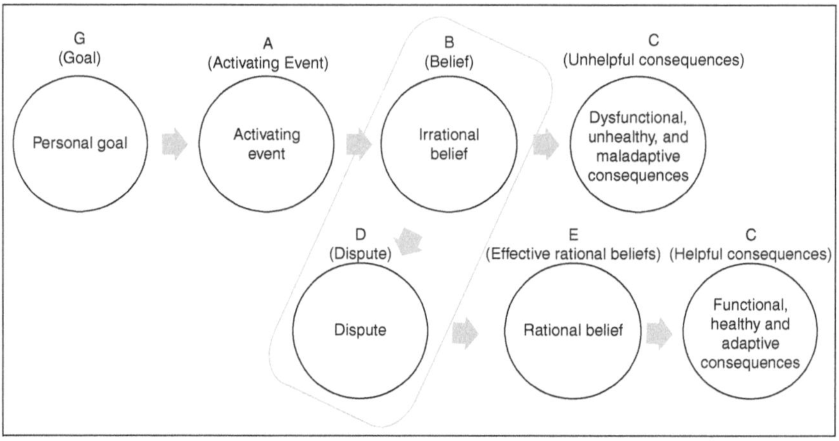

FIGURE 4.2 A schematic of the GABCDE framework central to the REBT process.

Branch, 2008). All humans to varying degrees are inherently irrational and rational, and those operating in elite sport are no exception (King et al., 2022). In REBT, the job is to help athletes dispute (D) their irrational beliefs and develop and strengthen effective new rational beliefs (E). The GABCDE framework thus in part captures the theory and application of REBT (Turner, 2022). This GABCDE framework helps to understand that thoughts, feelings, and actions are interrelated and interdependent (David, Miclea, & Opre, 2004; Turner, 2022), therefore changes in one element can lead to changes in the other elements. Thus, practitioners use a range of cognitive, emotional, and behavioural techniques to promote a functional and adaptive response to adversity.

Elite sport, like any other life of performance settings, is highly demanding and athletes face various organisational, competitive, and personal stressors in the pursuit of performance excellence (Fletcher, Hanton, & Wagstaff, 2012). To compound the challenges of elite sport, the context itself may implicitly encourage irrational beliefs (King et al., 2022; Turner, 2016a). Indeed, there may be a biological basis for irrationality, but irrational beliefs are influenced and driven by our socio-cultural environment (David & DiGiuseppe, 2010; Ellis, 1976). To illustrate, King et al. (2022) argued that we need to apply a whole-environment and whole-person perspective to irrational beliefs in athletes, because an athlete's micro-environment (e.g., comprised of daily communications and interactions) and macro-environment (e.g., which affect but do not directly contain the athletes), play a crucial role in shaping athlete beliefs. First, for some athletes, perceived self-worth is contingent on their ability to perform well and ultimately become successful (Kaplan & Flum, 2010), in turn disproportionately heightening the negative consequences of failure. For example, an athlete may perform in fear due to the belief that if they were to lose this would make them a complete failure and a worthless person. Athletes who are unable to accept themselves as fallible and imperfect human beings are also more susceptible to distress when encountering adversity, through harsh self-criticism and a focus upon personal inadequacies (Flett & Hewitt, 2005). Further, constant exposure to irrational language (e.g., "today is a must win game", "that was terrible today") entrenched into the sporting lexicon may further encourage an irrational approach to achievement (King et al., 2022; Turner, 2016a). Ultimately, the endorsement of irrational beliefs is detrimental to the psychological health of an athlete and hinders psychological resilience (i.e., ability to respond to adversity in a functional and adaptive manner; Dryden & Branch, 2008; Turner, 2016b).

Considering the abundance of research documenting the efficacy of REBT within clinical and non-clinical settings (see David et al., 2005) researchers have begun to evidence the potential value of REBT to understand and promote mental health in athletes (see Jordana et al., 2020 for a systematic review). Research has revealed that the detrimental effects of irrational beliefs on psychological health is overwhelming (David et al., 2005), with the evidence for this growing in sport literature (e.g., Jooste et al., 2022; Turner et al., 2019; Turner et al., 2022). Most notably, irrational beliefs predict increases in symptoms of burnout (i.e., emotional and physical exhaustion; Turner & Moore, 2015), whereas unconditional self-acceptance (a rational belief) has been associated with reduced self-blame and self-criticism (Hill, Hall, Appleton, & Kozub, 2008).

The application of clinical psychotherapeutic frameworks marks a shift in psychological interventions in sport. Using a case-example we aim to engage readers in an approach that moves beyond typical psychological-skills training as would be found with the Canon of sport psychology (i.e., relaxation, self-talk, imagery, goal setting, and concentration; Andersen, 2009), and expands the library of approaches from which sport psychologists are able to draw upon (see Turner et al., 2023, for a range of CBTs applicable to sport). In our chapter, we discuss intervention effects, professional competence, blurred boundaries between therapy and mental skills training, consultant's experience, and professional practice guidelines.

The client

Sarah (pseudonym) was a 42-year-old Paralympic athlete who at the time of the intervention had made the transition to a full-time podium performance programme, training four days a week with the national team. Whilst having ambitions to represent her nation at the upcoming Paralympics Sarah had contacted a Sport Psychologist (SP; Andrew Wood) via email to seek psychological support that would help her adjust to life as a full-time professional athlete, citing a variety of personal and competitive challenges during this transition. Furthermore, it was important to consider Sarah's personal history, specifically in relation to her disability. To respect client confidentiality and anonymity we will not provide explicit detail around her physical disability or medical history. Whilst there is a dearth of research with specialised population groups such as elite athletes with a disability (Barker, Mellalieu, McCarthy, Jones, & Moran, 2013), researchers have begun to put forth important considerations for practitioners. First, athletes with a disability will experience similar (e.g., incompatible coaching style, unfair selection, expectations for medal success) and differing (e.g., inaccessible venues, lack of disability specific coaching, disability classification) stressors to able-bodied athletes (Arnold, Wagstaff, Steadman, & Pratt, 2017). Second, Paralympic athletes will also have varying psychological experiences of disability that are influenced by their history, for example acquired versus congenital (i.e., impairment present from birth). For those athletes with an acquired disability their acquisition of a physical impairment may have been gradual, or after an acute traumatic incident. To illustrate, Skordilis, Skafida, Chrysagis, and Nikitaras (2006) explain that such individuals have to deal with sudden and prolonged psychological crises alternating between acknowledging their pre-disability identity and new "disability" identity. This can be shown in attempting super-human endeavours to portray the control, meaning, and identity they held prior to their injury. In addition, they are likely to only see themselves in a negative light, with diminished self-worth, and in some cases experience severe depression. In contrast, those with a congenital disability experience psychosocial adaptations associated with an impaired body and body image issues. Finally, researchers have also indicated that those with a physical disability are at greater risk to mental illness (e.g., depression; Fassberg et al., 2016).

Initial needs assessment

An intake interview was conducted as an appropriate means to explore Sarah's background, areas for development or concern, details of her sport, and life outside of sport, paying due care to attending to Sarah as a person and a performer (Aoyagi, Poczwardwski, Statler, Shapiro, & Cohen, 2017). No behavioural assessment strategies were implemented due to distance of Sarah's main training centre.

During the initial intake meeting with Sarah it became apparent that Sarah's history, personal events, and introduction to competitive life were inextricably linked, and were having detrimental effects upon her day-to-day functioning and performance. During training camps Sarah would excessively ruminate about personal issues and found it difficult to concentrate and fully immerse herself within training. Acknowledging the detrimental effects upon her training and competition performances, Sarah was angry and began to resent significant others in her personal life for not allowing her the opportunity to fulfil her potential. Subsequently, the resentment detracted from her ability to engage within the Paralympic programme. This dislike towards others was captured within her cognitive distortions such as overgeneralising (e.g., "they must be bad people") and over-personalisation (e.g., "they must be only doing it to me"; Dryden, 2012). Sarah was also becoming overtly concerned about what others thought of her and anxious that she was not meeting others' expectations (i.e., teammates or coaching staff).

During training Sarah was easily agitated and became pent up with anger towards teammates who would distract her from completing her pre-performance routine. For example, she used self-talk such as "don't worry what they do" and "stop thinking about what others are doing". As purported by the ironic processing theory (Wegner, 1994), the more she demanded that others should be more considerate, the more she noticed these transgressions and the harder it became to concentrate, leading to greater physical restlessness.

Much of her psychological unrest (e.g., anxiety, anger) was being externally attributed, and in Sarah's view her emotional disturbance (C) was directly a result of the adversity (A; e.g., others/events) rather than under her control. To compound the matter, the sport in which Sarah participated included minimal physical exertion, whereby success was largely attributed to psychological preparation. With the provision of full-time funding onto the performance programme Sarah was highlighted as a promising addition to the team. Nevertheless, during this transition to the senior team, she was struggling to cope (i.e., lack of concentration, easily angered, disheartened, feeling anxious) with the various personal, competitive, and organisational stressors she encountered, which have also been documented in literature (Fletcher, Hanton, & Mellalieu, 2006).

Based upon her use of irrational language, low levels of emotional control, and inability to cope effectively with challenges that transcended beyond her competitive life, a REBT intervention was selected as an appropriate framework to support and develop Sarah's needs. REBT practitioners are focussed on exploring the breadth of adversities (As) athletes may encounter, and whether their behaviours help or hinder goal achievement. It appeared Sarah held irrational beliefs that were having detrimental effects on her psychological health and ability to respond adaptively to challenges. Both Sarah's personal and sporting life were extremely important to her and she was eager to seek a resolution. Rather than unpicking each "problem", the application of REBT would offer a solution that allowed Sarah to respond in a healthy adaptive manner, irrespective of the situation. In other words, in REBT we try to ensure that the athlete leaves the work able to independently apply REBT to present and future adversity (Turner, 2022). Therefore, it would not just change Sarah's beliefs about one situation, but she would experience a shift towards a rational philosophy (i.e., the endorsement of rational beliefs that are supported empirically, logically, and pragmatically) that would in turn provide a pro-active approach that enhanced her psychological health and would allow her to achieve her respective goals (Turner, 2016a; 2022). A psychometric assessment of her irrational beliefs was conducted using the Shortened General Attitudes and Belief Scale (SGABS; Lindner, Kirkby, Wertheim, & Birch, 1999; see Figure 4.4), a scale that has been used with athletes in the past (Turner & Barker, 2013). Readers should also be aware that the use of the SGABS has been superseded by the irrational Performance Beliefs Inventory-2 (iPBI-2; Turner & Allen, 2018) which has been specifically validated for sport.

Nonetheless, SGABS scores indicated high total irrational beliefs and irrational beliefs related to the content areas of "demand for fairness" ("I must be treated fairly"), "other-downing" ("they are bad people for treating me badly"), and a "need for approval" ("I must be approved of"). It is important to state Sarah, like all humans, was not *wholly* irrational, and athletes will vary in the extent that they endorse both irrational and rational beliefs. The REBT intervention would provide a pro-active approach that not only reduced irrational beliefs but also bolstered a rational view of adversity. REBT is originally a psychotherapeutic intervention applied in clinical settings. In Sarah's case, the scope of the consultancy was not to address or treat a clinically diagnosed mental illness, but the aim was to rather use concepts and the framework of REBT (i.e., GABCDE framework) as a pro-active approach to bolster the foundations for wellbeing and effective functioning. Hence it was important to understand and be sensitive to the somewhat blurry lines of professional competence (Roberts, Faull, & Tod, 2016). To monitor the effects of REBT and changes in Sarah's irrational beliefs measures of total irrational beliefs, demand for fairness, other-downing, and a need for approval from significant others were collected on a weekly basis. To undertake social validation, a semi-structured interview was conducted with Sarah to ascertain the intervention effects, successful receipt, and practitioner evaluation.

REBT can of course be applied in conjunction with other approaches to sport psychology provision, such as the Canon of psychological skills (Andersen, 2009) given that both have their taxonomical roots buried in cognitive behaviourism (Turner, 2022). But, REBT is distinct from other approaches in the following ways:

1 **Getting Better and Staying Better** – Rather than just alleviating deleterious symptomology, REBT targets the root cause of athlete malaise (irrational beliefs & unhelpful behaviours; Dryden & Neenan, 2015). Rather than offering a short-term "sticky plaster", REBT aims to bring about meaningful and longer-term psychological change (i.e., self-efficacy, enjoyment, motivation, performance; Wood et al., 2017). Regular travel to national and international competitions was an inherent part of Sarah's sport engagement. By working through the GABCDE framework Sarah would

gain both psychological insight into her own behaviours and techniques to recognise, re-appraise, and reinforce new rational beliefs. Thus, once REBT was delivered sufficiently, Sarah would be autonomous and independent in maintaining a new rational view of adversity, and the role as a practitioner would become partially redundant.

2 **Fostering Adaptation** – Instead of adopting a deficit view, REBT offers a pro-active intervention that bolsters a rational philosophy towards both participation in competitive sport and how this fits into a person's life as a whole. In turn, athletes become resilient to the acute and chronic stressors that they will inevitably encounter (Deen, Turner, & Wong, 2017; Turner, 2016b). In Sarah's case the successful disputation of irrational beliefs with rational alternatives would foster a helpful and adaptive response to stressors across all aspects of her life, and not just restricted to sport.
3 **Active Acceptance of the Circumstances** – REBT does not *usually* dispute the adversity (A) but assumes it to be true. For example, an athlete may be extremely anxious about an important competition. Rather than disputing the athletes' inference that this is an important competition (e.g., trying to convince them that it is less important), practitioners dispute (D) their irrational beliefs (B) about the adversity (A) and aims to weaken them and help develop and strengthen rational alternatives (E). Essentially, athletes will become proficient in responding functionally irrespective of the circumstances, acknowledging the situation they face rather than telling themselves that this is not happening or burying their head in the sand. When faced with adversity the ability to shift her mindset from the situation (i.e., uncontrollable) to her own beliefs and response (i.e., controllable) was particularly important for Sarah; as much of what she found challenging in her personal or competitive lives were *unchangeable.*
4 **Changing Perceptions of Negative Emotions** – REBT advocates that negative emotions prior to, during, or after adversity are normal and vital on the path to goal attainment. Rather than focussing on emotional valence (positive vs. negative), the focus in REBT is on *unhealthy* vs *healthy.* In turn, this shift in perceiving negative emotions as helpful allows the athletes to then manage the situation and return to a normative or positive state in a somewhat swift fashion. Indeed, research indicates that greater irrational beliefs are related to the belief that stress is debilitative (Mansell, 2021). The process of normalising negative emotions would help Sarah prevent the development of meta-emotions when encountering adversity (i.e., not becoming depressed about being angry, or becoming more anxious about being anxious).

REBT intervention

REBT is perhaps most effective when delivered on a one-to-one basis, or at least, it is the one-to-one mode of delivery for which we have the most convincing evidence (Jordana et al., 2020). But group REBT has been shown to be effective (e.g., increasing performance under pressure; Nejati et al., 2022). In one-to-one REBT, practitioners are able to develop a strong working alliance whilst matching the pace, content, and delivery style to the client. Taking into consideration the contextual and pragmatic constraints, five one-to-one sessions and four homework tasks were delivered, each lasting for approximately forty-five minutes. The intervention was separated into an education, disputation, and reinforcement phase (see Turner & Barker, 2014 for an overview). The quality of relationship between the psychologist and the client is consistently shown as a leading factor towards successful intervention outcomes (Keegan, 2016; Woody & Adessky, 2002). A collaborative and empathetic approach is particularly pertinent to REBT delivery. Elements of the REBT process required Sarah to recall challenging events (i.e., education phase) whereby the success of the disputation phases requires a willingness to let go of deeply held irrational beliefs and replace them with healthy and rational alternatives. Therefore, it was and still remains central for those using REBT to develop a strong working alliance with the client from the onset of the intervention (Bernard & Dryden, 2019; Turner, 2022), whether it's through varying one's likeability, credibility, or through intentional self-disclosure (i.e., helping to normalise her position; Dryden & Neenan, 2015).

Education phase

The education phase was conducted over two sessions and aimed to show Sarah that it was her beliefs (B) that determined the functionality of feelings and actions (C) rather than the adversity alone (A). To begin, Sarah was asked to detail either the most recent or a poignant situation (A) that she had recently experienced and found challenging. Athletes will typically report an account that implicitly refers to the adversity (A) or their response (C), as well offer clues to what their underlying beliefs might be. Therefore, it is up to the practitioner to pinpoint and guide the client towards unpicking the example in a strategic fashion. A poignant adversity (A) for Sarah was not being able to voice her own needs, instead having to prioritise the needs of others and feeling at the maximum capacity as to what she could deal with. Sarah then detailed the corresponding unhealthy and dysfunctional feelings (i.e., anger, guilt), thoughts (i.e., resentment towards others), physical responses (e.g., somatic symptoms), action tendencies (e.g., what she wanted to do), and behaviours (i.e., acting out or avoiding conflict). Following this, Sarah described what a functional response to the same situation would look like (e.g., "when this situation arises again how would you like to respond?"). This was important as it highlighted that a negative feeling to the situation was normal, and that a negative yet functional alternative was possible. At this point it was important to agree upon a goal that Sarah would work towards if this situation were to arise again; Sarah wanted to find the balance between prioritising her own and other's needs. After checking in with Sarah to clarify her understanding at the end of the first session, she was asked to complete an A-C diary of any challenging moments that she might experience before our next session. The Sport Psychologist (SP) also asked her to ponder what she might be currently telling herself about the situation that led her to feeling and acting in this way. This was left purposefully vague, so that Sarah had the impetus to reflect on her own beliefs, typically a process people do not engage in in a typical day. It was important to tailor the pace of the education phase to Sarah's needs because sufficient understanding of the REBT framework lays the foundation for subsequent phases. Sarah was also encouraged to voice any doubts, concerns, or questions by the SP (Dryden & Branch, 2008). Over the course of the first session Sarah was open and engaged with the intervention content (i.e., GABCDE framework) and was curious as to what would be uncovered during the next session in a week's time.

At the beginning of session two, we began by reviewing Sarah's homework task (i.e., A-C diary). This provided an opportunity to check her understanding, as well begin to discuss the beliefs that Sarah held in this given situation. Here Sarah was asked "what are you telling yourself about the situation (i.e., having to prioritise others needs over her own) that was leading to responding in this way?". Sarah's response alluded to others not respecting or understanding her needs: For example, "I would like others to consider my needs as well as their own, therefore they must, and if they do not consider my needs, they are completely inconsiderate and I cannot tolerate these kinds of people". When asking clients about their underlying beliefs, it is only in exceptional cases where they will allude to their underlying beliefs straightway. Here an *inference chaining* exercise (Dryden, 1995) allowed the SP to explore the underlying irrational beliefs upon which Sarah based her inferences and evaluations of the adversity (A). This process involved asking Sarah what was so anger provoking about this adversity (e.g., "having to support others"), where she would reply with an inference (e.g., "not being able to prioritise herself and her sport"). The SP then continuously asked the same question for each inference before eventually reaching the critical A, which is the A that is most triggering of the athlete's core irrational belief. Whilst seemingly very specific, this belief is essentially underpinned by a sense of injustice and/or unfairness. If the SP was then able to alter her irrational beliefs when Sarah faced a sense of unfairness, in the future the new rational alternatives would be both applicable and ensured she responded in a healthy and functional manner. For the remainder of the second session, the SP worked with Sarah to enhance her self-awareness and familiarity of the REBT process by working through various ABC frameworks for various situations that she found challenging.

Disputation phase

The disputation phase is arguably the most important part of the REBT process. The main aim was to help Sarah to challenge her irrational beliefs and maladaptive behaviours and to help her develop and strengthen rational alternatives. Disputing beliefs can be a challenging and sensitive process, therefore it was important to manage Sarah's expectations, as well seek her permission to continue (Turner, 2022). Initially Sarah's irrational beliefs were challenged empirically (i.e., "where is it written that others must be considerate towards you"), logically (i.e., "just because you want them to be, does that mean they have to be?"), and pragmatically (i.e., "where has this belief got you so far?"). It was apparent from Sarah's mannerisms and verbal feedback that the didactic and directive nature of the disputation phase was unexpected but that she remained open to collaboratively discussing the definitions of an irrational belief. During REBT not only do we work to weaken irrational beliefs, but we endeavour to foster and enhance athlete endorsement of rational beliefs (see Figure 4.3 for an example). Based upon Sarah's four core irrational beliefs,

Aversity (A) *1st/2nd	
"Team-mates actions disrupting my performance"	
Irrational Beliefs (B) *4th	**Rational Beliefs (B) *5th**
I really want my teammates to be more considerate towards me, therefore they must be. I cannot tolerate it when they are inconsiderate, it is terrible, and makes them completely bad people.	I really want my teammates to be more considerate towards me, but that doesn't mean they have to be. Although difficult, I could tolerate it when they are inconsiderate, it is annoying but it certainly wouldn't be terrible, and doesn't make them completely bad people.
Unhealthy Negative Consequences (C) *1st/2nd	**Healthy Negative Consequences (C) *3rd**
Inward Anger Physical Tension Agitation Verbal Aggression Loss of Concentration	Slightly Annoyed. Acceptance of the situation and others. Find humour in the situation. Little resentment towards others. Able to deal with distractions and refocus on performance routines.

FIGURE 4.3 An example ABC framework formulation proforma completed with Sarah during the disputation phase.

* Indicates the order in which a practitioner will typically work through the framework.

four new rational alternatives were established: preference; anti-awfulizing; high-frustration tolerance; and unconditional self/life/other acceptance (see Figure 4.3). The newly established rational beliefs were then subjected to a similar disputation process (i.e., empirical, logical, and pragmatic arguments). This is good practice for the main reason irrational and rational beliefs are thought to exist on separate spectrums, where low levels of irrational beliefs do not signify high levels of rational beliefs (Ellis, David, & Lynn, 2010). Therefore, the disputation of rational beliefs reinforced the truth, logic, and helpful nature of her new rational beliefs. We have to hold both irrational and rational beliefs to the same standards of evidence, logic, and pragmatics. During the GABCDE framework practitioners will typically start by exploring either the adversity (A) or unhelpful negative consequences (C). Next, the helpful negative consequence and overarching goal will be outlined before the core irrational beliefs (B) are explored. Once the irrational beliefs have been agreed, the SP will help the athlete dispute (D) the irrational beliefs, and develop effective new rational beliefs E. Not restricted to one example, the GABCDE framework was repeated using pertinent and challenging adversities that Sarah experienced within and outside of sport.

Disputation and reinforcement phase

Continuing from the previous session, the disputation and reinforcement phase was conducted over two sessions and one homework task. Whilst the early phases of REBT can be quite formulaic within its delivery, the latter part allows the practitioner to be more flexible in the exercises (i.e., badness scale, reversal role-play), techniques (i.e., cognitive, emotive, or behavioural), and style (i.e., didactic or Socratic) suited towards the clients' needs. Whilst the disputation phases may represent a turning point, there would be occasions for Sarah to test her new ability to manage adversity, as such the current phases would help reaffirm Sarah's new rational view. For example, whilst away on an international competition, one night Sarah had little to no sleep due to a teammate who was speaking loudly on the phone for long periods of time. As a result, she had become extremely angry, resenting her teammate for not allowing her to rest appropriately, perpetuating her physical frustrations and anxiety that this would now hinder her ability to perform. These examples show how Sarah was able to reflect on and consider an alternative response for the future. The following non-exhaustive techniques were used over the last two sessions to help dispute and reinforce a rational philosophy.

To target Sarah's propensity to awfulise (i.e., "it is terrible when others treat me unfairly") and gain perspective during relatively trivial moments, a technique known as a "badness scale" was used (Ellis et al., 1997). By rating a situation as terrible Sarah was implying that there was nothing worse in this world than being treated unfairly, thus disproportionately magnifying the consequences of being treated unfairly. First, Sarah placed numerical percentage of badness on a scale from 0–100 using a variety of life and sporting adversities. Initially, the SP offered relatively trivial examples (e.g., losing a wallet, having a cold) that were scored low on the scale. Second, the SP then offered a range of adversities that he knew would resonate with Sarah's irrational beliefs (e.g., being treated unfairly, negative judgement from coaches); expectedly these examples were placed much higher (60–100%). Following this Sarah was provided with a series of major adversities (e.g., death of a loved one) at which she suddenly came to realise that whilst being treated unfairly is bad, it certainly is not terrible. Ultimately, REBT theory proposes nothing is 100% awful and the badness scale provides a way to help athletes adjust their perspective.

To target Sarah's tendency for self and/or other downing (i.e., they are completely bad for treating me this way), we completed a "Big I & Little I" task (Lazarus, 1977). Sarah was asked to draw a large I and inside it draw a variety of little i's. Here Sarah labelled each little i as an aspect of her life, the size representing its significance (i.e., family, friends, teammates). This exercise allowed Sarah to visually observe how we are unable to wholly rate people based on a single unfavourable action/outcome. We discussed famous examples in which people appear to be evil/bad people (i.e., dictators, serial killers), but in fact are not.

To further embed new rational beliefs, An Athlete Rational Resilience Credo (ARRC; Turner, 2016b) was used. A credo is defined as "a set of beliefs, which expresses a particular opinion and influences the way you live" (Dryden, 2007, p. 219). In Sarah's case, the ARRC was used to create a clear rational view that she was able to aim for and foster a rational philosophy of life. Initially, Sarah was asked to read and discuss elements of the credo. The SP then asked Sarah to personalise and re-write elements of the Credo for use whilst at home, training, or during competitions.

A behavioural technique was also used for Sarah's homework named "In vivo desensitization" (Froggat, 2005) or flooding (Ellis, 1980). Sarah was asked to seek out and approach challenging situations (e.g., facing evaluation from the coaches) rather than avoid them. Irrational beliefs are contextually sensitive and heightened in settings particularly important for the athlete (e.g., performance & family settings), and it was vital that Sarah could experientially test and challenge her old irrational beliefs, and reinforce them with rational beliefs in situations.

Intervention evaluation and lessons learned through self-reflection

Over the course of the final two sessions Sarah was making good progress and engaging with the homework tasks with utmost diligence. To illustrate the intervention effects and to draw together salient themes, the present section will be separated into 1) effects of REBT on Sarah's psychological resilience,

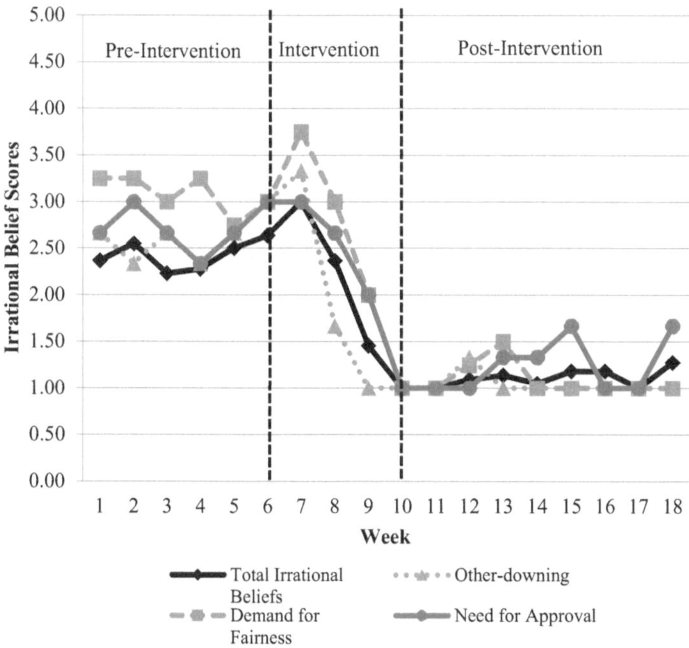

FIGURE 4.4 Meaningful and maintained reductions in irrational beliefs before and after the REBT intervention.

2) practitioner evaluation, and 3) lessons learned and professional practitioner insights gleaned during the consultancy process.

Healthy thoughts and feelings

The use of a questionnaire (i.e., the SGABS) offered a practical and validated measure of Sarah's irrational beliefs. Following this, a semi-structured interview provided a useful way to explore and understand if and/or how these changes impacted her on her ability to manage and overcome the various stressors that she faced, and thus become more resilient. Sarah first indicated changes in her thoughts when experiencing challenging moments. For example, during competitive events Sarah was able to concentrate on her performances instead of becoming embroiled within an inner dialogue – denigrating others for providing a distraction. Although subtle, Sarah was showing signs of emotional responsibility even though the situation (A) did not dictate one; rather she alone was responsible for the functionality of her response. The following quote highlights this eloquently:

> I don't get drawn into irritations on the shooting line anymore. I just ignore the nonsense going on around me, even deflecting what could be deliberate distractions and laughing them off in my head

As a result of the intervention, Sarah noted how her perception of others had shifted. Based on the core rational belief of unconditional self/other/life acceptance Sarah did not globally condemn significant others for a single action (e.g., "they are a completely bad person because they treated me unfairly"), but instead she rated their behaviour as opposed to them as a whole (e.g., "even though they have treated me unfairly that does not mean they are a completely bad person"). Looking beyond the performance benefits, a rational view of others helped Sarah to strengthen relationships, in turn enhancing her peer interaction and the social support she was able to seek. The following quote articulates this point well:

> My perception of others has changed, I think I look more kindly on people now. I always thought I saw the best in people, where people in the past I have thought no I don't want to talk to them they will talk my head off, I now think well actually they could with someone to talk to.

After making a rational shift and altering her perceptions of others, Sarah was also able to brush over minor stressors and return to a normative or positive state in a somewhat swift manner. Not to mistake this for indifference towards others' actions, she rather experiences a healthy negative emotion when encountering other people's challenging behaviour. Sarah noted:

> The intense frustration I used to experience has gone now, I might still think that's inconsiderate but it doesn't frustrate as much and I don't need five minutes in a quiet room.

Humour and anti-awfulising

When used with sensitivity, humour can be an important component of REBT. During the latter phases of the intervention, Sarah was encouraged to reflect on her old beliefs with a wry smile and take perspective on what used to be "awful" and "terrible" circumstances. For example, missing the first training session of a camp may have been awful, because this reflected badly upon her professionalism. In contrast Sarah could re-appraise challenging situations by using rational self-talk:

> I will say to myself that it isn't a catastrophe; it is just a bad day and then have a little chuckle about it. I did use the words awful and horrendous and catastrophic and it just isn't, and I have stopped using that now.

Rational philosophy and resilience

The social validation data indicated that Sarah responded to adversity in a healthy and adaptive manner that helped rather than hindered her respective goals, thus experiencing a shift towards a rational philosophy. Irrespective of the context, a rational view ultimately leads to healthy emotions, and an adaptive response facilitates goal achievement (Dryden & Branch, 2008). The GABCDE framework that Sarah now understood and used as a guiding framework presented a model of optimal human functioning and resilience. Indeed, researchers have highlighted the similarities between REBT and the concept of resilience (e.g., Deen et al., 2017; Turner, 2016b). Resilience is considered a process of adapting well in the face of adversity, whereby experiencing emotional distress is a part of becoming resilient (Turner, 2016b). Further, findings support the notion that resilience is a capacity that develops over time in the context of person-environment interactions (Egeland, Carlson, & Sroufe, 1993). Essentially, resilience is becoming an important predictor of wellbeing, mental health, and performance in sport (Sarkar & Fletcher, 2014), as such REBT presents an effective means to restore, maintain, and develop an athlete's psychological health. The following quotes eloquently highlight this rational shift:

> I feel these sessions have been incredibly helpful and I have gained tools that I will use for the rest of my life... . They have helped me to deal with everyday situations which would normally irritate, silly things which would get me down I don't have anymore. Yeah, I feel better in control of my emotions throughout the day, so it has helped.

Practitioner evaluation

Social validation showed that prior to the intervention showed that Sarah was concerned that the practitioner (myself) may be disinterested and would offer psychological support just by going through the motions. Nevertheless, by the end of the intervention process Sarah revealed:

> It was obvious from the outset that Andrew [the SP] was committed and friendly. I trusted him and he was incredibly enthusiastic about getting me to understand and enjoy the process of learning.

This notion was further validated using a Likert-scale from 1 (*Not at all*) to 7 (*Extremely*) whereby Sarah reported a 7, 6, and a 6 for motivation, effort, and enthusiasm in relation to the REBT intervention process. A central aim of REBT is to weaken irrational beliefs and strengthen rational alternatives; therefore, Sarah's endorsement of irrational beliefs were collected on a weekly basis. Using a single-case baseline design (Barker et al., 2013) Sarah reported meaningful short-term and long-term reductions in irrational beliefs between pre- and post-intervention phases (see Figure 4.4). These reductions indicated the effective application of REBT and a rational shift in the way Sarah viewed/perceived adverse situations.

Professional practice insights and lessons learned

As with any consultancy it was important to seek Sarah's feedback and reflect on elements of the intervention that could have been refined for future practice. First, Sarah was confused about the differentiation in healthy versus unhealthy negative emotions. This was further perpetuated by varying interpretations of REBT terminology. For example, the meaning I (practitioner) draw from the word "anxious" (e.g., unhealthy negative emotion) may have been different to Sarah's definition (a normal sensation before competition). To negate pitfalls in semantics it would be important to clarify terminology and use common language throughout the REBT process. For example, when using the term "frustration" this may represent a healthy negative emotion, whereas "rage" indicated a unhealthy alternative. To illustrate, Lindsay, Pitt, and Thomas (2014) discuss the conceptual confusions, misunderstandings, and misguided use of language that may hinder effective sport psychology practice.

Sarah also highlighted that having sessions delivered closely together allowed her to better sustain the momentum from previous sessions and apply the intersession tasks whilst the session content was still fresh within her thoughts. To outline this point Sarah noted:

> If the sessions can be bunched up together, that is better, so that you can remember what has happened each week, [and] so you can put it into practice that week then reinforce it when you sit back down. If there are three weeks between talking about it and talking about it again then you have forgotten some of the skills you were trying to learn, so it was much better being bunched up.

Targeting irrational beliefs and promoting rational alternatives can be a difficult process due to the often subconscious and deeply held nature of beliefs (Dryden & Neenan, 2015). Furthermore, all humans are inherently irrational and rational beings and whilst initially the participant may report reduced irrational beliefs, it is vital to continuously reinforce rational alternatives. In turn, such a rational view becomes a habituated and automatic response when encountering various challenges. Although not used in the present case, Turner and Wood (2019) developed and recommend a smartphone application that allows athletes to dispute and re-appraise challenging situations in situ; subsequently the brief and intuitive process provides the user with a set of rational beliefs for their given situation. To this end, the practitioner does not become a crutch, and athletes are provided with the autonomy to self-monitor and re-appraise challenging moments.

The present case shows the effectiveness and suitability of REBT as an intervention to bolster the psychological health of an elite athlete with a physical disability. As mentioned previously athletes with a disability will experience similar and additional stressors compared to able-bodied athletes (e.g., Arnold et al., 2017), further justifying the application of REBT as an approach to develop a rational view and psychological resilience. Nevertheless, it would be prudent to understand and/or make the following considerations. First, one should reflect on the biases and preconceptions that one may harbour regarding disability sport. Here, athletes are not defined by their disability, and shifts in terminology although subtle can clarify this point (e.g., athletes with disability, rather than disabled athletes). Second, one should find a balance between propagating autonomy, whilst making the necessary adjustments to meet their needs. Third, although in Sarah's case no amendments were made, consideration should be given to the delivery of the intervention (e.g., format, pace, resources). For example, there may exists complexities in the clients' history that will influence the athlete's willingness and/or ability to change.

The premise of REBT is simple yet powerful. The application of REBT to bolster mental health is not restricted just to elite sport, but can transcend other highly demanding settings (e.g., Healthcare, Military, Business, Emergency Services), essentially offering a framework of optimal functioning and resilience. Looking ahead, researchers are recommended to explore how irrational and/or rational beliefs are socialised, having implications for practitioners looking to foster rational environments in the pursuit of psychological health and performance.

References

Andersen, M. B. (2009). The "canon" of psychological skills training for enhancing performance. In K. F. Hays(Ed.), *Performance Psychology In Action: A Casebook for Working with Athletes, Performing Artists, Business Leaders, And Professionals in High-Risk Occupations* (pp. 11–34). Washington, DC: American Psychological Association.

Aoyagi, M. W., Poczwardwski, A., Statler, T., Shapiro, J. L., & Cohen, A. B. (2017). The performance interview guide: Recommendations for initial consultations in sport and performance psychology. *Professional Psychology: Research and Practice*, *48*, 352–360.

Arnold, R., Wagstaff, C. R., Steadman, L., & Pratt, Y. (2017). The organisational stressors encountered by athletes with a disability. *Journal of Sports Sciences*, *35*, 1187–1196.

Barker, J. B., Mellalieu, S. D., McCarthy, P. J., Jones, M. V., & Moran, A. (2013). A review of single-case research in sport psychology 1997–2012: Research trends and future directions. *Journal of Applied Sport Psychology*, *25*, 4–32.

Bernard, M. E., & Dryden, W. (2019). *Advances in REBT: Theory, Practice, Research, Measurement, Prevention And Promotion*. Switzerland: Springer Nature.

David, D., & DiGiuseppe, R. (2010). Social and cultural aspects of rational and irrational beliefs: A brief reconceptualization. In D David., S. J. Lynn & A Ellis (Eds.), *Rational and Irrational Beliefs: Research, Theory, and Clinical Practice* (pp. 49–61). London: Oxford University Press.

David, D., Miclea, M., & Opre, A. (2004). The information-processing approach to the human mind: Basics and beyond. *Journal of Clinical Psychology*, *60*, 353–368. doi:10.1002/jclp.10250

David, D., Szentagotai, A., Eva, K., & Macavei, B. (2005). A synopsis of rational-emotive behavior therapy (REBT): Fundamental and applied research. *Journal of Rational-Emotive & Cognitive-Behavior Therapy*, *23*, 175–221. doi:10.1007/s10942-005-0011-0

Deen, S., Turner, M. J., & Wong, R. S. (2017). The effects of REBT, and the use of credos, on irrational beliefs and resilience qualities in athletes. *The Sport Psychologist*, *31*(3), 1–39.

Dryden, W. (1995). *Brief Rational Emotive Behaviour Therapy*. Chichester: Wiley-Blackwell.

Dryden, W. (2007). Resilience and rationality. *Journal of Rational-Emotive & Cognitive-Behavior Therapy*, *25*, 213–226. doi:10.1007/s10942-006-0050-1

Dryden, W. (2012). The "ABCs" of REBT I: A preliminary study of errors and confusions in counselling and psychotherapy textbooks. *Journal of Rational-Emotive & Cognitive-Behavior Therapy*, *30*, 133–172.

Dryden, W., & Branch, R. (2008). *The Fundamentals of Rational Emotive Behaviour Therapy* (2nd ed.). Chichester: John Wiley & Sons, Ltd.

Dryden, W., & Neenan, M. (2015). *Rational Emotive Behaviour Therapy: 100 Key Points and Techniques*. Hove: Routledge.

Egeland, B., Carlson, E., & Sroufe, L. A. (1993). Resilience as process. *Development and Psychopathology*, *5*, 517–528. doi:10.1017/S0954579400006131

Ellis, A. (1957). Rational psychotherapy and individual psychology. *Journal of Individual Psychology*, *13*, 38–44.

Ellis, A. (1976). The biological basis of human irrationality. *Journal of Individual Psychology*, *32*(2), 145–168.

Ellis, A. (1980). *Rational-emotive therapy and cognitive behavior therapy: Similarities and differences. Cognitive Therapy and Research*, *4*(4), 325–340.

Ellis, A. (1994). *Reason and Emotion in Psychotherapy* (2nd ed). Carol Publishing Group.

Ellis, A., David, D., & Lynn, S. J. (2010). Rational and irrational beliefs: A historical and conceptual perspective. In D. David, S. J. Lynn, & A. Ellis(Eds.), *Rational and Irrational Beliefs in Human Functioning and Disturbances*. Oxford: Oxford University Press.

Ellis, A., Gordon, J., Neenan, M., & Palmer, S. (1997). *Stress Counselling: A Rational Emotive Behavior Approach*. Cassell.

Epictetus. (1948). *The Enchiridion*. Indianapolis: Bobbs-Merrill.

Epstein, R. (2001). *The Prince of Reason, an Interview with Albert Ellis*. Retrieved May 15, 2009, from www.psychologytoday.com/articles/200101/the-prince-reason

Fässberg, M. M., Cheung, G., Canetto, S. S., Erlangsen, A., Lapierre, S., Lindner, R., … Duberstein, P. (2016). A systematic review of physical illness, functional disability, and suicidal behaviour among older adults. *Aging & Mental Health*, *20*, 166–194.

Fletcher, D., Hanton, S., & Mellalieu, S. D. (2006). An organizational stress review: Conceptual and theoretical issues in competitive sport. InS. Hanton & S. D. Mellalieu (Eds.), *Literature Reviews in Sport Psychology* (pp. 321–373). New York, NY: Nova Science.

Fletcher, D., Hanton, S., & Wagstaff, C. R. (2012). Performers' responses to stressors encountered in sport organisations. *Journal of Sports Sciences*, *30*, 349–358.

Flett, G. L., & Hewitt, P. L. (2005). The perils of perfectionism in sports and exercise. *Cur-rent Directions in Psychological Science*, *14*, 14–18.

Froggatt, W. (2005). A brief introduction to rational emotive behaviour therapy. *Journal of Rational-Emotive and Cognitive Behaviour Therapy*, *3*, 1–15.

Hill, A. P., Hall, H. K., Appleton, P. R., & Kozub, S. A. (2008). Perfectionism and burnout in junior elite soccer players: The mediating influence of unconditional self-acceptance. *Psychology of Sport and Exercise*, *9*, 630–644. doi:10.1016/j.psychsport.2007.09.004

Jooste, J., Wolfson, S., & Kruger, A. (2022). Irrational performance beliefs and mental well-being upon returning to sport during the COVID-19 pandemic: A test of mediation by intolerance of uncertainty. *Research Quarterly for Exercise and Sport*. doi: 10.1080/02701367.2022.2056117

Jordana, A., Turner, M. J., Ramis, Y., & Torregrossa, M. (2020). A systematic mapping review on the use of Rational Emotive Behavior Therapy (REBT) with athletes. *International Review of Sport and Exercise Psychology*. doi: 10.1080/1750984X.2020.1836673

Kaplan, A., & Flum, H. (2010). Achievement goal orientations and identity formation styles. *Educational Research Review*, *5*, 50–67.

Keegan, R. J. (2016). *Being a Sport Psychologist: The Intake Process: Establishing a Relationship, Aims, Expectations, and Reality*. London: Palgrave Macmillan.

King, A., Barker, J. B., Turner, M. J., & Plateau, C. (2022). The socialisation of athlete irrational beliefs. *Journal of Rational-Emotive & Cognitive-Behavior Therapy*. https://doi.org/10.1080/1612197X.2022.2152852

Lazarus, A. A. (1977). Towards an egoless state of being. In A. Ellis & R. Grieger (Eds.), *Handbook of Rational-Emotive Therapy*. Springer Publishing Company.

Lindner, H., Kirkby, R., Wertheim, E., & Birch, P. (1999). A brief assessment of irrational thinking: The shortened general attitude and belief scale. *Cognitive Therapy and Research*, *23*, 651–663.

Lindsay, P., Pitt, T., & Thomas, O. (2014). Bewitched by our words: Wittgenstein, language-games, and the pictures that hold sport psychology captive. *Sport and Exercise Psychology Review*, *10*, 4.

Mansell, P. C. (2021). Stress mindset in athletes: Investigating the relationships between beliefs, challenge and threat with psychological wellbeing. *Psychology of Sport and Exercise*, *57*.

Nejati, M., Farsi, A., Moteshareie, E., Miller, A., & Turner, M. J. (2022). The effects of rational emotive behavior therapy (REBT) on performance under pressure in adolescent soccer athletes: A randomized control design. *International Journal of Sport and Exercise Psychology*. https://doi.org/10.1080/1612197X.2022.2152852

Roberts, C. M., Faull, A. L., & Tod, D. (2016). Blurred lines: Performance enhancement, common mental disorders and referral in the UK athletic population. *Frontiers in Psychology*, *7*, 1067.

Sarkar, M., & Fletcher, D. (2014). Psychological resilience in sport performers: A review of stressors and protective factors. *Journal of Sports Sciences*, *32*, 1419–1434.

Skordilis, E. K., Skafida, F. A., Chrysagis, N., & Nikitaras, N. (2006). Comparison of sport achievement orientation of male wheelchair basketball athletes with congenital and acquired disabilities. *Perceptual and Motor Skills*, *103*, 726–732. doi:10.2466/pms.103.3.726-732

Turner, M. J. (2016a). Rational Emotive Behavior Therapy (REBT), irrational and rational beliefs, and the mental health of athletes. *Frontiers in Psychology*, *7*. doi:10.3389/fpsyg.2016.01423

Turner, M. J. (2016b). Proposing a rational resilience credo for use with athletes. *Journal of Sport Psychology in Action*, *7*, 170–181. doi:10.1080/21520704.2016.1236051

Turner, M. J. (2022). *The Rational Practitioner: The Sport and Performance Psychologist's Guide To Practicing Rational Emotive Behaviour Therapy*. Routledge.

Turner, M. J., & Allen, M. (2018). Confirmatory factor analysis of the irrational Performance Beliefs Inventory (iPBI) in a sample of amateur and semi-professional athletes. Psychology of Sport and Exercise, 35, 126–130. https://doi.org/10.1016/j.psychsport.2017.11.017

Turner, M. J., Aspin, G., & Gillman, J. (2019). Maladaptive schema as a potential mechanism through which irrational beliefs relate to psychological distress in athletes. *Psychology of Sport & Exercise*, *44*, 9–16. https://doi.org/10.1016/j.psychsport.2019.04.015

Turner, M. J., & Barker, J. B. (2013). Examining the efficacy of Rational-Emotive Behavior Therapy (REBT) on irrational beliefs and anxiety in elite youth cricketers. *Journal of Applied Sport Psychology*, *25*(1), 131–147.

Turner, M. J., & Barker, J. B. (2014). Using rational emotive behavior therapy with athletes. *The Sport Psychologist*, *28*, 75–90. doi:10.1123/tsp.2013-0012

Turner, M. J., Jones, M. V., & Wood, A. G. (2023). Applying Cognitive Behavioural Therapeutic Approaches in Sport. Routledge.

Turner, M. J., & Moore, M. (2015). Irrational beliefs predict increased emotional and physical exhaustion in Gaelic football athletes. *International Journal of Sport Psychology*, *47*, 187–199.

Turner, M. J., Miller, A., Youngs, H., Barber, N., Brick, N. E., Chadha, N. J., Chandler, C., Coyle, M., Didymus, F. F., Evans, A. L., Jones, K., McCann, B., Meijen, C., & Rossato, C. J. L. (2022). "I must do this!": A latent profile analysis approach to understanding the role of irrational beliefs and motivation regulation in mental and physical health. *Journal of Sports Sciences*. doi: 10.1080/02640414.2022.2042124

Turner, M. J., & Wood, A. G. (2019). The Smarter Thinking App (Version 1.0.2). [Mobile app]. Google Play Store. https://play.google.com/store/apps/details?id=com.smarterthinkingprofile.smarterthinking&gl=GB

Vîslă, A., Flückiger, C., Grosse Holtforth, M., & David, D. (2016). Irrational beliefs and psychological distress: A meta-analysis. *Psychotherapy and Psychosomatics*, *85*, 8–15. doi:10.1159/000441231

Wegner, D. M. (1994). Ironic processes of mental control. *Psychological Review*, *101*, 34–52.

Wood, A. G., Barker, J., & Turner, M. J. (2017). Developing performance using Rational Emotive Behavior Therapy (REBT): A case study with an elite archer. *The Sport Psychologist*, *31*, 78–87.

Woody, S. R., & Adessky, R. S. (2002). Therapeutic alliance, group cohesion, and homework compliance during cognitive-behavioral group treatment of social phobia. *Behavior Therapy*, *33*, 5–27.

Further reading

Turner, M. J. (2016). Rational Emotive Behavior Therapy (REBT), irrational and rational beliefs, and the mental health of athletes. *Frontiers in Psychology*, *7*. doi:10.3389/fpsyg. 2016.01423

This article provides a review into the framework of REBT as an intervention to both understand and promote mental health in athletes.

Turner, M. J. (2022). *The Rational Practitioner: The Sport and Performance Psychologist's Guide To Practicing Rational Emotive Behaviour Therapy*. Routledge.

This book provides a detailed outline into applying REBT in athletes.

David, D., Cotet, C., Matu, S., Mogoase, C., & Stefan, S. (2017). 50 years of rational-emotive and cognitive behavioural therapy: A systematic review and meta-analysis. *Journal of Clinical Psychology*, *4*, 1–15.

This article provides a contemporary review as to the effectiveness and efficacy of REBT since its conception and the proposed mechanisms of change for practitioners.

Jordana, A., Turner, M. J., Ramis, Y., & Torregrossa, M. (2020). A systematic mapping review on the use of Rational Emotive Behavior Therapy (REBT) with athletes. *International Review of Sport and Exercise Psychology*. doi: 10.1080/1750984X.2020.1836673

This article provides a review as to the effectiveness and efficacy of REBT in sport specifically.

5

ENHANCING MENTAL HEALTH AWARENESS AND SELF-MANAGEMENT VIA MINDFULNESS-BASED EXERCISES

The State of Mind Ireland (SOMI) programme

Gavin Breslin, Tandy Jane Haughey and Stephen Shannon

Learning objectives

After reading this chapter you should be able to:

1 Identify the challenges faced by student athletes when transitioning from school to university/college.
2 Describe the content of the State of Mind Ireland (SOMI) mental health awareness and self-management programme, including the daily home-directed mindfulness meditation practices.
3 Understand the importance of psychological theory-based programme development and evaluation.
4 Consider athlete feedback and recommendations when designing mental health awareness and self-management programmes.

Introduction to the theme

Time at university is a period for personal and academic growth, characterised by opportunities for identity development, interpersonal relationship formation, and future career decision making (Arnett, 2016). It can also be a time of stress, brought on by instability and uncertainty due to academic need for achievement, financial hardship, and securing graduate employment (American College Health Association, 2018). Making the transition to university can be a challenging period for young people and is often overlooked in preparing students for new life experiences. Student-athletes who are prone to stress and mental health problems because of co-existing academic, social and sporting demands (Wilson & Pritchard, 2005; Bennet, 2007) are often overlooked

DOI: 10.4324/9781003291695-6

when it comes to mental health support (Breslin et al., 2021). Therefore, The State of Mind Ireland (SOMI) programme was developed in response to the lack of evidence and theory-based programmes designed to enhance mental health awareness of student-athletes (Breslin et al., 2018a). The aim of this chapter is to share the process we followed in developing, recruiting, delivering, and evaluating a third iteration of the SOMI mental health and awareness programme to student athletes (i.e., Shannon et al., 2019).

The primary aims of the original SOMI programme were to: (1) improve student self-knowledge of mental health; (2) reduce stigma about mental illness; (3) increase intentions to self-manage mental health and; (4) to increase well-being and resilience. The positive effects for achieving aims 1–3 are described in detail elsewhere (Breslin et al., 2018a; Breslin and Leavey, 2019; Breslin et al., 2021). However, the programme's ability in increasing athlete well-being (aim 4), had not been evidenced in the programme. Researchers have proposed that programmes of relatively short duration are unlikely to achieve substantial changes in well-being (Breslin et al., 2021). In version 1 (Breslin et al., 2018) and 2 (Breslin et al., 2021) of SOMI, while mental health promotion tools and coping techniques were offered to the student-athletes, supportive practices had not been followed up beyond the initial 90-minute workshop (Shannon et al., 2019). As such, this chapter provides a detailed description of how daily home directed mindfulness sessions were integrated into an enhanced third version of SOMI, detailing how the programme and its effects were informed using components of Self-Determination Theory (SDT) (Ryan & Deci, 2000). Some of the lessons learned in the reflection section will provide information on how to integrate a psychological theory of behaviour change into the design of a mental health awareness programme for student athletes.

Describe the client or group being targeted

Two hundred and thirty-eight student-athletes participated, with 108 in the SOMI intervention group, and 130 in the control group. Intervention participants were recruited through an open invitation to students studying Bachelor of Science Honours degrees in sport courses at university. Control participants were recruited by the research team from a range of sport centres, sports clubs, and university courses other than sport. There was no randomisation to the intervention or control group. The sports the athletes participated in included: Gaelic Football and Hurling (42%), Soccer (22.5%), Rugby (5.8%), Hockey (5.1%), Basketball (3.6%), Netball (2.9%) and other (18.1%; e.g., Athletics, Combat sports). The mean age of the sample was 20.47 years (SD=3.30); 57.6% percent were males and 42.4% were females (See Figure 5.1). Students had access to student support services for mental health within the university campus; the SOMI programme was delivered as an extension to existing services.

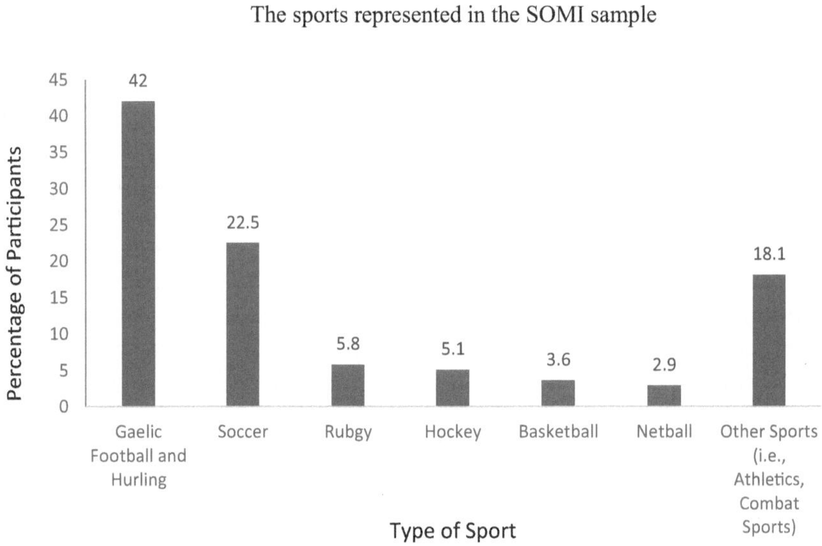

FIGURE 5.1 The sports represented in the SOMI sample.

Initial needs assessment

Well-being is defined as a state of optimal functioning (Ryan & Deci, 2017) and a key component of a two-continua model of mental health (Keyes, 2005), wherein well-being and ill-being (or mental illness) exist as two distinct, but correlated, factors. Stress, inversely related to well-being and often a precursor to mental ill-being (Keyes, 2005; Huppert, 2009; Diener, Lucas & Oishi, 2018), occurs when one feels overwhelmed or unable to cope because of pressures (Mental Health Foundation, 2018). Mental illness is the largest cause of ill health and disability in Northern Ireland (NI) and university students represent a high-risk group for the development of mental health problems (Dooley & Fitzgerald, 2013; McLafferty et al., 2017). For example, a study of Northern Ireland students (NUS-USI, 2017) indicated that 78% of the student population had experienced 'mental health worries' in the last year, with 51% not seeking support, indicating a need for bespoke mental health interventions (Karwig, Chambers, & Murphy, 2015).

Student-athletes (or collegiate athletes) are prone to increased stress because of co-existing academic, social, and sporting demands (Wilson & Pritchard, 2005; Bennet, 2007). It has been reported by student-athletes the pressure to achieve in both academic and sporting pursuits has resulted in a constrained social life and relationship difficulties (Gavrilova, Donohue & Galante, 2017). As such, student-athletes have higher clinical and sub-clinical risks for behavioural mental health problems (e.g., substance misuse, eating disorders, gambling) compared to non-athletes (Moreland, Coxe & Yang, 2018). Moreover, student-athletes are at least as, or sometimes more likely, to experience mood disorders compared to non-athletes (Donohue et al., 2018). In addition, the physical, and often aggressive nature of sport can lead to the student-athletes incurring physical injury and experiencing emotional and physical fatigue from competition and over-training (Putukian, 2016). Athletes may also experience performance pressures from coaches, teammates, and spectators, and often strive to succeed at the expense of personal well-being (Abedalhafiza, Altahaynehb & Al-Haliqc, 2010; Breslin et al., 2018b). When left untreated, such stressors can manifest in impaired functioning (Moreland, Coxe & Yang, 2018), highlighting the need for theory-based, athlete-specific mental health self-management interventions.

Michie and colleagues (2016) highlighted the need for theoretical mapping in health behaviour change interventions, such that the delivery techniques designed to improve the intended outcome (e.g., mental health) derive from a validated and logical psychological framework. In the case of mental health interventions, when theoretically derived constructs are applied and empirically measured, statistical modelling can be designed to elicit whether the assumed theoretical processes explain changes in mental health outcomes (Hagger & Chatzisarantis, 2014). One specific concept is mental health self-management. Mental health self-management refers to monitoring how one's mental health is impacting upon daily functioning, and utilization of strategies that protect and promote mental health (Wolf, 1996). Many student-athletes report that they lack the psychological skills, or resources to self-manage mental health, resulting in maladaptive coping strategies (e.g., substance misuse) (Eisenberg, Golberstein & Gollust, 2007; Hunt & Eisenberg, 2010). Mindfulness is an example of a self-management strategy available to athletes (Noetel, Ciarrochi, Van Zanden, & Lonsdale, 2017). Mindfulness is defined as a mental state characterised by an awareness of present events and experiences (Brown and Ryan, 2003), achieved mainly through meditative practices (Sappington & Longshore, 2015). Although mindfulness has traditionally been guided by practitioners in group-based or individual therapies (Langley, 2013), mindfulness programmes are widely available through auditory meditative guidance in smartphone applications (Howells, Ivtzan, & Eiroa-Orosa, 2016).

For athletes, most mindfulness interventions have been repurposed to improve performance-related outcomes (e.g., improving attention, concentration or psychological flow during performance) (Sappington & Longshore, 2015; Noetel, Ciarrochi, Van Zanden, & Lonsdale, 2017). While mindfulness intervention studies for improving mental health outcomes among athletes offer an accessible option, and are promising (e.g., Vidic, Martin & Oxhandler, 2017; Glass, Spears, Perskaudas & Kaufman, 2018), theoretical mechanisms of change that may explain the benefits experienced are not well explored. To ascertain how or what changes occur during mindfulness programmes, theoretical constructs are modelled to assess the indirect effect of a treatment (X) on an outcome (Y) through one or more mediators (M) (Kok, Schaalma, Ruiter, Van Empelen & Brug, 2004). This statistical modelling analysis was used in the current SOMI programme.

Relevant to the monitoring and ability components of the mental health self-management construct (Wolf, 1996), it is proposed that when one perceives mental health competence, one can cope adaptively, regulate stress, and experience a positive sense of well-being (Gustafsson & Skoog, 2012). SDT (Ryan & Deci, 2000) posits that competence, an innate psychological need and feeling a sense of effectiveness in one's environment, is essential for optimal well-being. Of the three core psychological needs in SDT (i.e. competence, autonomy, relatedness) the perception of competence has been shown to have clear theoretical links with self-management, and indeed, a comprehensive body of research indicates that competence satisfaction is robustly related to positive mental health (Ryan & Deci, 2017), including enhanced well-being (Mikolajczak et al., 2015) and reduced stress (Jex, Bliese, Buzzell & Primeau, 2001). Therefore, given clear theoretical links, mental health competence can be operationalised in a self-management intervention aiming to promote well-being.

In this chapter we demonstrate how the inclusion of mindfulness practices in the SOMI mental health awareness programme may play a significant part in promoting mental health competence and subsequent well-being among student athletes. The intervention was analysed through a regression model comprising theory-driven hypotheses. Well-being was designated as the dependent variable (Y), with participation in the intervention as the independent variable (X). Competence satisfaction (i.e., in self-managing mental health) was designated as the primary mediator [M1], mindfulness was designated as mediator 2 [M2], and stress as mediator 3 [M3] (See Figure 5.2). The intervention was hypothesised to directly increase competence (Hypothesis 1; H1), and was in turn hypothesised to partially mediate the effects of the intervention on mindfulness (Hypothesis 2; H2). Considering stress has been

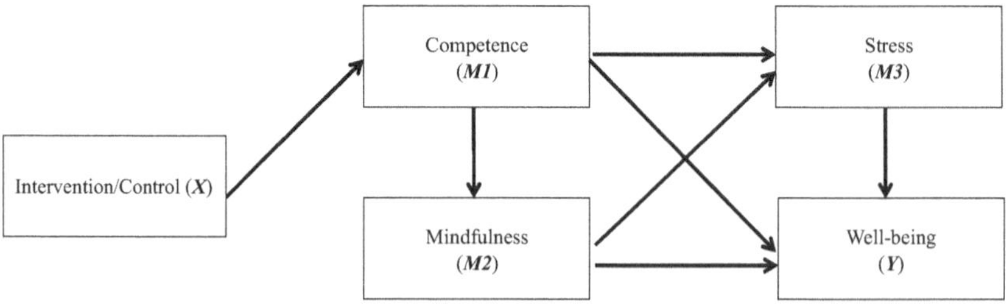

FIGURE 5.2 Theoretical model hypothesising direct and indirect effects of the SOMI programme on competence, mindfulness, stress and well-being.

inversely related to both mindfulness and competence, the intervention was hypothesised to indirectly effect stress through competence (Hypothesis 3; H3), and through competence and mindfulness in sequence (Hypothesis 4; H4). Lastly, the SOMI intervention's effects on well-being were hypothesised to be indirectly influenced through a combination of sequential mediating pathways (Hypothesis 5; H5) (e.g., intervention>competence> well-being; intervention>competence>stress>well-being).

Framework and intervention for delivery

The SOMI programme (Lawlor, Rae, Kelly, & Moriarty, 2015) was developed in response to the need to do more in university sport settings to enhance mental health awareness and the well-being of student athletes. SOMI (Lawlor et al., 2015) is an experiential and skill-enhancing programme that is delivered on a university campus during scheduled class time by experienced mental health and well-being tutors in partnership with students and student support services. Previous versions of the SOMI programme (Lawlor et al, 2015; Breslin et al., 2018a; Breslin et al., 2019) comprised a 90-minute instructional workshop on mental health, whereas the present version (Shannon et al., 2019) entailed the instructional workshop plus a home-directed mindfulness training programme (see Table 5.1).

The SOMI programme was delivered by a psychiatrist and a student counsellor with extensive mental health course delivery experience. The workshop content and delivery were designed using SDT principles (Stone, Deci & Ryan, 2009), to the extent that the activities and tutor delivery-style were provided through a needs-supportive environment that acknowledged participant input through open-ended questions, included regular positive instructional feedback, and empathetic communication. The first half of the workshop introduced mental health as a positive concept, and asked participants to reflect on common life stressors, and discuss their knowledge of mindfulness as a mental health self-management technique. Participants reviewed vignettes of prominent athletes who practice meditation, and then considered how a mindful state may improve participants' competence to manage stressors and promote mental health both in sport and university life contexts.

The second half of the workshop comprised instructions on the mindfulness home programme, which was delivered via a mobile telephone application (app) designed by an online healthcare company specialising in meditation. The application included fourteen daily sessions comprising auditory and visual guidance, such as mindful body scanning for physical sensations, counting inhalations and exhalations, and noting thoughts and feelings. As part of the workshop participants engaged in a one-minute guided taster session before being asked to practice daily.

TABLE 5.1 Core content of the mental health workshop and mindfulness application

Intervention component	*Key themes*	*Tasks*
Mental health workshop part 1	Introduction to mental health concepts (i.e. stress, mindfulness, 5 steps to well-being, Connect, Be active, Take notice, Keep learning, Give.	Group-based and participant-led discussions on positive framing of mental health, practical ways to complete the five steps to well-being, and mindfulness as a tool.
Mental health workshop part 2	Instructions of how to use the mindfulness application.	A taster mindfulness meditation session, download and try-out of the application.
Home-directed mindfulness programme	Non-judgmental awareness of thoughts and the present moment	Guided practices on counting breaths, body scanning and noting thoughts and feelings.

Using needs-supportive communication, the workshop deliverers encouraged the participants to complete the daily sessions as much as possible during the two-week period, with the application allowing for self-selection of the session durations (i.e., 5, 10, 15 or 20 minutes in length). Further positive instructional reminders were sent to participants through email and SMS to enhance the use of the mindfulness app.

Intervention evaluation and lessons learned through self-reflection

Four outcome measures were used to assess the SOMI programme. Mindfulness was measured using the validated Attention Awareness Scale (MAAS; Brown and Ryan, 2009), a 15-item questionnaire designed to assess attention to, and awareness of, day-to-day experiences. An example item from the MAAS is: 'I could be experiencing some emotion and not be conscious of it until sometime later'. The valid and reliable Perceived Competence Scale (PCS; Williams, & Deci, 1996) was used to measure the participants' competence with respect to self-managing mental health. An example item was: 'I feel confident in my ability to manage my mental health'. Stress was measured using the 10-item Perceived Stress Scale (PSS) (Cohen, Kamarck, & Mermelstein, 1994). The PSS assesses the appraisal of stress in day-to-day experiences and demonstrates excellent psychometric properties (Roberti, Harrington & Storch, 2006; Lee, 2012). Well-being was measured using the 14-item Warwick-Edinburgh Mental Well-being Scale (WEMWBS) a validated and reliable instrument (Tennant et al., 2007). These questionnaires were completed by student athletes at two time points; prior to the programme (T1) and two-weeks after the training (T2). For the control group, similar time points for the completion of the questionnaire were utilised: before a regularly scheduled lecture session and two-weeks later.

Results revealed support for the study hypotheses (see Figure 5.3). Specifically in comparison to the control group, the intervention had a direct positive effect on changes in competence satisfaction difference scores (H1). Further support was revealed to the extent that indirect effects were found for the intervention on mindfulness through competence satisfaction (H2); on stress through competence satisfaction (H3), and; on stress through competence satisfaction and mindfulness in sequence (H4). In respect of H5, the intervention indirectly effected changes in well-being through competence satisfaction, mindfulness, and stress in sequence. Factoring in all of the variables in the model resulted in a significant proportion of variance predicted for changes in well-being (R^2=.54), in addition to stress (R^2=.17), mindfulness, (R^2=.14) and competence (R^2=.04).

Overall, results indicated that mindfulness training can foster perceptions of competence in mental health self-management, which may be beneficial to stress regulation and well-being promotion (Ryan & Deci, 2017). However, effect sizes were generally small, and as such, we now discuss findings with a view of advancing mental health interventions for the athlete population.

The intervention's effects were modelled through SDT using competence satisfaction and mindfulness as primary and secondary mediators. This approach enabled an empirical inquiry into the mechanisms of change in the programme, specifically the temporal nature of the relationship between competence and mindfulness, and their salutary effects, which is considered a crucial step in developing a theoretical underpinning for mental health promotion through mindfulness (Sedlmeier, Losse & Quasten, 2018). The finding that improvements in mindfulness were indirectly predicted by the intervention's direct effect on competence satisfaction (H1), suggests that engaging with mindfulness practices and instructions can facilitate improved perceptions of competence in mental health self-management, which in turn, enables an individual to be mindful and attend to the present (Olafsen, 2017).

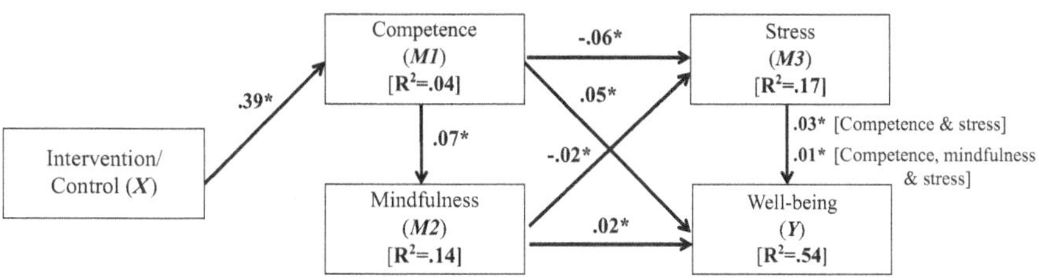

FIGURE 5.3 Intervention model analysis showing effects on the study outcome of well-being through competence, mindfulness, and stress.

The indirect effects found for the intervention on reducing stress through competence satisfaction (H3), and competence satisfaction and mindfulness in sequence (H4), supports evidence that mindfulness-based interventions can reduce stress through self-regulatory mechanisms (Vidic, Martin & Oxhandler, 2017; Gu, Strauss, Bond, & Cavanagh, 2015). Specifically, findings are theoretically aligned with a SDT perspective (Ryan & Deci, 2017) to the extent that improved competence satisfaction can result in better self-regulation of environmental stressors (Weinstein & Ryan, 2011). Indeed, research studies have shown that competence independently predicts reduced stress and improved well-being (Jex, Bliese, Buzzell & Primeau, 2001; Mikolajczak et al., 2015). Given student-athletes experience multiple social, academic and sporting stressors, and often report a lack of ability in self-regulating stressors (Moreland, Coxe & Yang, 2018), improving competence through provision of mindfulness training may be of value. Such efforts may be aided by longer-lasting interventions that provide sufficient time to directly improve mindfulness skills (Cayoun, 2011).

Lastly, changes in competence, mindfulness and stress indirectly predicted the interventions positive effects on well-being. The specific skills taught to the participants through the mindfulness programme, including improving awareness of the concept of mindfulness, and the relationship between thoughts, breathing and attention, may have improved student-athlete's well-being through competence needs satisfaction (Brown & Ryan, 2003; Weinstein & Ryan, 2011). Mindfulness and stress both accompanied the intervention's indirect effects on well-being through competence, supporting the view that mindfulness-based programmes can help individuals feel effective at self-regulating stressors related to mental health (Creswell, 2017).

In conclusion, implementation of an enhanced SOMI intervention comprising daily mindfulness meditation sessions suggests that mental health competence was enhanced in comparison to the control group. This finding related to indirect effects on mindfulness awareness, reduced stress, and enhanced well-being. As such, SOMI could be integrated into university courses to promote mental health among student-athletes. Overall, we propose that mindfulness-based mental health interventions may offer a way to promote mental health among athletes, with the caveat that attention is given to the promotion of competence in such programmes. Given this study was conducted over a two-week period, we support other researchers in suggesting that longer-lasting programmes tailored for sports culture are warranted (Gavrilova, Donohue & Galante, 2017). Those involved in programme design should consider intervention accessibility and sustainability, adherence, duration and intensity of mindfulness sessions, in addition to theoretical application by session facilitators (Creswell, 2017). Moreover, researchers may consider conducting such interventions adopting a longitudinal group design, in which allocation to groups are randomised. Finally, we continue to modify the SOMI programme for various contexts not only for university athletes but other settings beyond the university to include; schools, sports clubs, young offender centres, workplaces, and prisons utilising the available research, theory, and practices which are available.

References

Abedalhafiz, A., Altahayneh, Z., & Al-Haliq, M. (2010). Sources of stress and coping styles among student-athletes in Jordan universities. *Procedia-Social and Behavioral Sciences*, 5, 1911–1917.

American College Health Association (ACHA). (2018). *American College Health Association-National College Health Assessment II: Undergraduate Student Reference Group Executive Summary*. Retrieved from www.acha.org/documents/ncha/NCHA-II_Spring_2018_Undergraduate_Reference_Group_Executive_Summary.pdf

Arnett, J. J. (2016). College students as emerging adults: The developmental implications of the college context. *Emerging Adulthood*, 4(3), 219–222. Doi: 10.1177/2167696815587422.

Bennett, G. (2007). The role of a clinical psychologist in a Division I athletics program. *Journal of Clinical Sport Psychology*, 1(3), 261–269.

Breslin, G., Haughey, T., O'Brien, W., Caulfield, L., Robertson, A., & Lawlor, M. (2018a). Increasing athlete knowledge of mental health and intentions to seek help: The State of mind Ireland (SOMI). *Pilot Program. Journal of Clinical Sport Psychology*, 12(1), 39–56.

Breslin, G., Shannon, S., Ferguson, K., Devlin, S., Haughey, T., & Prentice, G. (2018b). Predicting athletes' mental health stigma using the theory of reasoned action framework. *Journal of Clinical Sport Psychology*, *13*(1), 1–23.

Breslin, G., Haughey, T. J., Shannon, S., Neill, D., & Lawlor, M. (2019). The State of Mind Ireland Programme for Student Athletes. In: Breslin, G. & Leavey, G. *Mental Health and Well-being Interventions in Sport: Research, Theory and Practice* (2019: pg63–74). Routledge.

Breslin, G. and Leavey, G. (2019). *Mental Health and Well-Being Interventions in Sport*. London: Routledge. https://doi. org/10.4324/9781315147703

Breslin, G., Shannon, S., Haughey, T., Sarju, N., Neill, D., Leavey, G., & Lawlor, M. (2021). Athlete and nonathlete intentions to self-manage mental health: applying the integrated behavior change model to the state of mind program. *Journal of Applied Sport Psychology*, 33(1), 83–97

Brown, K. W., & Ryan, R. M. (2003). The benefits of being present: Mindfulness and its role in psychological well-being. *Journal of Personality and Social Psychology*, 84(4), 822.

Brown, K. W., & Ryan, R. M. (2009). The mindfulness attention awareness scale (MAAS). *Acceptance and Commitment Therapy. Measures Package*, 82, 82–84.

Cayoun, B. A. (2011). *Mindfulness-Integrated CBT: Principles and Practice*. John Wiley & Sons.

Cohen, S., Kamarck, T., & Mermelstein, R. (1994). Perceived stress scale. *Measuring Stress: A Guide for Health and Social Scientists*, *10*(2), 235–283.

Creswell, J. D. (2017). Mindfulness interventions. *Annual Review of Psychology*, 68, 491–516.

Diener, E., Lucas, R. E., & Oishi, S. (2018). Advances and open questions in the science of subjective well-being. *Collabra: Psychology*, 4(1).

Donohue, B., Gavrilova, Y., Galante, M., Gavrilova, E., Loughran, T., Scott, J., Chow, G., Plant, C.P. & Allen, D.N. (2018). Controlled Evaluation of an Optimization Approach to Mental Health and Sport Performance. *Journal of Clinical Sport Psychology*, pp.1–42.

Dooley, B., & Fitzgerald, A. (2013). Methodology on the My World Survey (MWS): A unique window into the world of adolescents in Ireland. *Early Intervention in Psychiatry*, 7(1), 12–22.

Eisenberg, D., Golberstein, E., & Gollust, S. E. (2007). Help-seeking and access to mental health care in a university student population. *Medical care*, 45(7), 594–601.

Gavrilova, Y., Donohue, B., & Galante, M. (2017). Mental health and sport performance programming in athletes who present without pathology: A case examination supporting optimization. *Clinical Case Studies*, 16(3), 234–253.

Glass, C. R., Spears, C. A., Perskaudas, R., & Kaufman, K. A. (2018). Mindful sport performance enhancement: Randomized controlled trial of a mental training program with collegiate athletes. *Journal of Clinical Sport Psychology*, 1–34.

Gu, J., Strauss, C., Bond, R., & Cavanagh, K. (2015). How do mindfulness-based cognitive therapy and mindfulness-based stress reduction improve mental health and wellbeing? A systematic review and meta-analysis of mediation studies. *Clinical psychology review*, 37, 1–12.

Gustafsson, H., & Skoog, T. (2012). The mediational role of perceived stress in the relation between optimism and burnout in competitive athletes. *Anxiety, Stress & Coping*, 25(2), 183–199.

Hagger, M. S., & Chatzisarantis, N. L. (2014). An integrated behavior change model for physical activity. *Exercise and Sport Sciences Reviews*, 42(2), 62–69.

Howells, A., Ivtzan, I., & Eiroa-Orosa, F. J. (2016). Putting the 'app'in happiness: a randomised controlled trial of a smartphone-based mindfulness intervention to enhance wellbeing. *Journal of Happiness Studies*, 17(1), 163–185.

Hunt, J., & Eisenberg, D. (2010). Mental health problems and help-seeking behavior among college students. *Journal of Adolescent Health*, 46(1), 3–10.

Huppert, F. A. (2009). Psychological well-being: Evidence regarding its causes and consequences. *Applied Psychology: Health and Well-Being*, 1(2), 137–164.

Jex, S. M., Bliese, P. D., Buzzell, S., & Primeau, J. (2001). The impact of self-efficacy on stressor–strain relations: Coping style as an explanatory mechanism. *Journal of applied psychology*, 86(3), 401.

Karwig, G., Chambers, D., & Murphy, F. (2015). Reaching out in college: Help-seeking at third level in Ireland. Reach Out Ireland.

Keyes, C. L. (2005). Mental illness and/or mental health? Investigating axioms of the complete state model of health. *Journal of consulting and clinical psychology*, 73(3), 539.

Kok, G., Schaalma, H., Ruiter, R. A., Van Empelen, P., & Brug, J. (2004). Intervention mapping: protocol for applying health psychology theory to prevention programmes. *Journal of health psychology*, 9(1), 85–98.

Langley, M. (2013). The Mindfulness Workbook. Hodder and Stoughton, United Kingdom.

Lawlor, M., Rae, M., Kelly, N., & Moriarty, P. (2015). State of mind Ireland: Towards a skills for life passport. In Proceedings of the CRSI Conference. Retrieved from www. stateofmindireland. com/crsi/resources.

Lee, E.H., 2012. Review of the psychometric evidence of the perceived stress scale. *Asian nursing research*, 6(4), pp.121–127.
Mental Health Foundation (2018). Stress: are we coping?. Available at: www.mentalhealth.org.uk/a-to-z/s/stress (accessed February 2019).
McLafferty, M., Lapsley, C. R., Ennis, E., Armour, C., Murphy, S., Bunting, B. P., … O'Neill, S. M. (2017). Mental health, behavioural problems and treatment seeking among students commencing university in Northern Ireland. *PloS One*, 12(12), e0188785.
Michie, S., Carey, R., Johnston, M., Rothman, A., Kelly, M., Davidson, K., & de Bruin, M. (2016). From theory-inspired to theory-based interventions: Linking behaviour change techniques to their mechanisms of action. *European Health Psychologist*, 18(S), 395.
Mikolajczak, M., Avalosse, H., Vancorenland, S., Verniest, R., Callens, M., Van Broeck, N., Fantini-Hauwel, C. & Mierop, A. (2015). A nationally representative study of emotional competence and health. *Emotion*, 15(5), 653–751.
Moreland, J. J., Coxe, K. A., & Yang, J. (2018). Collegiate athletes' mental health services utilization: A systematic review of conceptualizations, operationalizations, facilitators, and barriers. *Journal of Sport and Health Science*, 7(1), 58–69.
National Union of Students – Union of Students Ireland (NUS-USI) . (2017). NI student wellbeing survey report. Retrieved from http://nus-usi.org/campaigns/education-welfare/nus-usi-student-wellbeing-survey-report/
Noetel, M., Ciarrochi, J., Van Zanden, B., & Lonsdale, C. (2017). Mindfulness and acceptance approaches to sporting performance enhancement: a systematic review. *International Review of Sport and Exercise Psychology*, 12(1), 139–175.
Olafsen, A.H. (2017). The implications of need-satisfying work climates on state mindfulness in a longitudinal analysis of work outcomes. *Motivation and Emotion*, 41, 22–37.
Putukian, M. (2016). The psychological response to injury in student athletes: a narrative review with a focus on mental health. *British Journal of Sports Medicine*, 50(3), 145–148.
Ryan, R. M., & Deci, E. L. (2000). Self-determination theory and the facilitation of intrinsic motivation, social development, and well-being. *American Psychologist*, 55(1), 68.
Ryan, R. M., & Deci, E. L. (2017). Self-determination theory: Basic psychological needs in motivation, development, and wellness. Guilford Publications.
Roberti, J. W., Harrington, L. N., & Storch, E. A. (2006). Further psychometric support for the 10-item version of the perceived stress scale. *Journal of College Counseling*, 9(2), 135–147.
Sappington, R., & Longshore, K. (2015). Systematically reviewing the efficacy of mindfulness-based interventions for enhanced athletic performance. *Journal of Clinical Sport Psychology*, 9(3), 232–262.
Sedlmeier, P., Loße, C. & Quasten, L.C. (2018). Psychological effects of meditation for healthy practitioners: an update. *Mindfulness*, 9(2), 371–387.
Shannon, S., Breslin, G., Haughey, T., Sarju, N., Neill, D., Lawlor, M., & Leavey, G. (2019). Predicting Student-Athlete and Non-Athletes' Intentions to Self-Manage Mental Health: Testing an Integrated Behaviour Change Model. *Mental Health & Prevention* 13, 92–99, https://doi.org/10.1016/j.mhp.2019.01.006.
Stone, D.N., Deci, E.L. & Ryan, R.M. (2009). Beyond talk: Creating autonomous motivation through self-determination theory. *Journal of General Management*, 34(3), 75–91.

Tennant, R., Hiller, L., Fishwick, R., Platt, S., Joseph, S., Weich, S., … & Stewart-Brown, S. (2007). The Warwick-Edinburgh mental well-being scale (WEMWBS): Development and UK validation. *Health and Quality of Life Outcomes*, 5(1), 63.

Vidic, Z., St. Martin, M., & Oxhandler, R. (2017). Mindfulness Intervention with a US women's NCAA Division I basketball team: impact on stress, athletic coping skills and perceptions of intervention. *The Sport Psychologist*, 31(2), 147–159.

Weinstein, N., & Ryan, R. M. (2011). A self-determination theory approach to understanding stress incursion and responses. *Stress and Health*, 27(1), 4–17.

Pritchard, M., & Wilson, G. (2005). Comparing sources of stress in college student athletes and non-athletes. *Athletic Insight: The Online Journal of Sports Psychology*, 5(1), 1–8.

Williams, G. C., & Deci, E. L. (1996). Internalization of biopsychosocial values by medical students: a test of self-determination theory. *Journal of Personality and Social Psychology*, 70(4), 767.

Wolf, H. (1996). Self-management and mental health, in Bährer-Kohler, S. (2012). *Social determinants and mental health*. Nova Science Publishers.

Further reading

Breslin, G., Shannon, S., Cummings, M., & Leavey, G. (2022). An updated systematic review of interventions to increase awareness of mental health and well-being in athletes, coaches, officials and parents. *Systematic Reviews, 11*(1), 1–29.

This systematic review article critically evaluates available psycho-educational programmes for athletes, coaches and officials.

Donohue, B., Gavrilova, E., Danlag, A., Perry, J., Kuhn, C., Allen, D. N., & Benning, S. D. (2021). A comprehensive examination of factors impacting collegiate athletes' utilization of psychological assessment and intervention services. *Psychology in the Schools, 58*(3), 458–474.

This recent article describes challenges faced by athletes when accessing support and completing assessments.

Gavrilova, E., Donohue, B., Kalita, J., Paul, M., Pharr, J., & Allen, D. (2022). Empirical Justification for the Involvement of Athletes' Supportive Others When Conducting Sport Specific Mental Health Interventions. *Sport Social Work Journal, 1*(1), 1–12.

This article describes how student-athletes can be better supported if we include their supportive significant others in interventions programmes. It appears that by including significant others engagement in services is improved, as is a willingness to breakdown perceived barriers to seeking help.

Sutcliffe, J. T., Graupensperger, S., Schweickle, M. J., Rice, S. M., Swann, C., & Vella, S. A. (2021). Mental health interventions in non-elite sport: a systematic review and meta-analysis. *International Review of Sport and Exercise Psychology, 1–24.*

This systematic review and meta-analysis summarise mental health interventions for non-elite athletes and highlights the need for further programme development and scalability of programmes.

6

AHEAD OF THE GAME

International scale-up of evidence-based mental health programming

Stewart A. Vella, Sarah K. Liddle, Matthew J. Schweickle, Christian Swann, Angelina Lim, Emily Arnold and Caitlin Liddelow

Learning objectives

After reading this chapter you should be able to:

1 Understand the way in which evidence builds the case for implementation of mental health programming.
2 Critically examine the role of formative research and community involvement in intervention development.
3 Appreciate and justify the processes required to implement a comprehensive mental health programme within a sport club.
4 Understand and describe the key lessons learned from attempts to scale up a programme internationally.

Introduction to the theme

This chapter reports on the design, evaluation, and international translation of the Ahead of the Game (AOTG) programme. AOTG is a comprehensive multi-level, multi-component programme for adolescent males delivered through community sporting clubs and organisations. The aims of the programme are to: (1) increase mental health literacy among adolescents and their social support systems; (2) increase help-seeking intentions and attitudes that facilitate help-seeking among adolescent male sport participants; and (3) increase resilience and factors which prevent the onset of mental health problems, including wellbeing. To achieve these aims, the programme includes four components, two interventions for adolescents targeting mental health literacy (Help Out a Mate) and resilience (The Challenge), a parent

DOI: 10.4324/9781003291695-7

mental health literacy intervention (Number One Supporter), and a coach mental health literacy intervention (Got Your Back for Coaches). These four distinct interventions are complemented by a mental health messaging campaign that is rolled out at playing fields and clubhouses of participating clubs and organisations. AOTG is primarily a mental health promotion and prevention programme that also promotes early intervention for mental illness and available support services. The programme was designed and evaluated in Australia, and has undergone translation for international contexts including Canada and the United Kingdom (UK).

Targeting mental health literacy, help-seeking, stigma, and resilience in adolescent males is important for a number of reasons. Mental illnesses among children and young people are one of the leading causes of years of life lived with disability and disability-adjusted-life-years, particularly in developed nations such as across Europe and the Americas (Baranne & Falissard, 2018). This is true of both diagnosed mental disorders, as well as sub-threshold mental disorders, both of which are associated with a meaningful burden of disease among adolescents (Roberts et al., 2015). The estimated prevalence of any mental disorder was 16.1% among adolescents globally, along with an estimated prevalence of subthreshold disorders of 42.3% (Roberts et al., 2015). Both the prevalence and burden of mental health disorders among children and adolescents were exacerbated during the coronavirus pandemic in 2020–2021 (Hossain et al., 2022). In Australia, suicide is currently the leading cause of death among young people aged 15 to 24 years (Australian Institute of Health and Welfare, 2020a), with a disproportionate rate among males (Australian Institute of Health and Welfare, 2020b).

Preventative programmes can provide protection against the onset of mental health problems. Specifically, preventative programmes aimed at adolescents can reduce and prevent the detrimental long-term impact of adolescent mental disorders which reduce the likelihood of completing school, gaining employment, and engaging as a productive member of society (Lawrence et al., 2015). Community sports may be a particularly beneficial context in which to implement such preventative programmes. For example, community sports programmes provide access to a large percentage of the population, particularly among high-income countries where approximately two-thirds of all young people participate in organised sports (Aubert et al., 2018). Young people also spend a large amount of time in organised sports. In Australia, the average time spent by adolescents in organised sports is over seven hours each week (Vella, Cliff, Okely, Scully, & Morley, 2013), and this environment is an engaging avenue for mental health programming (Swann et al., 2018). In addition, sports participants also express additional barriers to seeking help, such as the potential impact on playing time, and being perceived as mentally weak or lacking commitment (Breslin, Shannon, Haughey, Donnelly, & Leavey, 2017; Trojian, 2016). Many sports cultures celebrate mental toughness, masculinity, and disapproval of weakness disclosure (Bauman, 2016; Doherty, Hannigan, & Campbell, 2016), potentially perpetuating the negative effects of mental illness and increasing stigma. Stigma is an important issue because it may result in problems being hidden and could prevent young people from appropriately seeking help and receiving support (Trojian, 2016). When compared to more general public health programmes, interventions that are specifically developed and tailored to the culture of sport may be particularly relevant and beneficial in the promotion of mental health and wellbeing, especially among athletes (Breslin et al., 2022).

Describe the client or group being targeted

The AOTG programme targets adolescent males aged 12–17 years who participate in organised sports from community grass-roots level through to elite academy level. In the initial development and evaluation phase, a total of 1675 adolescent males with an average age of 14.51 years participated in the programme across all implementation phases, with 283 participating in the final evaluation phase of the programme. All participating sport clubs were from a range of suburbs with ranging social-economic status from eastern New South Wales, Australia. In addition, the AOTG programme aimed to include the parents and coaches of adolescent male sport participants in distinct, complementary interventions. All interventions that comprise the AOTG programme were delivered through, and most often in conjunction with, community sporting clubs and organisations. Since the initial development and evaluation phase, many thousands more adolescents have participated in the AOTG programme through initiatives such as the Rugby League World Cup 2021/22. Importantly, in these large-scale initiatives to scale-up the programme, it has been delivered to both adolescent boys and girls, including across some of the most deprived areas of the UK (Rugby League World Cup, 2022). These scale-up efforts have been undertaken in conjunction with funding partners (i.e., Movember), charity and delivery partners (i.e., Rugby League Cares), and within the broader context of the Mental Fitness Charter of the Rugby League World Cup 2021/22.

Initial needs assessment

Consistent with the Community-Based Participatory Research framework (Minkler & Wallerstein, 2003), development of the AOTG programme first went through a rigorous community-based needs assessment and exploration stage (Fixsen, Naoom, Blase, Friedman, & Wallace, 2005). This stage involved extensive engagement with the extended community and consultation with key stakeholders. In total 16 focus groups were conducted with adolescent male sport participants (n = 55), 10 with their parents (n = 46) and five with coaches (n = 20). The research team also facilitated a two-day workshop in conjunction with their research partners, five national sporting organisations, and local sporting representatives to assess the feasibility of implementation approaches and potential barriers at a policy, regional, and local level. These steps were also repeated when scaling the AOTG programme internationally. Key messages, content, and branding were tested in focus groups to ensure that the final version was culturally appropriate and engaging.

The most salient outcomes of the initial needs assessment, which in large part dictated the AOTG programme content, were that: (1) adolescent males desired more information about mental health problems, how to recognise them, and how to provide help to their friends if they are experiencing a mental health problem (Swann et al., 2018); (2) adolescent males desired information that would help them to increase their wellbeing and prevent the onset of mental health problems (Swann et al., 2018); (3) parents of adolescent males were not adequately knowledgeable, prepared, or confident to assist children who experience a mental health problem (Brown, Deane, Vella, & Liddle, 2017; Hurley, Swann, Allen, Okely, & Vella, 2017); (4) there was significant variation in the role that coaches believed that they should play in adolescent athlete mental health, with most coaches not willing to take an active role (Ferguson et al., 2018) and (5) coaches were interested in content regarding adolescent motivation and wellbeing, as opposed to mental health (Ferguson et al., 2018). A full description of the formative research findings is provided below.

Adolescent males

We aimed to understand adolescent males' existing knowledge, previous experience, and perceived needs regarding mental health. Additionally, their perceptions of organised sport as a vehicle for supporting mental health, and preferences for mental health interventions in sport were explored. A detailed description of the methods and results of this qualitative study can be found elsewhere (Swann et al., 2018).

Six key dimensions emerged from that initial needs assessment with adolescent males. First, they reported broadly understanding mental health as a "state of mind", with most having some experience with mental illness – either personally or through someone close to them. Adolescents also reflected that perceived masculinity was an important factor in stigmatised attitudes towards male mental health. Second, there was variation in adolescents' opinion on the relationship between sport and mental health. For some, sport was perceived as positive for mental health, especially when the primary motivation was enjoyment or fun. However, for others, sport was perceived as a negative influence on mental health, particularly when the primary motivation was performance. Third, adolescents reported that coaches could play an important role in their life, such as acting as an important avenue of support if they were struggling with a mental health problem. In addition, adolescents also reported that, in some cases, they would prefer if coaches changed their approach to focus less on winning and more on enjoyment of sport. Fourth, adolescents expressed that family is particularly important in supporting mental health through sport. However, adolescents felt that parents need to receive more information about mental health and mental illness, and that it was important that they learnt about it together. Fifth, adolescents reported a range of interests in learning about mental health. Specifically, adolescents wanted to gain knowledge around how to help a friend, and further, learn to better recognise and empathise with those who experience mental health issues. Adolescents also highlighted a desire to learn how to manage adversity, which could be used both within sport and to protect their mental health more broadly. Lastly, adolescents suggested that sport could provide an engaging environment for discussing mental health especially when compared to the school environment, further describing the utility of the group and team context in sport as a facilitator of mental health promotion. However, adolescents also reported that the success of mental health discussions within their teams may depend on how connected individuals feel to their club or team. Furthermore, adolescents expressed an interest in learning about elite athletes' mental health and also in learning about mental health from someone with lived experience of mental illness.

Parents

We aimed to investigate and understand sport parents' existing knowledge, beliefs, attitudes and perceptions of the role sport clubs play in mental health promotion and disorder prevention, and the factors that might promote or limit their participation in (and effectiveness of) mental health-focused interventions. Parents play an important role in recognising young people's mental health symptoms, providing emotional support and facilitating professional help-seeking (Mendenhall & Frauenholtz, 2015; Rickwood, Deane, & Wilson, 2007). Parents are a key source of support in adolescent sport participation (Harwood & Knight, 2015), and parent behaviour has been targeted in the youth sport environment as a mechanism to increase support and warmth and reduce conflict and pressure (Dorsch, King, Dunn, Osai, & Tulane, 2017). A detailed description of the methods and results of the qualitative study are available elsewhere (see, Hurley et al., 2017).

In summary, the majority of parents reported limited ability to recognise the presence or potential development of mental health disorders in their child. Parents' reported particular confusion about how to distinguish between possible symptoms of mental illness and "normal" male adolescent behaviours such as moodiness or oversleeping. Parents reported having insufficient knowledge about help-seeking services and treatment options and lacked the capacity and confidence to effectively communicate, support and intervene in the face of a mental health problem. These parents had favourable attitudes towards receiving education on adolescent mental health but expressed mixed views on the role of the sport club in promoting positive mental health. The sport club provided a forum for parents to talk, share advise and discuss parenting as well as look out for each other's children as a supportive community, but it was not seen as having an explicit role in mental health promotion.

Findings of the needs assessment with parents suggested that the intervention should target symptom identification, provide clear guidelines and strategies on how to respond to and manage adolescent mental health disorders and how to communicate about mental health with adolescents. This would serve to ease parents' concerns about their current lack of knowledge, skills and confidence to support and protect adolescent mental health. In addition, according to the parents, interventions should build on the existing supportive social networks among sport parents, and be brief, convenient and accessible to allow for parents' reported time constraints.

Coaches

We aimed to understand coaches' existing knowledge, attitudes and beliefs regarding supporting adolescent athletes with mental health problems and the promotion of mental health and wellbeing. Additionally, coaches' preferences for coach education, including format and modality, were also explored. A detailed description of the methodology and results of the coach needs assessment has been provided elsewhere (Ferguson et al., 2018).

Coaches perceived their role as a youth sport coach to be diverse and included the promotion of athlete wellbeing. Consistent with previous research, coaches agreed that their role does include the promotion of mental health (Brown et al., 2017; Mazzer & Rickwood, 2015; Vella, Oades, & Crowe, 2011). For some coaches, this role extends to targeted actions to facilitate professional help-seeking, however, this view was not shared by all coaches. Despite the variation in the extent to which coaches described their willingness to act regarding athlete mental illness, all coaches articulated some form of role in the identification, referral and prevention of mental health problems. Notably, some coaches expressed a preference to work directly with athletes, while others preferred to notify parents. Coaches expressed a preference to receive education face-to-face, and to include practical components. These coaches preferred supplementary information to be delivered online, and for sessions to be short.

Given large discrepancies in coaches' willingness to be involved in the prevention of mental illness, we decided to build on coaches' universal belief that the promotion of wellbeing was part of their role. In particular, an intervention was designed based on self-determination theory (Ryan & Deci, 2000) that would allow coaches to: i) facilitate good quality (self-determined) motivation that would decrease the risk of mental health problems associated with the prioritisation of performance; ii) increase athlete wellbeing by increasing self-determined motivation; and, iii) lead to higher retention rates in youth sport, which have been associated with lower risk for mental health problems (Vella, Cliff, Magee, & Okely, 2015). However, this programme was not attractive to coaches, as evidenced by the very small numbers of coaches who completed the programme (Vella et al., 2020). Following feedback from coaches after the study, we created a 75-minute coach version of the mental health literacy program being run with adolescents and parents. The programme focuses on identifying the warning signs of depression and anxiety, the ways to start a conversation, and help seeking options. More specifically, the coach programme aims to communicate key messages, including: athletes' changes in behaviour may be as important as the behaviour itself; coaches are not responsible for solving the 'problem', and merely need to start a conversation; and, navigating the coach-athlete-parent triad is difficult, but being transparent is important. This version of the programme was piloted in Canada among (ice) hockey coaches, and appeared to be feasible in its delivery, acceptable in its content, and showed some evidence of effectiveness (Drew et al., 2022).

Framework and intervention delivery

Based on the above findings, four distinct intervention components and a supporting messaging campaign were developed to meet the needs of all stakeholders (including adolescent sport participants, their parents, coaches, clubs and regional sporting bodies), in the most feasible and engaging manner. A detailed description of the entire AOTG programme content has been reported elsewhere (Vella et al., 2018). However, this description does not include the updated coach mental health literacy programme, which is described in more detail below. Briefly, AOTG comprises two distinct interventions for adolescent male sports participants targeting mental health literacy and resilience, respectively. A single intervention for parents targets parental mental health literacy. Finally, a coach mental health literacy intervention is included for coaches of adolescent sport participants. These four interventions are supplemented by a club-based mental health messaging campaign that reinforces the key messages contained within the Ahead of the Game intervention components.

Adolescent mental health literacy: Help Out a Mate

Help Out a Mate (HOAM) is a brief 45-minute face-to-face sports-based mental health literacy intervention. The intervention is delivered by trained volunteer presenters and aims to: increase mental health literacy among adolescent males (specifically in regard to depression and anxiety); increase their skills and confidence to help a peer showing signs of a mental health problem; increase helping behaviour and supportive actions; increase appropriate help-seeking among young males at risk of mental health problems; and decrease stigmatising attitudes. The intervention was intentionally designed to be brief so that it could be presented at sports clubs to a team or group of adolescent males in or around a regularly scheduled training session. Specifically, participants are taught the HOAM action plan with regard to the provision of help to somebody else: *ask how they are; listen without judgement; ask about supportive adults; suggest sources of help;* and *check again later.* Presentation slides followed a consistent theme of a sepia-toned cartoon which had been concept-tested. Participants' confidence and intentions to help someone experiencing a mental health problem were reinforced through three brief role-plays based on the HOAM action plan.

The HOAM intervention involved the following components: (i) a description of what is mental health and mental illness; (ii) dispelling myths about mental illness; (iii) a description of depression; (iv) what is anxiety?; (v) how to provide help; and (vi) where to get reliable information. Additional resources provided to adolescents include a business card sized "Man Card", which lists key steps on how to help a friend (the HOAM Action Plan), and a list of mental health resources.

Mental health literacy refers to the knowledge, attitudes and beliefs about mental health and disorders, and the effectiveness of potential actions to benefit personal or others' mental health through symptom recognition, management and prevention (Jorm, 2012; Jorm et al., 1997). HOAM addresses these components with the content and structure developed following a review of the literature and existing programmes and materials (Black Dog Institute, 2014; Hart, Mason, Kelly, Cvetkovski, & Jorm, 2016; Kitchener & Jorm, 2002; Ross, Hart, Jorm, Kelly, & Kitchener, 2012) and consultation with a Mental Health First Aid Trainer. Depression and anxiety are covered as these are the most common mental health problems among youth (Lawrence et al., 2015). Clarifying when signs and symptoms of depression or anxiety move from being a part of normal experience to becoming problems likely to require help-seeking is a key part of the workshop content. Other mental illnesses or the effectiveness of various treatments were not addressed due to the time limitations on the workshop. The focus was on developing the knowledge to recognise when a friend is struggling and the skills to offer support, particularly with help-seeking.

The HOAM programme underwent a cluster-randomised controlled trial in Australia (Liddle et al., 2021). Compared to the waitlist control group, adolescent male sport participants who took part in the HOAM programme showed improvements in mental health literacy for depression and anxiety, as well as higher intentions to provide help along with sustained improvements in attitudes that promote help-seeking and reduce stigma. A qualitative evaluation of the programme showed that the workshop was a positive experience that led to increases in confidence to seek and provide help for mental health, and that community sports was an engaging setting for the delivery of the programme (Wynters et al., 2021).

Adolescent resilience: Your Path to Success in Sport

The original AOTG programme contained a resilience component named Your Path to Success in Sport (YPTSS). YPTSS is a brief 45–60-minute face-to-face workshop supported by six internet-based (website/mobile application) modules. The primary aim of YPTSS is to increase psychological resilience: the mental processes and behaviour which promote personal assets and protect an individual from the potential negative effect of stressors (Fletcher & Sarkar, 2013). The face-to-face workshop is facilitated by trained presenters and delivered at the sports club to groups of up to 30 adolescents. The content of the workshop focuses on "expectations vs reality" in the process of achieving goals (i.e., the "path to success"). This acts to identify inevitable challenges, obstacles and adversity that adolescents are likely to face in and outside of sport. The workshop then focuses on the need to build key skills through which adolescents can overcome adversity, which can be learnt via the internet-based resources.

The internet-based component of the intervention contains six modules, each of which take approximately 10–15 minutes to complete, and are designed to be completed in order. Informed by sport-based resilience literature (Fletcher & Sarkar, 2012, 2013; Galli & Gonzalez, 2015; Sarkar & Fletcher, 2014a, 2014b), the modules are: (i) problem-solving; (ii) controlling the controllables; (iii) managing your thoughts; (iv) keeping your cool; (v) playing to your strengths; and (vi) appreciating your team. These skills are communicated through informational videos, infographics, reflective activities and exercises to try at the end of each module. An additional recap module is also available to participants who completed the six preceding modules. Upon completion of YPTSS, adolescents will have had the opportunity to develop more adaptive beliefs about managing adversity and increasing their psychological resilience.

However, the scale-up of the programme in the UK and Australia has incorporated a revised resilience programme. Based on the same theory and principles of resilience, the workshop and online components have been updated to increase engagement and interest. The programme – renamed The Challenge – now follows the story of one 'main character' (an adolescent male rugby player in the UK version, and an Australian Rules Footballer in the Australian version) who comes up against adversity in the form of an injury and a critical performance failure. The programme follows his journey to deal with those setbacks and incorporates the key skills described above over a number of online modules.

Parents

The parent intervention is a brief 60-minute face-to-face intervention with supplementary print content. The intervention aims to increase parents' knowledge and self-efficacy in dealing with mental health problems by increasing knowledge and confidence to help, reducing stigmatising attitudes and increasing engagement in actual help-seeking and support strategies. All components of mental health literacy were targeted including: 1) knowledge awareness and help-promoting positive attitudes; 2) capacity to recognise the development or signs of a mental health disorder; 3) knowledge about professional help-seeking and treatment options; 4) capacity to help and support; and finally 5) knowledge of preventive and self-help strategies.

Workshops took place at local community sport club facilities, community centres, and on a university campus and were scheduled at convenient times for parents (e.g., while son is training). Workshops were led by a member of the research team who had mental health first aid certification and experience in delivering mental health workshops. Following the workshop, parents received a pamphlet containing key information and resources from the workshop and were also directed to online resources should they require or want more information. Printed material focussed on how to tell the difference between "normal" teenage behaviour and potential warning signs of mental health problems.

The content of the parent intervention was designed to be engaging, utilising a mix of parent reflection, discussion, scenarios, presentation and some brief videos. Materials were developed and adapted from Mental Health First Aid guidelines (Fischer, Kelly, Kitchener, & Jorm, 2013; Morgan & Jorm, 2009), or used with permission from mental health organisations and parenting organisations. The content of the intervention workshop was assessed for relevance and accuracy by a Mental Health First Aid Trainer.

A controlled trial of the parent programme showed that while there were no significant improvements in the intervention group compared to a control in depression or anxiety literacy, parents in the intervention group were more likely to seek formal help for themselves, had increased confidence and knowledge to help someone experiencing a mental health disorder, experienced reduced psychological distress, and perceived more support from other parents in their sport club, relative to the control group (Hurley et al., 2021). A qualitative evaluation of the programme showed that: parents reported increased awareness and knowledge of mental health disorders and help-seeking options; parents perceived increased confidence and preparedness to assist someone experiencing a mental health issue; the intervention stimulated conversation about mental health within sport club communities; parents made use of intervention information and resources to help others; and, community sport clubs were perceived as an acceptable setting to discuss mental health among parents.

Coaches

The coach component of the programme was based on the existing mental health literacy interventions for parents and adolescents. It is delivered via a 75-minute face-to-face workshop that covers seven key components. These components include: (1) a brief introduction where presenters are introduced and video of popular coaches talking about mental health is used to set the scene; (2) an exploration of the concept of mental health as existing on a continuum akin to physical health and injury; (3) a 'myth or reality' section designed to provoke discussion among the group, such as 'it is better not to know if my athlete has a mental health problem'; (4) signs and symptoms of depression; (5) signs and symptoms of anxiety; (6) how to provide help using the framework of ask, listen, encourage action, and check in again later, which also includes role plays and; (7) a discussion of the coach's role in mental health promotion, including creating a psychologically safe environment. The programme was designed to engage coaches with the use of multimedia (e.g., videos), discussion (e.g., on topical issues such as whether it is better not to know if an athlete has a mental health problem), and role plays (e.g., with other coaches to practice key skills around starting a conversation).

This version of the programme was piloted in Canada among (ice) hockey coaches. Quantitative evidence showed that coaches who participated in the pilot programme reported improvements in depression literacy, intentions to seek help for oneself and their athletes, and knowledge and confidence to provide help. In addition, in a qualitative evaluation of the pilot programme coaches reported positive impressions of the workshop and provided concrete examples of programme content application across sport and other domains of life (Drew et al., 2022).

Intervention evaluation and lessons learned through self-reflection

The AOTG programme was implemented over three distinct phases (Vella et al., 2019). Phase I included an initial pilot implementation which involved the collection of preliminary data on contextual variables, as well as any local adaptations within sporting clubs that were required. Phase II included programme and intervention implementation and development which involved the collection of data on the dose, reach, fidelity and cost of the programme. Phase III included the programme's full implementation which involved a robust formative evaluation of the effectiveness of the programme implementation, and the contextual information including its cost-effectiveness and possible mechanisms of change (Stetler et al., 2006). A full description of the implementation phases and the lessons learned is given elsewhere (Vella et al., 2019). We will focus here on the fourth Phase of programme implementation – global scale up.

To move forward in the most cost-effective manner, and in recognising the limitations of the research team in delivering an effective global scale-up of the AOTG programme, the implementation model during the scale-up phase centred on working with delivery partners. For example, AOTG was delivered as part of the Rugby League World Cup 2021/22 as a partnership between the funding body (i.e., Movember) and the delivery organisation (Rugby League Cares). The delivery partner was responsible for the delivery of AOTG programme across the UK. To enable delivery, a 'train the trainer' programme was undertaken to train the programme facilitators from with the delivery partners (i.e., ex rugby league players who would be facilitating the workshops). The delivery partner was responsible for contacting local rugby league clubs, as well as organising and delivering sessions. The lessons learned from formal and informal self-reflection on the global scale-up process are presented below.

In choosing a partner to work with, we emphasise the need for values alignment an at organisational level. Our reflection has been that partners who are aligned on their values make for a smoother implementation process. For example, delivery partners who genuinely want to improve the mental health of young people, value the potential of community sport to make a meaningful difference to mental health, and are willing to engage in genuine partnership for mutual benefit have been the hallmarks of our most successful partnerships. In this sense, it is also important to find a delivery partner who is invested in the programme and is prepared to invest in the programme in some meaningful way. Similarly, it is also important that delivery partners have some influence over the target audience (i.e., an ability to recruit participants and facilitate programme delivery), with some certainty that they will be willing to leverage that influence for the purposes of delivering the programme.

Once a partner has been chosen, the ways of working with a partner is important and has also been the subject of a lot of reflection. Fundamentally, a delivery partner should be empowered to 'own' the programme, as opposed to the perception that they are simply delivering somebody else's programme.

As such, it is important to facilitate ownership of the programme on behalf of partners by making changes to the programme where appropriate, its delivery model, and/or other programme materials. One way to ensure that the delivery partner can own the programme is provide them with some autonomy to deliver the programme in a way that suits their organisational resources, processes, and strengths. Ideally, this means that the programme can be embedded within the partner organisation which we hold to increase sustainability of the programme. A final reflection here is to provide some accountability to delivery partners around key outcomes which could be the number and quality of programmes delivered.

The train the trainer programme – wherein people are trained from within the delivery partner to be able to deliver the programme effectively and with fidelity – is a critical step in ensuring the success of the scale up process. The train the trainer programme is the key touch point with those people who will become the face of the programme, will have the face-to-face contact with the target population, and are primarily responsible for fulfilling the promise of the programme to facilitate change. As such, one of the primary outcomes of the train the trainer programmes should be to ensure buy-in on behalf of the people who will deliver the programme. The other outcomes that would ideally be the result of the train the trainer programme are people who become advocates for the programme, who are well-prepared to delivered the programme, and who have high levels of confidence in their ability to deliver the programme including their ability to navigate any potential problems. In addition, the train the trainer programme should lead to programme deliverers who are intrinsically motivated, and who are given the flexibility and permission to deliver the programme in a manner that feels authentic to them while also ensuring high levels of fidelity.

Ultimately, the delivery of the programme should reflect the funder, the delivery partner, and the programme facilitator. While this is a tall order, the processes described above could be used to ensure that ownership and identity are high among these three key stakeholders. This includes a programme that can be delivered in line with the values of each organisation/partner. Ultimately, there will be some difficulties in scaling up a programme in partnership, so open lines of communication between the partners is critical. Further, when the programme can be embedded within each partner organisation it leads to a smoother process for overcoming key difficulties.

Finally, where meaningful and lasting change are desired, a systems-based approach to programme scale up may be beneficial (Vella et al., 2022). In line with this approach, partnership across all components of the sports system is held to lead to greater and longer lasting change. In order to achieve a system-wide partnership, we need a recreational sport system that acknowledges and values the opportunity to deliver mental health programming in sport. We also need a system whereby all of its components (e.g., national sports organisations, sports clubs, teams, individuals) can buy-in and work in genuine partnership and coordination.

In conclusion, there have been many important lessons learned from formal and informal reflection on the global scale up process undertaken with the AOTG programme. In order to achieve that global scale up a partnership model was necessary. The vast majority of the key lessons learned are related to the manner in which partners are selected, empowered, and trained, as well as how they should deliver the programme. We hold that these lessons are the key to successful scale up of programmes across multiple countries. Of course, many years of programme design and evaluation were necessary before embarking on a scale up process, and the large evidence base that underpins AOTG provides the foundation upon which scale up can be justified.

References

Aubert, S., Barnes, J. D., Abdeta, C., Abi Nader, P., Adeniyi, A. F., Aguilar-Farias, N. .... Tremblay, M. S. (2018). Global matrix 3.0 physical activity report card grades for children and youth: Results and analysis from 49 countries. *Journal of Physical Activity and Health, 15*(s2), S251–273.

Australian Institute of Health and Welfare. (2020a). *Deaths in Australia*. www.aihw.gov.au/reports/life-expectancy-death/deaths-in-australia

Australian Institute of Health and Welfare. (2020b). *Deaths by Suicide over Time (Suicide & Self-Harm Monitoring)*. www.aihw.gov.au/suicide-self-harm-monitoring/data/deaths-by-suicide-in-australia/suicide-deaths-over-time

Baranne, M. L., Falissard, B. (2018). Global burden of mental disorders among children aged 5–14 years. *Child and Adolescent Psychiatry and Mental Health 12*, 19 (2018). doi: 10.1186/s13034-018-0225-4

Bauman, N. J. (2016). The stigma of mental health in athletes: Are mental toughness and mental health seen as contradictory in elite sport? *British Journal of Sports Medicine, 50*, 135–136. doi:10/gc95g7

Black Dog Institute. (2014). Youth Programs. Retrieved from www.blackdoginstitute.org.au

Breslin, G., Shannon, S., Haughey, T., Donnelly, P., & Leavey, G. (2017). A systematic review of interventions to increase awareness of mental health and well-being in athletes, coaches and officials. *Systematic Reviews, 6*, 177–192. doi:10/gc95g8

Breslin, G., Shannon, S., Cummings, M., & Leavey, G. (2022). An updated systematic review of interventions to increase awareness of mental health and well-being in athletes, coaches, officials and parents. *Systematic Reviews, 11*(1), 1–29.

Brown, M., Deane, F. P., Vella, S. A., & Liddle, S. K. (2017). Parents views of the role of sports coaches as mental health gatekeepers for adolescent males. *International Journal of Mental Health Promotion, 19*, 1–13. doi:10/gc95hf

Doherty, S., Hannigan, B., & Campbell, M. J. (2016). The experience of depression during the careers of elite male athletes. *Frontiers in Psychology, 7*, 1–11. doi:10/f8wgg9

Dorsch, T. E., King, M. Q., Dunn, C. R., Osai, K. V., & Tulane, S. (2017). The impact of evidence-based parent education in organized youth sport: A pilot study. *Journal of Applied Sport Psychology, 29*, 199–214. doi:10/gc95hk

Drew, B. J., Sutcliffe, J. T., Liddle, S. K., Bruner, M. W., McLaren, C. D., Swann, C., Schweickle, M. J., & Vella, S. A. (2022). Mental health literacy workshop for youth sport coaches: A mixed-methods pilot study. *International Sport Coaching Journal, 10*(1), 91–101.

Ferguson, H., Swann, C., Liddle, S. K., & Vella, S. A. (2018). Investigating youth sports coaches' perceptions of their role in adolescent mental health. *Journal of Applied Sport Psychology, 31*(2), 1–16. doi:10.1080/10413200.2018.1466839

Fischer, J. A., Kelly, C. M., Kitchener, B. A., & Jorm, A. F. (2013). Development of guidelines for adults on how to communicate with adolescents about mental health problems and other sensitive topics: A Delphi study. *SAGE Open, 3*, 1–15. doi:10/gc95hj

Fixsen, D. L., Naoom, S. F., Blase, K. A., Friedman, R. M., & Wallace, F. (2005). *Implementation Research: A Synthesis of the Literature*. Tampa, FL: University of South Florida.

Fletcher, D., & Sarkar, M. (2012). A grounded theory of psychological resilience in Olympic champions. *Psychology of Sport and Exercise, 13*, 669–678. doi:10/bcg4

Fletcher, D., & Sarkar, M. (2013). Psychological resilience. *European Psychologist, 18*, 12–23. doi:10/bwr7

Galli, N., & Gonzalez, S. P. (2015). Psychological resilience in sport: A review of the literature and implications for research and practice. *International Journal of Sport and Exercise Psychology, 13*, 243–257. doi:10/bcg5

Hart, L. M., Mason, R. J., Kelly, C. M., Cvetkovski, S., & Jorm, A. F. (2016). "teen Mental Health First Aid": A description of the program and an initial evaluation. *International Journal of Mental Health Systems, 10*, 1–18. doi:10/gc95g9

Harwood, C. G., & Knight, C. J. (2015). Parenting in youth sport: A position paper on parenting expertise. *Psychology of Sport and Exercise, 16*, 24–35. doi:10/gc95hm

Hossain, M. M., Nesa, F., Das, J., Aggad, R., Tasnim, S., Bairwa, M., … & Ramirez, G. (2022). Global burden of mental health problems among children and adolescents during COVID-19 pandemic: An umbrella review. *Psychiatry Research, 317*, 114814.

Hurley, D., Swann, C., Allen, M. S., Okely, A. D., & Vella, S. A. (2017). The role of community sports clubs in adolescent mental health: The perspectives of adolescent males' parents. *Qualitative Research in Sport, Exercise and Health, 9*, 372–388. doi:10/gc95hn

Hurley, D., Allen, M. S., Swann, C., & Vella, S. A. (2021). A matched control trial of a mental health literacy intervention for parents in community sports clubs. *Child Psychiatry & Human Development, 52*, 141–153.

Jorm, A. F. (2012). Mental health literacy: Empowering the community to take action for better mental health. *American Psychologist, 67*, 231–243. doi:10/fbjbqw

Jorm, A. F., Korten, A. E., Jacomb, P. A., Christensen, H., Rodgers, B., & Pollitt, P. (1997). Mental health literacy: A survey of the public's ability to recognise mental disorders and their beliefs about the effectiveness of treatment. *Medical Journal Australia, 166*(4), 182–186.

Kitchener, B. A., & Jorm, A. F. (2002). Mental health first aid training for the public: Evaluation of effects on knowledge, attitudes and helping behavior. *BMC Psychiatry, 2*, 1–6. doi:10/cfd9rh

Lawrence, D., Johnson, S., Hafekost, J., Boterhoven de Haan, K., Sawyer, M. G., Ainley, J., & Zubrick, S. R. (2015). *The Mental Health of Children and Adolescents: Report on the Second Australian Child and Adolescent Survey of Mental Health and Wellbeing*. Canberra, ACT: Department of Health.

Liddle, S. K., Deane, F. P., Batterham, M., & Vella, S. A. (2021). A brief sports-based mental health literacy program for adolescent males: A cluster-randomized controlled trial. *Journal of Applied Sport Psychology*, *33*, 20–44.

Mazzer, K. R., & Rickwood, D. J. (2015). Mental health in sport: Coaches' views of their role and efficacy in supporting young people's mental health. *International Journal of Health Promotion and Education*, *53*, 102–113. doi:10/gc95hc

Mendenhall, A. N., & Frauenholtz, S. (2015). Predictors of mental health literacy among parents of youth diagnosed with mood disorders. *Child & Family Social Work*, *20*, 300–309. doi:10/f7ksk4

Minkler, M., & Wallerstein, N. (2003). Part one: Introduction to community-based participatory research. In *Community-Based Participatory Research for Health* (pp. 5–24). San Francisco, CA: Jossey-Bass.

Morgan, A. J., & Jorm, A. F. (2009). Self-help strategies that are helpful for sub-threshold depression: A Delphi consensus study. *Journal of Affective Disorders*, *115*, 196–200. doi:10/cbhzgb

Rickwood, D. J., Deane, F. P., & Wilson, C. J. (2007). When and how do young people seek professional help for mental health problems? *Medical Journal of Australia*, *187*, S35–S39.

Roberts, R. E., Fisher, P. W., Blake Turner, J., & Tang, M. (2015). Estimating the burden of psychiatric disorders in adolescence: The impact of subthreshold disorders. *Social Psychiatry and Psychiatric Epidemiology*, *50*, 397–406. doi:10.1007/s00127-014-0972-3

Ross, A. M., Hart, L. M., Jorm, A. F., Kelly, C. M., & Kitchener, B. A. (2012). Development of key messages for adolescents on providing basic mental health first aid to peers: A Delphi consensus study. *Early Intervention in Psychiatry*, *6*, 229–238. doi:10/fxw2kc

Rugby League World Cup 2021. (2022). *Blazing a trail: Making a positive social impact: The story so far*. Rugby League World Cup 2021. www.rlwc2021.com/uploads/docs/SI_InterimReport_Digital.pdf

Ryan, R. M., & Deci, E. L. (2000). Self-determination theory and the facilitation of intrinsic motivation, social development, and well-being. *American Psychologist*, *55*(*1*), 68–78. doi:10/c48g8h

Sarkar, M., & Fletcher, D. (2014a). Ordinary magic, extraordinary performance: Psychological resilience and thriving in high achievers. *Sport, Exercise, and Performance Psychology*, *3*, 46–60. doi:10/gc95hh

Sarkar, M., & Fletcher, D. (2014b). Psychological resilience in sport performers: A review of stressors and protective factors. *Journal of Sports Sciences*, *32*, 1419–1434. doi:10/bchc

Stetler, C. B., Legro, M. W., Wallace, C. M., Bowman, C., Guihan, M., Hagedorn, H., … Smith, J. L. (2006). The role of formative evaluation in implementation research and the QUERI experience. *Journal of General Internal Medicine*, *21*(2), S1–S8.

Swann, C., Telenta, J., Draper, G., Liddle, S. K., Fogarty, A., Hurley, D., & Vella, S. A. (2018). Youth sport as a context for supporting mental health: Adolescent male perspectives. *Psychology of Sport and Exercise*, *35*, 55–64. doi:10/gc5922

Trojian, T. (2016). Depression is under-recognised in the sport setting: Time for primary care sports medicine to be proactive and screen widely for depression symptoms. *British Journal of Sports Medicine*, *50*, 137–139. doi:10/gc95hb

Vella, S. A., Oades, L., & Crowe, T. (2011). The role of the coach in facilitating positive youth development: Moving from theory to practice. *Journal of Applied Sport Psychology, 23*, 33–48. doi:10/cmbw92

Vella, S. A., Cliff, D. P., Okely, A. D., Scully, M. L., & Morley, B. C. (2013). Associations between sports participation, adiposity and obesity-related health behaviors in Australian adolescents. *International Journal of Behavioural Nutrition and Physical Activity, 10*, 113. doi:10/bqr8

Vella, S. A., Cliff, D. P., Magee, C. A., & Okely, A. D. (2015). Associations between sports participation and psychological difficulties during childhood: A two-year follow up. *Journal of Science and Medicine in Sport, 18*(3), 304–309. doi:10/gc95hv

Vella, S. A., Swann, C., Batterham, M., Boydell, K. M., Eckermann, S., Fogarty, A., … Miller, A. (2018). Ahead of the game protocol: A multi-component, community sport-based program targeting prevention, promotion and early intervention for mental health among adolescent males. *BMC Public Health, 18*, 1–12. doi:10/gc95hg

Vella, S. A., Swann, C., Boydell, K. M., Eckermann, S., Fogarty, A., Hurley, D., Liddle, S. K., Lonsdale, C., Sanders, T., Schweickle, M. J., Telenta, J., & Deane, F. P. (2019). Sports-based mental health promotion in Australia: formative evaluation. *Psychology of Sport & Exercise, 45*, 101560.

Vella, S. A., Swann, C., Batterham, M., Boydell, K. M., Eckermann, S., Ferguson, H., Fogarty, A., Hurley, D., Liddle, S. K., Lonsdale, C., Miller, A., Noetel, M., Okely, A. D., Sanders, T., Schweickle, M. J., Telenta, J., & Deane, F. P. (2020). An intervention for mental health literacy and resilience in organised sports. *Medicine & Science in Sports & Exercise, 53*(1), 139–149.

Vella, S. A., Schweickle, M. J., Sutcliffe, J., Liddelow, C., & Swann, C. (2022). A Systems theory of mental health in recreational sport. *International Journal of Environmental Research and Public Health, 19*(21), 14244.

Wynters, R., Liddle, S. K., Swann, C., Schweickle, M. J., & Vella, S. A. (2021). Qualitative evaluation of a sports-based mental health literacy program for adolescent males. *Psychology of Sport & Exercise, 56*, 101989.

Further reading

Vella, S. A., Swann, C., Batterham, M., Boydell, K. M., Eckermann, S., Fogarty, A., … Miller, A. (2018). Ahead of the game protocol: A multi-component, community sport-based program targeting prevention, promotion and early intervention for mental health among adolescent males. *BMC Public Health, 18*(390), 1–12.

This article provides a thorough explanation of the intervention and research protocol of the Ahead of the Game programme, and will expand in detail on the description provided in this chapter.

Schweickle, M. J., Graupensperger, S., Liddelow, C. R., Sutcliffe, J. T., Swann, C., & Vella, S. A. (2023). Potential moderators and mediators of intervention effects in a sport-based mental health literacy and resilience program for adolescent men. *Journal of Applied Sport Psychology*, 1–20. doi: 10.1080/10413200.2023.2208632

This article provides information on moderators and mediators of intervention and would be of interest to those readers considering theory development.

Drew, B., Bruner, M. McLaren, C., Swann, C., Schweickle, M., & Vella, S. A. (2022). Mental health literacy workshop for youth sport coaches: a mixed-methods pilot study. *International Sport Coaching Journal, 10*(1), 91–101.

This article will be of interest to coaches and those interested in developing mental health literacy workshops.

Wynters, R., Liddle, S. K., Swann, C., Schweickle, M. J., & Vella, S. A. (2021). Qualitative evaluation of a sports-based mental health literacy program for adolescent males. *Psychology of Sport and Exercise, 56,* 101989.

This article will be of interest to those designing a qualitative evaluation of mental health awareness programmes.

7

NAVIGATING MENTAL ILLNESS AND BRAIN INJURY IN AMATEUR RUGBY

A Sport Psychiatry case study

Thomas McCabe

Learning objectives

After reading this chapter you should be able to:

1. Describe the importance of holistic care when considering therapeutic interventions in mental illness
2. Critically consider first line options and practical considerations of medication use for athletes
3. Critically consider practical obstacles to optimised and joined up care and support in amateur sport

Introduction to the theme

Creating informed policy and sourcing expertise in a timely fashion for those in need of mental health support can be difficult for sporting administrators, with differing challenges encountered at the amateur when compared to the elite level. Out width the highest level of sport, access to practitioners with the necessary skills in diagnosis and management of psychological issues can vary. Uncertainty and inconsistent practices can contribute to increased morbidity and delayed presentation if support for a player cannot be sourced at the optimal time. As with other areas of medicine, prevention and intervention at the earliest appropriate opportunity, can prevent longer term poorer outcomes. Cultivation of multi-disciplinary teams in amateur levels of sport can be difficult compared to elite level where mental health support is much more readily available as part of a 'backroom' team (McEwan, 2020).

DOI: 10.4324/9781003291695-8

Mental illness continues to be overshadowed by more recognisable physical disease processes in other parts of the body. This applies to both the general population but also the sporting environment. Focus on the physical rehabilitation from injury, for example to lower limbs, can be easier to envisage for sportspersons with well recognised pathways back into training and competition – however little thought can be given to psychological response to injury, forced time away from the sporting environment, resultant contractual issues, and disrupted training and games schedule. Prevalence studies from throughout elite level sport are consistent in suggesting physical injury to be associated with the most well recognised mental health symptomology (Schuring, 2017; Wood, 2017).

The impact of mental health stigma is well documented and is a recognised barrier to those seeking 'help' (Clement, 2014). Traditionally this has been amplified in many contact sports such as Rugby Union, where any disclosure of mental frailty may be viewed as weakness by others (e.g., coaches, players, spectators), hence creating an environment of not sharing mental health challenges or experiences. However, there appears to be a sense of change in attitude from society when viewing those suffering with mental illness, particularly so in sport. Some theories behind this include a softening of attitudes in society in general during the recent COVID-19 pandemic when mental distress and uncertainty with regards the future were experienced by many. Also, high profile sports stars have described their experiences with mental illness in detail to media outlets and have promoted sources of mental health support (Kitson, 2022; Payten, 2022; BBC Sport, 2017). These factors along with public mental health campaigns such as those in the United Kingdom (UK) with tag lines such as '#itsoknottobeok' have combined to contribute to normalisation of mental illness (Lawrence, 2021).

There appears to be increased awareness from players and practitioners in terms of identification and subsequent reporting of rugby related traumatic brain injury/concussion (Miller, 2021). The brain is reported to be one of the most common sites of the body to be injured within the elite level and community rugby games for men and women, with concussion reported as taking longer to recover from within women's sport (World Rugby, 2022a; World Rugby, 2022b; The Irish Rugby Injury Surveillance Project Steering Group, 2022; Bretzin, 2021).

Recent media coverage has further highlighted some of the issues around identification and management of concussion and reported variable practices between different sports for apparently the 'same' injury. Rugby Union would appear to be a leader in terms of effort to trying to reduce frequency of concussion. However, given the dearth of evidence within the medical literature, many of these are changes of policy without a strong scientific basis and can be met with resistance in terms of acceptance. Furthermore, at present diagnosis of a concussion or mild traumatic brain injury is partly dependant on neurocognitive testing and self-report patient questionnaire, which are open to bias and may be subject to variability in how information is sourced (Echemendia, 2017). Until reliable objective testing is available and standardised, or a biomarker is discovered – as well as a change of culture and realisation of potential longer term health issues, concussion will continue to present challenges for sport medicine and psychiatry clinicians working within the field.

What follows is a description of a traumatic sports related brain injury and the associated outcomes. Psychological distress and outcomes are described, some of which could have been avoided with clarity around the patient's diagnosis and an early, comprehensive management plan. The assessment is that of a psychiatrist and although is not the real-life experience of one individual or team, is based on the writer's experiences within the field of sport psychiatry.

Introduction to the patient

Background

SL is a 26 year old semi-professional Rugby Union player. He is an established first team player within the highest division in a Tier 1 country. SL has played national age group rugby up until the age of 19 when he was not offered a professional contract, thereafter choosing to combine his future playing career with university studies.

SL suffers a facial injury after making a tackle during an important match for his team. He is assessed by the team physiotherapist for a suspected facial fracture, which is initially not identified and it is felt that he is safe to play on. Ten minutes later in the same game, he goes into another heavy contact. He is observed to try to get up but is dazed and sits back down on the pitch awaiting attention. SL is noted by coaching staff to be unsteady on his feet which is clearly communicated through to the medical team who attend the player promptly. SL eventually gets up slowly and jogs away from the physiotherapist to get back into position as the game is still going on – but is noted to be going in the wrong direction from where he would be expected to be defending when compared to where the play has moved onto. The referee does not stop the game immediately, as it appears the physiotherapist is still reviewing SL. Eventually when this long passage of play stops, he is assessed by the physiotherapist who attempts to ask him some orientation-based questions but the player appears agitated and focused on the next move in the game. The physiotherapist informs the referee of his concerns and insists on a Head Injury Assessment requiring evaluation in the changing rooms, much to the disappointment of SL. Any injury to the face is not immediately apparent on inspection and is denied by SL.

In the changing room, SL appears agitated and reluctant to engage with the proposed assessment. He challenges the physiotherapist without obvious foundation and his focus appears still to be on the game. It is difficult to get SL to concentrate on answering questions. It is apparent the initial facial injury is possibly a fracture given the tenderness and swelling which has now developed – it is decided he requires brain imaging in the local hospital accident and emergency department. SL settles to a degree when he realises he isn't getting back on the pitch to continue the game but with a focus on his facial injury rather than that of an injured brain. He complains of headache, admits to double vision, a painful area around his chin and feels there is a malalignment of his mandible (jaw bone) when clenching his teeth – this is now his focus after being taken off from the field of play. A basic examination suggests no damage to the eye socket and his eye movements appear normal, however he is tender on palpation (touch) over the 'jaw line' and it appears there is likely a fracture. A short period of time passes, and the physiotherapist attempts to find SL's baseline Sport Concussion Assessment Tool 5 (SCAT5) evaluation given events on the pitch and reported headache. SL says he may have had one completed during preseason however the folder of completed assessments has been misplaced – all the team assessments are usually kept within the medical room amongst other notes. This is not beside the changing room and is kept locked during the game. This delay, when the physiotherapist is away to attempt to find SCAT5, irritates SL.

SL's father comes into the dressing room, informs the physiotherapist it looks like there is another serious injury to one of his team's players and suggests he takes his son straight away off to the accident and emergency department. The physio rushes off and says he will contact SL after the match. SL gets changed out of his match gear and his father takes him to the hospital – during transfer headache largely resolves and SL says he feels more 'with it.' In the accident and emergency department he has a 3 hour wait to be seen, has some food and although reports he feels 'lousy' – seems to be brighter and more alert. He is keen to get home and his teammates are encouraging him to get back to the rugby club for celebratory post-match drinks. SL is eventually assessed and following an Xray of his mandible – will be followed up as an outpatient with a view to surgical correction of a fracture by the maxillofacial team. He is advised he has a 'concussion' and given an advice leaflet – there is little explanation offered but told to expect any symptoms to subside over the next 48 hours. He is strongly encouraged not to drink alcohol or drive. SL is advised to be in the company of others over the next 48 hours, but doesn't think this is possible as his parents live in another city and his girlfriend is at a social event. SL is told not go back to rugby 'for a week or 2' and rest over the next 72 hours. He is advised he should be feeling better within a week and appropriate safety advice is put into place with regards reasons to return to the accident and emergency department should his condition deteriorate.

SL's father is adamant he should have his brain scanned but an explanation is offered as to why this is not advised at present, which he accepts.

SL is followed up by the maxillofacial surgeons and a straightforward surgical correction of the fracture is carried out in the week that follows without any complications.

Presenting complaint

SL presents to his General Practitioner (GP) reporting a variety of symptoms in the weeks since injury, different to that which he initially experienced. His GP is content his mandibular injury has largely healed. However he recommends onward referral given symptoms from a likely 'concussion' are lingering – which now have a likely mental illness focus. With assistance of funding from the rugby club as well as his parents, he is referred to a local sports psychiatrist. SL is initially reviewed by a psychiatrist approximately 2 months following injury.

Two months after the head injury, SL reports to the psychiatrist fatigue, poor sleep pattern, 'being on edge all the time,' 'jumpy' and 'expecting the worst' since being discharged from hospital. He is unable to give accurate timelines of events, has little recollection of the day of original injury, how the intensity of these symptoms have varied or how they may have impacted on each other. At times, SL feels he gets a burst of energy just after lunch when he feels full of confidence but otherwise feels 'in a blur' for most of the day and has taken to napping on the couch in early evening because 'I am so worn out.' This pattern of being tired and lethargic has led to irritability with his family and girlfriend, whom he lives with. They have paused their previously active social life and SL is reluctant to leave the house for any length of time – due to 'being bored' and 'just can't be bothered.'

SL describes getting over to sleep easily but wakening up usually 2 hours after going to bed at around 11:30. He 'tosses and turns' thereafter and feels his thoughts 'get messy' when awakes – he is unable to expand on this. SL feels unrefreshed in the morning, sometimes with a headache. He describes being 'at his wits end' and desperate for any kind of help. He last had a good night sleep before his most recent concussion, and usually sleeps a regimented 9 hours a night when feeling 'well.'

SL denies any twitching, abnormal movements, nightmares, flashbacks or visual symptoms.

History of presenting complaint

SL has suffered from concussion on a seasonal basis since the age of 17. None of these have resulted in hospitalisation or prolonged periods away from the game. Rather, he has usually returned to the field of play within a fortnight without any formal return to play rehabilitation or active intervention. SL denies having an obvious mental illness symptomology following these previously although describes an intermittent tension-type headache persisting for 1 month following his last injury, in the season prior. He has worn a scrum-cap since being a teenager with a presumption that this would help 'protect him' from further injury after his grandfather had bought him it for a Christmas present and this has added to his confidence in going into contact. As the years have gone on, coaches and family have commented he doesn't seem as robust or physical as he was in his earlier years of rugby.

SL denies feeling depressed when directly asked but rather 'fed up with all this.' He has avoided any socialisation and has struggled looking at his computer screen for prolonged periods of time. This is an important year for him at university and he has real concern over his ability to pass his final assignments. His usual high calorie intake in order to meet training requirements as a result of training and gym work has tailed off and he thinks he has lost muscle definition and weight. He feels regretful at getting angry at his girlfriend over, in hindsight, relatively trivial matters and she has been sleeping in the spare room. SL is worried she might leave him despite having a stable relationship before now.

From a mental state perspective – SL presented wearing a loose fitting t-shirt, woolly hat, tracksuit bottoms and trainers with some food stains apparent on his clothes. He was not cleanly shaven and there is a faint smell of body odour. SL is tall and well built. He has well healed scarring around cheeks and forehead, presumably from previous rugby related injuries. He smiled and appeared bright in the initial stages of the assessment, however appeared more fatigued and displayed psychomotor retardation as the assessment progressed. SL appeared tearful at one stage when discussing some of the more challenging aspects of his presentation, including his relationship with his girlfriend. He shrugged his shoulders in response to some questions as if he 'couldn't be bothered' to answer – but not in an obnoxious or rude fashion and overall engaged well in the process. There was no abnormal movements or tremor. He kept reasonable eye contact although spent some short periods of time staring aimlessly at the ground. SL did not present overtly anxious. His speech when in flow – was normal in terms of rhythm, rate and tone – conversely at times was hesitant and monotonous.

SL described his mood as being low, at 2 out of 10. He appeared low in mood. He denies any thoughts or plans for suicide. Thought processes were largely organised and in reality without anything to suggest delusional thought content or psychotic features. There was slight preoccupation with events around most recent events at rugby however this was not thought to be pathological and very much at the centre of SL perception of where his problems stem from. Mini Mental State Examination scored 10/10. Insight, which is defined as having understanding on one's own mental state and how this affects the environment around the patient, was judged to be intact.

In terms of risk assessment, SL denied any ongoing thoughts of harm to himself or others. However, he described two instances lately when he felt like 'banging my head off the wall' in order to try to get himself some relief from his situation. SL was aware that this would be unlikely to help. He felt at times over the past fortnight he has pent up aggression and energy without any outlet for his feelings – previously this would have been 'offloaded' during rugby. SL admitted he clenches his fists at these times and removes himself from any company he may be in. He did feel impulsive at times and at times 'blurts stuff out' verbally which usually is hurtful towards his girlfriend. He regrets these shortly after. SL denied having access to significant amounts of medication and weapons which he would consider harming himself with. SL admits to feeling out of control for short periods of time. He believes in his own worth and doesn't feel a burden on family, friends or medical staff. SL has protective factors surrounding him, including his girlfriend, family, medical staff and a supportive club which are contributing from a sporting perspective and also helping fund specialist assessment as part of his rehabilitation programme. He is aware of how to contact this support, usually has company for vast majority of the day and is aware of a variety of crisis support telephone lines. SL engages well when agreeing a short safety plan for when he feels overwhelmed by some of the psychological symptoms he is experiencing.

Initial needs assessment

Case formulation

SL is a university student and rugby player whose diagnosis is most suited to mixed anxiety and depressive disorder International Classification of Diseases-10 (ICD10) code F43.23. This is evidenced by symptoms of low mood, poor sleep, irritability, lethargy, hopelessness, somatic features of anxiety and anhedonia with significant knock-on effect on social and educational functioning. The symptoms have been persisting for 2 months following sports related brain injury, which may be viewed as a precipitant or causative factor. His symptoms have largely been left untreated from a purely mental health perspective over this time period and indeed the symptoms described above appear to be his primary concern given relative resolution of cognitive symptomology – although this has not necessarily been monitored or tested by way of standard assessment tools. SL has historical experience with sports related brain injury through rugby participation which is likely to have left him vulnerable to further injury and added to this, has had maladaptive coping mechanisms as a result of these previously being untreated.

SL has positive support from his partner and family – who appear to be attempting to understand his experience and interacting with health professionals in order to assist. He has a positive relationship with his tutors in university and they are understanding of his present challenges. His sole being and identity is not based around that of his sporting interests and he has managed to shift focus onto other interests when unable to participate in rugby. SL does not have any significant family history of mental disorder or in environments where mental illness is noticeably prevalent.

Framework and intervention for delivery

The biopsychosocial model of care (Papadimitriou, 2017) is the most commonly used way of understanding and creating formulation within mental health care in the United Kingdom. It minimises focus on purely biomedical factors which influence the way we think and behave in the context of or absence of stress. The biopsychosocial model allows for holistic medicine to be practiced and patients to feel that they are being listened to, understood and taking control of their care management plan alongside their clinician. In some situations, environmental factors and intensity of symptoms can change within a relatively short period of time and this model of care allows for change in focus to different aspects of management in order to reduce risk of deterioration in an already fragile, mental state.

The three main elements of the model, which are all intertwined, are 1) Biological, which considers factors such as age, physical co-morbidity, neurochemistry and genetics 2) Psychological, which considers thoughts, emotions, behaviour, cognitive domains (such as memory, attention and concentration) and stress management, and 3) Social, which considers environments, social identity, economic status, community belonging, interpersonal relationships, education and patient background

Prevalence rates, rugby risk factors

Outside of the professional game of rugby, rates of concussion are difficult to estimate due to lack of and variation with reporting standards and practice. Rugby Union is partly reliant upon winning the contact area, be that tackle or ruck, as well as competition of balls 'in the air' with potential for contact with others as well as uncontrolled fall to the pitch. The tackle area is the part of the game which carries the highest risk of brain injury. Players are getting bigger and stronger when compared to the elite but amateur game of the early 1990s and before (Tucker, 2021; Smart, 2013). There have been a variety of on and off field factors proposed as putting players at greater risk of concussion (Abrahams, 2013; McGroarty, 2020). On field factors such as previous concussion, age, sex, tackle height, velocity into contact and playing position have been raised as potential risk factors. Some of these have been addressed and minimised to a degree with interventions such as law changes and minimisation of 'heavy' training contact sessions. Off field factors such as poor quality sleep, existing mental health diagnosis such as Attention Deficit Hyperactivity Disorder (ADHD) and neck strength have been proposed as contributing to an increased risk of brain injury (Collins, 2014; Cook, 2020).

Participation in sporting activity is generally viewed of as being beneficial from a cardiovascular and overall health perspective. Longer term neurocognitive outcomes of rugby players are yet to definitively described within medical literature (Russell, 2022). However, lessons from other contact sports such as soccer or American football suggest higher rates of progressive mental illness disease in later life, albeit with a different presumed mechanism of injury (Mackay, 2019). Rugby Union is a relatively 'young sport' in a professional sense, with players only being officially employed (and hence training) full time since 1995. With this, it has been suggested the game changed around this time with strength, fitness, intensity and force transmitted in contact all having increased. The evidence is unclear as to whether frequency of contact with the head has increased, stayed at similar levels or decreased. Time for 'ball in play' has increased, so opportunities for head impact has likely increased too. To date, there have not been any unequivocal prospective cohort studies to examine the possible consequences of participation in professional or amateur rugby – mostly due to relatively small numbers of professional players, allowing time for chronic disease states to develop and agreed definition and diagnosis of concussion or equivalent.

Sports Concussion Assessment Tool – Version 5 (SCAT5) (Echemendia, 2017) is the most widely used assessment tool in rugby and is promoted by World Rugby (the global authority on the game) as well as many of the main rugby administrations. The authors attempt to update this tool every 4 years. SCAT5 centres on self-report of a variety of symptoms as well as neurocognitive tests in order to assist with diagnosis of 'concussion' and thereafter, guide management. Step 2 of the SCAT5 requires players to rate symptoms from 0–6 'at this time' and calculate an overall score thereafter. Some of the mental illness symptoms within this list includes 'more emotional' 'sadness' 'nervous or anxious' 'trouble falling asleep' and 'fatigue or low energy.'

Despite an apparent consensus, there is still little to indicate the optimal time(s) to complete and ensure maximal validity of SCAT5 – be that from a cognitive or mental health perspective. Traditionally, the tool would be utilised in the first 48 hours following injury. Symptoms such as anxiety or depression tend to present 'later' than the cognitive symptoms and may take time to develop (Bunt, 2020) with significant differences between sexes. There can be variability in completion of base line testing and players may still attempt to 'beat' the assessor by rehearsing answers or being unable to give full disclosure on symptomology. Added to this, there would appear to be raised scores in some elements of mental health reported symptomology at baseline as well as a positive effect on exercise on scoring outcomes. Thus, SCAT5 in its existing form is inadequate to screen for emerging mental health symptoms following head impact based on the factors described and a somewhat vague, incomplete and disorganised approach to implementation of the tool. Furthermore, it is not clear how proposed symptoms within the self-report section have been formulated and chosen. This should be an area of focus for future versions of SCAT and of concern for clinicians, given depression is viewed of one of the most common features of 'prolonged' concussion.

Mild traumatic brain injury has been described as a major public health issue (Rauchman, 2022). Traumatic brain injury has been positively associated with depressive disorder and post-traumatic stress disorder in certain selected cohorts of patients, typically those who have been in conflict affected regions of the world or military personnel (Bryan, 2013). To a lesser degree, associations have been made with anxiety related disorders and various dependence syndromes, albeit with the multifactorial aspect of causation considered. Replication of such prevalence studies have largely been lacking within rugby medical literature at the elite level, instead relying on self-report questionnaires reporting of symptomology of the common mental health disorders, often with low participation engagement rates (Gouttebarge, 2017). Despite this, similarly designed studies from other sport would largely correlate with the suggested prevalence rates presented here. However, clinicians must continue to be cognisant of many isolated symptoms of mental illness being simply a normal human reaction to life events and thereby avoid labelling or 'over diagnosis.'

The absence of pathological changes on CT head should not lessen the potential for harm or persistent disability from a sports related traumatic brain injury, if not identified and managed effectively. Although not reflected in the medical literature – there has been many prominent international level players who have been forced to retire from the game as a result of 'head injuries' and persisting symptomology thereafter (Merchant, 2020; Stuff, 2018). Unless there is focal neurological signs on examination or other red flags on initial assessment or evolving thereafter, typically there is nothing abnormal noted on CT or MRI of the apparent 'injured brain.' When symptoms persist beyond expected, this can be anxiety provoking and there might be thoughts from the patient of 'something else going' which may lead to an expectation of requirement of brain imaging to confirm or otherwise. This is potential to strain the doctor: patient relationship, if patient expectations or wishes are not accounted for. Thus, clinicians should prioritise prehabilitation and psychoeducation with athletes and pay close consideration to diverse and evolving symptoms in the days and weeks following injury.

Concussive head injury causes the brain to experience a mechanical shake or twisting by virtue of the action of the acceleration and deceleration forces transmitted to the brain immediately after the impact. Typically, the brain tissue does not impact to the inside of the skull bone. This movement initiates a complex cascade of subsequent neurochemical and neurometabolic events with resultant inflammatory response. The sudden stretching of the neuronal and axonal membranes initiates an indiscriminate flux of ions through previously regulated ion channels and transient physical membrane defects. Furthermore, disruption of the Blood Brain Barrier and function occurs following brain injury with the protective element of this organ compromised, leading to altered permeability.

The use of pharmacological intervention with patients suffering from affective or mood related disorder following head injury is not necessarily standardised and practices may vary slightly between clinicians. We know little with regards psychotropic medication use specific to that in elite level sport, however general principles of prescribing would still pertain for this population. The perception of elite level athletes being ‘healthier’ than the general population might suggest typical medications are indeed ‘safer’ given the relative good health baseline that many sporting young adults possess. However, clinicians will be mindful of such issues such as how elite athletes’ metabolism and pharmacokinetics may vary in and out of competition, as well as the less well understood potential interaction with dietary supplementation or performance enhancing substances. Selective serotonin reuptake inhibitors (SSRIs) continue to be recommended as first-line management option for depressive disorder in expert consensus clinical practice guidelines (Silverberg, 2019). Within the UK, there are currently no licenced pharmacological options to prevent neurocognitive disorders as a result of brain trauma.

Risk assessment is a dynamic process of identification of, and managing risk, based on factors associated with the patient who may be considering harm to themselves or others. It is used to identify and explore practical and therapeutic strategies that the patient should be offered to lessen the likelihood of harm occurring. The responsibility for risk minimisation as a result of risk assessment should be everyone’s business who is involved in the care of athlete in distress, be that medic, family physician, physiotherapist, carers, family and close associates. However, experience tells us that it is usually the medic or in this case, the sport psychiatrist, who takes ownership for completing, documentation of and monitoring of risk assessment. In all cases, the information and strategies gleaned should be communicated to others within the realms of agreed level of confidentiality.

Although suicidality did not appear to be an immediate issue for SL, the topic should be broached with sensitivity and within each mental health assessment. It usually requires ‘lead up’ questions which psychiatrists should be familiar with and routinely use with confidence. Some patients may find it a surprise to be asked about their darkest of thoughts and may not have had these thoughts. Others will not have told anyone about their suicidal thoughts or indeed, plans they have made to carry these out. There can be a sense of relief when allowed to share such information with someone who cares and has heard similar accounts before. In some sporting populations of contact sport athletes with a history of concussion or traumatic brain injury, there has been a reported increased risk of suicide (Nguyen, 2019). These studies have been complicated by low numbers and the multifactorial aspects of suicidality, meaning direct causation is almost impossible to conclude from a scientific perspective at the present time. Nonetheless, there would be a direct association between suicidality and the most common of mental health disorders (Cavanagh, 2003).

Progress and delivery

SL agreed to complete a Patient Health Questionnaire – 9 for depression (PHQ9). Overall, he scored 21/27, suggesting a 'severe' depressive episode. SL scored a maximal 3/3 on the following questions – Feeling down, depressed, or hopeless? Trouble falling or staying asleep, or sleeping too much? Feeling tired or having little energy?

Providing explanation to SL with regards his presentation was carried out over two, hour long sessions. This allowed summary reflections made in order to allow the patient to provide information and share with his family – which he was keen to do. SL was also provided with video links to online resources in order to attempt to consolidate learning. Sports related brain injury was described as an injury affecting the brain due to a direct blow or sudden jolt – causing movement and/or twisting of the brain with resultant inflammation and biochemical changes with stretching and damage to exposed and fragile brain cells. SL was concerned with regards the structural architecture or the brain and whether there were bleeding or contusions. Explanation was offered that these structural changes are rarely seen on brain imaging and hence why Computer Tomography (CT) or Magnetic Resonance Imaging (MRI) are usually not indicated (Some exceptions to this are when atypical features with focal neurology or signs of cerebral irrational become prominent, suggesting the need to consider concurrent or underlying diagnosis including that of skull fracture. Certain mechanisms of injury as well as observable acute signs necessitate imaging).

The 2nd part of the psychoeducation was provided with regards some of the theories behind depression and how a depressive episode impacts on activities of daily living. Although being challenged by some of late (Moncrieff, 2022) – the serotonin theory was explained, as well as cognitive approach theory (Beddington, 1985). Similarly to previous, SL was given resources to look up – he preferred to watch short 5 minute videos online with basic animations rather than read at length with regards these theories. Some of these videos evolved into the basis of cognitive behavioural therapy (Mor, 2009).

Psychoeducation is viewed as a low level, early intervention psychotherapeutic strategy, providing a base and framework in order to progress from (Motlova, 2017). It is usually carried out early, whenever formulation is established and is aimed at providing information to the patient with regards their symptoms and thereby increasing understanding of illness, prognosis and treatment options. If the patient responds well to psychoeducation, it can be a significant factor at increasing adherence to the management plan further into treatment and allows for measured response to variations in mental state.

Psychoeducation is an integral part of the 'brief intervention management plan' at the 3a stage of The Sport Mental Health Assessment Tool 1 (SMHAT-1) tool and to the writer's knowledge, the only area within the sports medicine literature where it is specifically recommended (Gouttebarge, 2020). The SMHAT tool is the first mental health screening tool designed for athletes. It was created by a group of experts from the International Olympic Committee (IOC) and originally published in 2020 in the British Journal of Sports Medicine. Screening is the concept within medicine of identification of illness in its early stages with a test which is acceptable to the population, thought to be at risk from the illness. Screening is aimed at a significant health issue which has potential to be treated in the early stages and to prevent deterioration. It can also give clues with regards more serious stages of illness requiring urgent review e.g. suicidality in PHQ9. The SMHAT 1 has two recognisable stages and in the first part uses the Athlete Psychological Strain Questionnaire (Rice, 2019), with a score of 17 or more necessitating need to progress to the 2nd stage. Six further questionnaires are used at this point for those reaching threshold – including General Anxiety Disorder-7 (GAD-7) (Kertz, 2012): Patient Health Questionnaire-9 (PHQ-9) (Ford, 2020), Athlete Sleep Screening Questionnaire (ASSQ) (Bender, 2018), Alcohol Use Disorders Identification Test Consumption (AUDIT-C) (Reinert, 2007), Cutting Down, Annoyance by Criticism, Guilty Feeling, and Eye-openers Adapted to Include Drugs (CAGE-AID) (Dhalla, 2007) and Brief Eating Disorder in Athletes Questionnaire (BEDA-Q) (Martinsen, 2014). Although not necessarily covering mental health problems such as post traumatic stress disorder, attention deficit hyperactivity disorder or cognitive deficits – this stage would expect to pick up the main symptoms in depressive episodes, some anxiety disorders, harmful alcohol use, disordered eating and poor sleep. Meeting or exceeding threshold with any of these tests necessitates formal referral for psychiatric assessment. A score not meeting the specified threshold would indicate the need for monitoring or low-level interventions, such as psychoeducation, mindfulness training, counselling or sleep hygiene. Of concern, these interventions are very much at the discretion of the clinician administrating the tool and without any data driven evidence base.

Progress and intervention 2

During subsequent reviews and despite initial improvement, SL was frustrated at the lack of progress with his overall presentation and wanted to 'feel normal' again quickly. He raised the possibility of medication as an option for his situation and was aware of some family and friends on 'depression meds' to help with their mental health. His health anxiety has been raised, after one evening reading a social media post about a professional rugby player who had to retire from the game as a result of a concussive injury and didn't want 'my life to be over' as a result of his situation. He was concerned about being on medication long term and if he would be addicted and 'zonked' as a result. It was within subsequent reviews that the issue of the connection between brain injury and his mental health symptomology became more prominent for SL. He was aware of other high-profile cases described in the media of professional rugby players suffering from 'early onset of dementia' and considering legal action against their former employers. SL had also seen some fund-raising events for ex-players who were now in wheelchairs and unable to speak. SLs girlfriend had phoned ahead of the appointment asking to speak to the psychiatrist to inform them that last week, SL had been 'in a panic' with regards these things which he had read about. He had 'opened up' and began to cry in front of his family. They were partially successful in reassuring him with regards this and diverting his thoughts to something else. He had written out some questions in order to address at the next meeting.

The psychiatrist explained the basis and theoretical background of medication use in terms of monoamine neurotransmission and how it is proposed that by maximising serotonin and norepinephrine for postsynaptic uptake, there is enhanced transmission between cells. Medication would be expected to work, but not immediately and suitability could not be assessed for 2 weeks at the earliest – albeit some patients are shown to have a likely placebo effect or quicker response. Added to this, the most commonly experienced side effects were outlined and included a paradoxical increase in anxiety, gastrointestinal upset, sexual dysfunction, sweating and irritability. SL was reassured that these would be closely monitored, and any medication would be started at a low dose in order to reduce the likelihood of any emerging side effects. The psychiatrist emphasised that there was little in terms of empirical evidence on how medication use would translate to any on – field sport specific recovery and the somewhat complicated history of untreated brain injury. The psychiatrist also reiterated the need to consider the wider management plan and take focus away from one sole element of the management as a 'cure' for his symptoms. SL was given a patient information leaflet to consider his options and reviewed again by the psychiatrist one week later.

Options for medication were considered – these were sertraline and mirtazapine. The common benefits and side effect profile was described for both. In sertralines case – it was one tablet daily, at a starting dose of 100 mg daily (lower dose of 50mg daily is available) with a view to increasing after 1 month based on tolerability and efficacy. The most common side effects were stated as gastrointestinal upset, sweating and a small risk of paradoxical increase in anxiety and insomnia. Mirtazapine was described as a medication aimed at reducing anxiety and symptoms of low mood, as well as aiding sleep. It would be started at a dose of 15mg once daily and taken at night prior to going to bed. At that dose it would expected to work as a sleep aid. The most common side effects were described as a 'hungover' effect first thing in the morning, increased appetite (which may be beneficial to some patients with reduced oral intake as a result of mood or affective disorder) and weight gain (the latter pair of these could well be related). It was emphasised to SL however of the potential benefits of these medication, which alongside psycho-social interventions and close monitoring would be expected to work well for him. He was given a reputable evidence based website to do any further reading on the medication and a telephone call organised 3 days later to make a decision.

Decisions around psychotropic medication should be taken alongside the patient with information on choices and open conversations had with regards benefits, timelines and side effects. Perhaps one of the most pressing issues for athletes is how medication will impact on onfield performance. Some psychotropic medication can alter elements of cognition such as concentration, alertness or attention. Impact on other important sport related factors such as weight or cardiovascular function should be considered too as all have potential to compromise training potential or competition. Sexual dysfunction, although a rare side effect, should be highlighted in such a population of patients. For a patient who is actively engaged in training or competition and therefore expending significant amounts of energy, one should consider how metabolic or potential electrolyte disturbance may impact on a patient particularly so with medications such as selective serotonin receptors inhibitors and lithium. Conversely the patient and doctor should be aware of how performance may suffer as a result of the impact of an undertreated mental health disorder and the chances of side effects occurring – which if occurring at all, would likely be mild and easily reversed. The doctor-patient relationship can be influenced by 'success' or otherwise of some decisions considered above. Therefore, giving the patient autonomy over their body is a key aspect to cultivate this relationship, and this principle forms the basis of the Self-Determination Theory, as described by Deci and Ryan (2004).

Within the United Kingdom, selective serotonin reuptake inhibitors (SSRIs such as sertraline or fluoxetine) or mirtazapine are widely accepted as 'first line' antidepressants to be used in significant mood or affect disorders. SSRIs are thought to work on the hypothesis that increasing the serotonin level in the brain by preventing reuptake in the presynaptic neurons, allowing the hormone to remain available to bind to postsynaptic neurons and thereby increasing transmission. SSRIs are generally thought of as 'safe' medication options amongst young fit people. A survey of sports psychiatrists (Reardon, 2016) showed a preference for the use of fluoxetine or venlafaxine, a serotonin and noradrenaline reuptake inhibitor (SNRI) antidepressant (with similar mechanism of action to SSRIs), perhaps due to being regarded as being weight 'neutral.' Limited evidence base exists for such medications within athletic populations. Added to the above and illustrated within this case, athletes do not necessarily have access to professionals with expertise in prescribing and stigma continues to exist around psychotropic medication and perceived side effects associated.

Timing of starting medication should be considered alongside the athlete. For example, if in the run up to an important competition or with a patient who would be judged as having a high risk of experiences side effects, commencing medication could be delayed. However, decisions about starting should not be delayed beyond what is reasonable – medication is an important intervention in moderate and severe depressive and anxiety disorders – withholding without due reason is difficult to justify.

After 2 months SL agreed to repeat a PHQ9. Overall, he scored 11/27 suggesting a 'moderate' depression. SL scored a maximal 3/3 on the following questions – Trouble falling or staying asleep, or sleeping too much? Feeling tired or having little energy? This was a marked improvement on previous.

Return to play protocols were attempted by the club physiotherapist after spontaneous resolution of any lingering symptoms of balance impairments and cognition – albeit these weren't necessarily documented around time of injury. Given SL's injury to his mandible, he was rarely at practice in the fortnight following his injury and the physiotherapist was only employed by the club on Saturdays for games and one weekday evening. The physiotherapist attempted to leave messages for SL via Whatsapp and expected the player to complete various exercise interventions himself. Without clear direction and instruction, SL struggled to follow these without any consistency or report back on progress or regression. He admitted apathy towards exercise interventions and he wasn't 'in the mood' to do any 'half baked' moderate exercise and didn't see the point. There was no follow up SCAT5 carried out. Eventually the physiotherapist gave up trying to contact him as the season had ended and it appeared an opinion from a psychiatrist was being sought – this was now where the primary focus of ongoing care was.

Outcomes

After reviews by the psychiatrist and overall improvement noted by both the patient and psychiatrist, SL agreed to discharge back to general practice care. He contributed to the discharge planning and had extensive notes summarising his experiences and learnings from the sessions. His family engaged in this process and met with the psychiatrist alongside SL where events were summarised and discussions had, with regards how the future may look and warning signs to look out for to indicate a decline in mental state. Clear advice was given with regards stopping medication in the future and that this should be done in conjunction with medical personnel with caution and what other supportive structures were available. With SL's agreement, a summary of the assessment and recommendations were forwarded to his general practitioner. If he decided to return to rugby, it was made clear that he should disclose his experiences to the club and personnel involved with care, given that he would be viewed of being 'high risk' of further brain or other physical injury.

Stopping playing rugby or 'forced retirement' was a challenging time for SL. He occasionally returned to the club to watch some games but his interest in this waned shortly after. SL admitted he was never really a keen watcher of the game and preferred playing. In the evenings, when training would have been on, SL began to focus more on university studies as concentration gradually improved – there was an increased requirement for 'laboratory preparation' as part of his studies and longer-term coursework/assignments which acted as a motivator to him. Alongside his girlfriend, he continued to go to the gym regularly and had started running with a local running group – with a plan to work up to a half marathon. This gave the couple a shared goal and made their relationship stronger. This transition although ultimately enforced upon SL, was partially planned and SL had taken ownership of this, with minimal prompting from the psychiatrist.

Events involving SL allowed the rugby club to reflect upon events and optimise practices. There was a sense that the club could have done more to support their player during a difficult time, but the hierarchy of the club did not necessarily know where it had went wrong and the situation had been largely been taken out of the medical teams hands. Firstly, guidance around concussion practices were improved with coaches and medical staff instructed and facilitated to go on training courses. Players and significant others (e.g., family) were then given information from this and 2 sessions were incorporated into the preseason schedule so everyone within the wider club was in no doubt as to when removal of a player from competition would happen and what the aftercare protocol thereafter was. Basic infographics were put up around the club in prominent places such as the changing room, physiotherapy room and bar area to reinforce the 'no risk' message. This was clearly reemphasised and 'practiced' during any contact training and 'buy in' particularly from the senior players or leadership group was sought. From a purely mental health perspective, the club worked proactively with the governing union to provide information sessions, screening with onward referral and a basic cognitive behavioural therapy model delivered on a group basis for the team.

Conclusions

This case of SL highlights the importance of early intervention from a psychological perspective when considering brain injury in sport. The attitude toward brain injury in sport appears to be changing to that of caution and concern, as the evidence base slowly filters through into clinical practice. Previously, a lack of knowledge or access to medical expertise may have been a barrier to preventative strategies, getting to identification and an initial diagnosis with management plan. However, the stigma associated with this now appears to be lifting. The basics of removal from play and time away from full contact participation with potential for compromise of mental health is now widely acceptable to those within the game.

Multidisciplinary care is now the cornerstone of medicine. It allows differing approaches and skills to be harnessed in order to achieve the best possible outcomes for the patient. This was illustrated in the above case, where initially physiotherapy and emergency medicine largely managed the case – with requirement of input from general practice and psychiatry thereafter. Each had an important role to play, at differing stages of the illness as symptoms evolved.

Interventions in the above case were not necessarily standardised and may have been dependant on which professional was consulted for their views and practices. In particular, pharmacological management was an important part of the psychiatrist's management plan for the patient but may not have been considered by a general practitioner, sports medic or a clinical psychologist. Nonetheless, all of the above professionals would recognise the importance of holistic care demonstrated in this case and that particularly so in athletes and young adults, focus on social aspects of care and interactions with those around the patient, in this case the family, is of the upmost importance. In the case study, initial anxiety with regards medication use was eased by shared decision making and likely enhanced adherence resulting. Given the media coverage and at times sensationalism around brain injury in sport, there is potential for narratives to be taken as applicable to all situations and confusing for those reading first-hand accounts of difficult experiences faced. In reality, every patients presenting complaint, past history and approach to illness are different. Hence in this instance, such a strong focus was put towards the psychoeducation aspect of care to allow the patient and his family to understand the clinical situation and allow for autonomy thereafter. Psychoeducation is something which requires more than basic knowledge to carry out effectively and should be tailored to recipient(s) to achieve maximal effect.

Finally, sadly situations similar to this sometimes occur and prompt change to occur, more so when practices have been established for many decades. The patients experience led to changes around the club structures to brain injury and mental illness. As a rugby community, we must ensure we are listening to those around us and adapting to ensure well-being is put before any on field performance outcomes to further protect our athletes.

References

Abrahams, S., Fie, S. M., Patricios, J., Posthumus, M., & September, A. V. (2013). Risk factors for sports concussion: An evidence-based systematic review. *British Journal of Sports Medicine*, 48(2), 91–97. https://doi.org/10.1136/bjsports-2013-092734

Bebbington, P. (1985). Three cognitive theories of depression. *Psychological Medicine*, 15(4), 759–769. https://doi.org/10.1017/s0033291700004992

Bender, A., Lawson, D., Werthner, P., & Samuels, C. (2018). The Clinical validation of the athlete sleep screening questionnaire: An instrument to identify athletes that need further sleep assessment. *Sports Medicine – Open*, 4(1). https://doi.org/10.1186/s40798-018-0140-5

Bretzin, A. C., Esopenko, C., D'Alonzo, B. A., & Wiebe, D. J. (2021). Clinical recovery timelines after sport-related concussion in men's and women's collegiate sports. *Journal of Athletic Training*, 57(7), 678–687. https://doi.org/10.4085/601-20

Bryan, C. J., Clemans, T. A., Hernandez, A. M., & Rudd, M. E. (2013). Loss of consciousness, depression, posttraumatic stress disorder, and suicide risk among deployed military personnel with mild traumatic brain injury. *Journal of Head Trauma Rehabilitation*, 28(1), 13–20. https://doi.org/10.1097/htr.0b013e31826c73cc

Bunt, S. C., Didehbani, N., Tarkenton, T., Rossetti, H., Hicks, C., Vargas, B. B., Silver, C. H., Nakonezny, P. A., Bell, K. R., Batjer, H. H., & Cullum, C. M. (2020). Sex differences and reporting of SCAT-5 concussion symptoms in adolescent athletes. *Clinical Journal of Sport Medicine*, 31(5), e229–e234. https://doi.org/10.1097/jsm.0000000000000788

Cavanagh, J., Carson, A., Sharpe, M., & Lawrie, S. M. (2003). Psychological autopsy studies of suicide: A systematic review. *Psychological Medicine*, 33(3), 395–405. https://doi.org/10.1017/s0033291702006943.

Clement, S., Schauman, O., Graham, T., Maggioni, F., Evans-Lacko, S., Bezborodovs, N., Morgan, C., Rüsch, N., Brown, J. S. L., & Thornicroft, G. (2014). What is the impact of mental health-related stigma on help-seeking? A systematic review of quantitative and qualitative studies. *Psychological Medicine*, 45(1), 11–27. https://doi.org/10.1017/s0033291714000129

Collins, C. L., Fletcher, E. L., Fields, S. K., Kluchurosky, L., Rohrkemper, M. M., Comstock, R. D., & Cantu, R. C. (2014). Neck strength: A protective factor reducing risk for concussion in high school sports. *The Journal of Primary Prevention*, 35(5), 309–319. https://doi.org/10.1007/s10935-014-0355-2

Cook, N. E., Iaccarino, M. A., Karr, J. E., & Iverson, G. L. (2020). Attention-deficit/hyperactivity disorder and outcome after concussion: A systematic review. *Journal of Developmental and Behavioral Pediatrics*, 41(7), 571–582. https://doi.org/10.1097/dbp.0000000000000808

Deci, E. L., & Ryan, R. M. (2004). *Handbook of Self-Determination Research*. http://ci.nii.ac.jp/ncid/BA85081503

Dhalla, S., & Kopec, J. A. (2007). The CAGE questionnaire for alcohol misuse: A review of reliability and validity studies. *Clinical and Investigative Medicine*, 30(1), 33. https://doi.org/10.25011/cim.v30i1.447

Echemendia, R. J., Meeuwisse, W. H., McCrory, P., Davis, G. A., Putukian, M., Leddy, J. J., Makdissi, M., Sullivan, S., Broglio, S. P., Raftery, M., Schneider, K. J., Kissick, J., McCrea, M., Dvořák, J., Sills, A. K., Aubry, M., Engebretsen, L., Loosemore,

M., Fuller, G., Herring, S. A. (2017). The Sport Concussion Assessment Tool 5th Edition (SCAT5). *British Journal of Sports Medicine*, bjsports-097506. https://doi.org/10.1136/bjsports-2017-097506

Ford, J. E., Thomas, F., Byng, R., & McCabe, R. (2020). Use of the Patient Health Questionnaire (PHQ-9) in Practice: Interactions between patients and physicians. *Qualitative Health Research*, 30(13), 2146–2159. https://doi.org/10.1177/1049732320924625

Gouttebarge, V., Hopley, P., Kerkhoffs, G., Verhagen, E., Viljoen, W., Wylleman, P., & Lambert, M. I. (2017). Symptoms of common mental disorders in professional rugby: An international observational descriptive study. *International Journal of Sports Medicine*, 38(11), 864–870. https://doi.org/10.1055/s-0043-114010

Gouttebarge, V., Bindra, A., Blauwet, C. A., Campriani, N., Currie, A., Engebretsen, L., Hainline, B., Kroshus, E., McDuff, D. R., Mountjoy, M., Purcell, R., Putukian, M., Reardon, C. L., Rice, S. M., & Budgett, R. (2020). International Olympic Committee (IOC) Sport Mental Health Assessment Tool 1 (SMHAT-1) and Sport Mental Health Recognition Tool 1 (SMHRT-1): Towards better support of athletes' mental health. *British Journal of Sports Medicine*, 55(1), 30–37. https://doi.org/10.1136/bjsports-2020-102411

Kertz, S. J., Bigda-Peyton, J. S., & Björgvinsson, T. (2012). Validity of the Generalized Anxiety Disorder-7 Scale in an Acute Psychiatric Sample. *Clinical Psychology & Psychotherapy*, n/a. https://doi.org/10.1002/cpp.1802

Kitson, R. (2022, October 19). Players' union urges action on mental health after Kearnan Myall speaks out. *The Guardian*. www.theguardian.com/sport/2019/aug/20/rugby-players-union-mental-health-kearnan-myall

Lawrence, R. (2021, April 28). 'It's OK to not be OK' is a nice hashtag, but does it really help? *The Guardian*. www.theguardian.com/commentisfree/2021/apr/28/its-ok-to-not-be-ok-hashtag-mental-illness

Mackay, D. F., Russell, E., Stewart, K., Maclean, J., Pell, J. P., & Stewart, W. J. (2019). Neurodegenerative disease mortality among former professional soccer players. *The New England Journal of Medicine*, 381(19), 1801–1808. https://doi.org/10.1056/nejmoa1908483

Martinsen, M., Holme, I., Pensgaard, A. M., Torstveit, M. K., & Sundgot-Borgen, J. (2014). The development of the brief eating disorder in athletes questionnaire. *Medicine and Science in Sports and Exercise*, 46(8), 1666–1675. https://doi.org/10.1249/mss.0000000000000276

McEwan, H. (2020). *Mental Health in Performance Sport: An Interdisciplinary Approach*. https://dspace.stir.ac.uk/handle/1893/33177

McGroarty, N. K., Brown, S. M., & Mulcahey, M. K. (2020). Sport-Related concussion in female athletes: A systematic review. *Orthopaedic Journal of Sports Medicine*, 8(7), 232596712093230. https://doi.org/10.1177/2325967120932306

Merchant, K. (2020, December 9). Concussions forced me to quit professional rugby – now I'm worried about my future. *The Independent*. www.independent.co.uk/voices/rugby-concussion-steve-thompson-dementia-b1768596.html

Miller, J. M., Stein, K. S., Moon, T. J., Trofa, D. P., Kerr, H. A., Bottiglieri, T. S., & Ahmad, C. S. (2021). Concussion-reporting behavior in rugby: A national survey of rugby union players in the united states. *Orthopaedic Journal of Sports Medicine*, 9(1), 232596712097214. https://doi.org/10.1177/2325967120972141

Moncrieff, J., Cooper, R. E., Stockmann, T., Amendola, S., Hengartner, M. P., & Horowitz, M. (2022). The serotonin theory of depression: A systematic umbrella review of the evidence. *Molecular Psychiatry*. https://doi.org/10.1038/s41380-022-01661-0

Mor, N., Haran D. (2009) Cognitive-behavioral therapy for depression. Israel *Journal of Psychiatry and Related Sciences*, 46(4), 269–73.

Motlová, L. B., Balon, R., Beresin, E. V., Brenner, A. M., Coverdale, J. H., Guerrero, A. P. S., Louie, A. K., & Roberts, L. W. (2017). Psychoeducation as an opportunity for patients, psychiatrists, and psychiatric educators: Why Do We Ignore It? *Academic Psychiatry*, 41(4), 447–451. https://doi.org/10.1007/s40596-017-0728-y

Nguyen, V. K., Zafonte, R., Chen, J. T., Kponee-Shovein, K. Z., Paganoni, S., Pascual-Leone, A., Speizer, F. E., Baggish, A. L., Taylor, H. A., Nadler, L. M., Courtney, T. K., Connor, A., & Weisskopf, M. G. (2019). Mortality Among Professional American-Style Football Players and Professional American Baseball Players. *JAMA Network Open*, 2(5), e194223. https://doi.org/10.1001/jamanetworkopen.2019.4223

NZ-born Ireland centre Jared Payne forced to retire due to concussion symptoms. (2018, May 28). Stuff. www.stuff.co.nz/sport/rugby/international/104283232/nzborn-ireland-centre-payne-forced-to-retire-due-to-concussion-symptoms

Papadimitriou, G. I. (2017). The 'Biopsychosocial Model': 40 years of application in Psychiatry. *Psychiatrikī*, 28(2), 107–110. https://doi.org/10.22365/jpsych.2017.282.107

Payten, I. (2022, August 5). Hooper leaves Wallabies tour for break after admitting 'mindset' struggle. *The Sydney Morning Herald*. www.smh.com.au/sport/rugby-union/hooper-to-leave-wallabies-tour-take-break-after-admitting-mindset-struggle-20220806-p5b7qk.html

Rauchman, S. H., Albert, J., Pinkhasov, A., & Reiss, A. B. (2022). Mild-to-Moderate traumatic brain injury: A review with focus on the visual system. *Neurology International*, 14(2), 453–470. https://doi.org/10.3390/neurolint14020038

Reardon, C. L., & Creado, S. (2016). Psychiatric medication preferences of sports psychiatrists. *The Physician and Sportsmedicine*, 44(4), 397–402. https://doi.org/10.1080/00913847.2016.1216719

Reinert, D. F., & Allen, J. F. (2007). The alcohol use disorders identification test: An update of research findings. *Alcoholism: Clinical and Experimental Research*, 31(2), 185–199. https://doi.org/10.1111/j.1530-0277.2006.00295.x

Rice, S. M., Parker, A. G., Mawren, D., Clifton, P., Harcourt, P., Lloyd, M., Kountouris, A., Smith, B. J., McGorry, P. D., & Purcell, R. (2019). Preliminary psychometric validation of a brief screening tool for athlete mental health among male elite athletes: the Athlete Psychological Strain Questionnaire. *International Journal of Sport and Exercise Psychology*, 18(6), 850–865. https://doi.org/10.1080/1612197x.2019.1611900

Russell, E., Mackay, D. F., Lyall, D. M., Stewart, K., Maclean, J., Robson, J., Pell, J. P., & Stewart, W. J. (2022). Neurodegenerative disease risk among former international rugby union players. *Journal of Neurology, Neurosurgery, and Psychiatry*, 93(12), 1262–1268. https://doi.org/10.1136/jnnp-2022-329675

Schuring, N., Kerkhoffs, G. M. M. J., Gray, J., & Gouttebarge, V. (2017). The mental wellbeing of current and retired professional cricketers: an observational prospective cohort study. *The Physician and Sportsmedicine*, 45(4), 463–469. https://doi.org/10.1080/00913847.2017.1386069

Silverberg, N. D., & Panenka, W. J. (2019). Antidepressants for depression after concussion and traumatic brain injury are still best practice. *BMC Psychiatry*, 19(1). https://doi.org/10.1186/s12888-019-2076-9

Smart, D. J., Hopkins, W. G., & Gill, N. (2013). Differences and changes in the physical characteristics of professional and Amateur Rugby union players. *Journal of Strength and Conditioning Research*, 27(11), 3033–3044. https://doi.org/10.1519/jsc.0b013e31828c26d3

The Irish Rugby Injury Surveillance Project Steering Group. (2022). *The Irish Rugby Injury Surveillance Project*. Season Report 2021-2022. extension://elhekieabhbkpmcefcoobjddigjcaadp/https://d19fc3vd0ojo3m.cloudfront.net/irfu/wp-content/uploads/2023/01/18112219/IRIS-Clubs-Season-Report-2122-web.pdf

Tucker, R., Lancaster, S., Davies, P., Street, G., Starling, L., De Coning, C., & Brown, J. H. (2021). Trends in player body mass at men's and women's Rugby World Cups: a plateau in body mass and differences in emerging rugby nations. *BMJ Open Sport & Exercise Medicine*, 7(1), e000885. https://doi.org/10.1136/bmjsem-2020-000885

Wood, S., Harrison, L. K., & Kucharska, J. (2017). Male professional footballers' experiences of mental health difficulties and help-seeking. *The Physician and Sportsmedicine*. https://doi.org/10.1080/00913847.2017.1283209

World Rugby. (2022a). *Global Injury Surveillance Research in Community Rugby*. extension://elhekieabhbkpmcefcoobjddigjcaadp/https://resources.world.rugby/worldrugby/document/2022/05/04/4005431b-5a3e-4e86-a877-841c504b1847/Global-injury-surveillance-research-in-community-rugby-union-2022.pdf

World Rugby. (2022b). *Global Injury Surveillance in Elite Rugby Union*. extension://elhekieabhbkpmcefcoobjddigjcaadp/https://resources.world.rugby/worldrugby/document/2022/05/04/00203aa6-bb54-491d-9ea7-afbc26aec39a/Global-injury-surveillance-research-in-elite-rugby-union-2022.pdf

Further reading

Mistry, A. D., McCabe, T., & Currie, A. (Eds.). (2020). *Case Studies in Sports Psychiatry*. Cambridge University Press. ISBN 110880201X, 9781108802017.

The first book of its kind to describe what a mental health assessment looks like for an elite sportsperson. Each chapter combines the viewpoints of psychiatrists, sports medics and athletes with multiple choice questions being used to explore the themes raised.

Cross, M. J., Tucker, R., Raftery, M., Hester, B., Williams, S., Stokes, K. A., … & Kemp, S. (2019). Tackling concussion in professional rugby union: A case–control study of tackle-based risk factors and recommendations for primary prevention. *British journal of sports medicine*, 53(16), 1021–1025.

This research article summarises the evidence base around reduction in head impacts within rugby union.

Kelly, J. P., Priemer, D. S., Perl, D. P., & Filley, C. M. (2023). Sports concussion and chronic traumatic encephalopathy: Finding a path forward. *Annals of Neurology*, 93(2), 222–225.

The topic of long-term brain health outcomes within contact sports is an area of focus for researchers. This paper summarises what is already known and suggests ways in which this influences the future direction of the area of study.

8

SUPPORTING SPORTS OFFICIALS' MENTAL HEALTH AND WELL-BEING USING THE TRAUMA-INFORMED PRACTICE DEVELOPMENTAL MODEL

Noel Brick, Gavin Breslin, Mikel Mellick and Tom Webb

Learning objectives

After reading this chapter you should be able to:

1. Appreciate the stressors and mental health challenges faced by sports officials.
2. Understand the impact of sport-specific stressors, such as verbal and physical abuse, on sports officials' mental health and retention in the sport.
3. Understand and critically evaluate the value of using psychological theory-based interventions to support sports officials' mental health.
4. Consider and critically evaluate research and practice recommendations when designing and implementing interventions to support sport officials' mental health and to increase their recruitment and retention.

Introduction to the theme

Sports officials (i.e., referees, judges, umpires) are integral to organised sport. By applying the rules of sport and adjudicating to maintain competitive fairness, sports officials facilitate participation in sport for millions of people worldwide (Cunningham et al., 2022; Hancock et al., 2021). Not only can this participation benefit the health of participants and competitors (e.g., Eime et al., 2013; Oja et al., 2015), officiating can also promote positive physical health and psychosocial health benefits for those involved in the role. Many individuals are attracted to officiating because of a strong affiliation with their sport and perceive officiating as an enjoyable pursuit that enhances both physical

DOI: 10.4324/9781003291695-9

activity levels and positive relationships with fellow officials (e.g., Cuskelly & Hoye, 2013; Kellett & Shilbury, 2007). Yet despite these positive aspects, officiating can also be a stressful and in some cases a harmful endeavor for those involved. Sports officials can experience distress from non-performance (e.g., constrained social lives, managing family demands with referee time schedule demands) and performance-related sources (e.g., unfamiliarity with game situations, making critical decision errors, over analysis of negative performance, deselection, negative evaluations by coaches, players, spectators, and media scrutiny) (García-Santos et al., 2020; Hill et al., 2016). More so, the experience of interpersonal conflict and abuse – either verbal, physical or via social media – are amongst the primary sport-specific sources of distress for sports officials (Mojtahedi et al., 2022; Webb et al., 2020a). Importantly, the abuse experienced by both male and female sports officials from spectators, coaches and players is associated with higher distress, poorer mental health, and greater intentions to quit their role as a sports official (Brick et al., 2022; Tingle et al., 2021).

Despite the valuable, intricate role of sports officials and sport governing organizations being aware of these concerns, the mental health of sports officials has received scant research attention (Gorczynski & Webb, 2020; 2021) when compared with evidence available for athletes and coaches (see Breslin et al., 2022; Prior et al., 2022 for reviews). Indeed, only a handful of studies to date have explored the mental health of sports officials. Despite the relative paucity of literature, those few studies provide an important insight into the prevalence and incidence of mental ill-health symptomology amongst sports officials. Specifically, prevalence rates for common mental health disorders have ranged between 4.8% and 5.3% for moderate or more severe anxiety, and between 5.5% and 10.1% for moderate or more severe depression (Brick et al., 2022; Carson et al., 2020; El Bakry, 2013; Lima et al., 2022). When including mild symptomology, Lima and colleagues (2022) reported an additional 18.7% and 24.5% prevalence of mild anxiety and depression, respectively, in their sample of Turkish soccer referees. Furthermore, Gouttebarge et al. (2017) noted the incidence of symptoms for mental health disorders over one season was 9.6% for distress, 16.3% for anxiety/depression, 14.1% for sleep disturbance, 28.9% for eating disorders, and 8.1% for adverse alcohol use amongst a sample of 391 professional European soccer referees. Further analysis of these data indicated that those referees exposed to severe injuries or that reported lower satisfaction with social support received, were more likely to report symptoms of anxiety/depression and eating disorders (Kilic et al., 2018). Collectively, the figures for common mental health disorders are equivalent to those reported for athlete populations for anxiety (3.7% to 36.5%; Gorczynski et al., 2017) and depression symptomology (6.0% to 14.6%; Du Preez et al., 2017; Reardon et al., 2019). As such, these similarities in prevalence, coupled with the small number of research studies on mental health within sports officials, highlight a pressing need for further exploration of mental health issues within this group (e.g., Gorczynski & Webb, 2020).

In addition to the paucity of research exploring sports officials' mental health prevalence, even less is known about mental health and well-being interventions to support sports officials. To emphasise this point, a recent systematic review of interventions to increase awareness of mental health and well-being in athletes, coaches, officials and parents (Breslin et al., 2022) included only one study that focused on sports officials. This multiple-baselines-across-participants research design study (Slack et al., 2015) evaluated the effectiveness of a mental toughness education and training intervention with a sample of three early-career, English Football League referees. The intervention occurred over a single season and consisted of six workshops delivered monthly. Underpinned by situational Stress Inoculation Training (e.g., Meichenbaum, 1985), the authors described the programme as consisting of pressurised role-play and behaviour modelling methods, coupled with the use of Cognitive-Behavioural Therapy techniques, to develop referee-specific mental toughness attributes, behaviours and cognitions. The intervention also targeted refereeing performance as measured by a subjective rating from the official match-day referee-assessor report. The findings indicated that referees' sport-general mental toughness (e.g., control of emotions, interpersonal confidence), referee-specific mental toughness (e.g., coping with pressure, awareness of own and players' emotions), and subjectively assessed performance-levels (e.g., decision-making, management of game and players, teamwork and communication with other match-officials) were all enhanced as a result of the intervention. Relevant to the present chapter, neither the referees' mental well-being nor mental ill-health outcomes were reported in the study. As such, the development of evidence-based, psychological theory informed interventions that help sports officials deal with the distress experienced in their role and that support their mental health are urgently required. Responding to the gap in the evidence, this chapter will provide an insight into, and evaluation of, a theory-based mental health intervention with sports officials. Furthermore, we will provide lessons learned and recommendations that researchers and practitioners could consider when designing interventions to support sports officials' mental health and well-being.

The client group

The University of Gloucestershire Match Officials (MO) scholarship cohort served as the population for this intervention. This is the only United Kingdom Higher Education programme of its kind and was established under the direction of the former International Rugby Union Football Referee, Chris White. Chris combines this role with his work as the Full-time Head Coach, Elite Match Officials for England Rugby. The purpose of the MO scholarship is to support and develop MOs as they progress their academic careers. The aim is to provide well developed, mentally fit and curious MOs who go on to serve their respective sporting community with purpose and passion and with a positive engagement within a supportive peer network. A strong focus of the MO scholars' group is also on the promotion of a collaborative high performing team ethos that develops transferable coping skills and resources between high performance sport and life. The Scholarship is open to referees, umpires and judges from all sports, but typically members are drawn from rugby football union, association football, netball, field hockey, cricket and boccia. As part of their funding, MO scholars are required to commit to weekly bespoke strength and conditioning fitness sessions, a nutritional programme, sports psychology workshops, and individual positive psychology well-being / mental health coaching sessions. The current MO scholarship group consists of 10 members across five sports of various levels from international to national and regional leagues and competitions.

One of the authors (MM) has a well-established ten-year sport psychology and positive psychology coaching role with the referee scholars' programme. As a former elite rugby referee with Rugby Australia, a former national match official development manager for England Rugby, and as a Registered Practitioner Psychologist who has worked extensively in supporting elite match officials across a variety of sports, this author is very familiar with the practice community and the associated mental health and well-being demands of officiating. This author's engagement with the programme came via his professional association with Chris White and is focused on the provision of performance psychology training, referee well-being mental health literacy workshops, and one-on-one positive psychology coaching sessions.

Initial needs assessment

The present needs of the group from a mental health and well-being context were screened through a series of 10 individual intake interviews with first year MO scholars. Question themes were framed using the *International Society of Sport Psychology* consensus statement on improving the mental health of athletes (Henriksen et al., 2020). The interviews asked each MO about their current level of perceived openness to discussing mental health within the scholar's group and within the MO practice community more broadly. Further questions probing the MOs on their awareness for existing structures and/or resources they felt promoted early identification and effective support when their well-being was threatened were also asked. This allowed for some interpretation of the level of perceived mental health / psychological well-being literacy. The intake interview also provided the MO scholars an early opportunity to disclose any personal testimonials / lived experience of mental health / well-being difficulties that may already have arisen from challenging refereeing or major life event experiences. This further permitted identification of any previous awareness for referee practice community support for help-seeking for psychological distress and/or existing referee governing body educational initiatives in place to improve mental health literacy and well-being.

The emergent need identified was a desire for the MO scholars programme to explicitly acknowledge the 'typical' referee well-being threats associated with the role. These centred upon incidents of maltreatment and typically involved dealing with major transition events (e.g., injury, promotion, professional selection) and coping with external performance judgments (e.g., social media criticism, de-selection, verbal abuse). A core recommendation arising was a desire for the programme to offer MO specific mental health awareness training and increased opportunities to hold peer and mental health professional conversations about mental health demands and MO challenges faced. At an individual level, scholars wanted to know when and how to access appropriate mental health issue support in a timely manner.

A further 'want' from the programme was to provide the MOs with knowledge on specific protective factors and techniques that could be used to better maintain well-being across a season and or when at a major tournament. To gain greater detail around this, a focus group was undertaken with six members of the cohort. Its purpose was to explore the group's awareness for, and/or previous use of, positive psychology techniques/interventions. This discussion was framed using Seligman's PERMA (Positive emotion, Engagement, Relationships, Meaning, and Accomplishment) model of well-being (Seligman, 2011).

The guided discussion focused on what MO self-care practices were perceived to look like and how they are used as means to cope with stressful/traumatic refereeing experiences. Specifically, the focus group explored cognitive and behavioural strategies that the referees believed to result in their increased well-being. To facilitate the discussions, example interventions were presented which included the role of grateful thoughts, feelings, and actions in promoting positive effects on mental health. The focus group demonstrated the significant role that perceived and actual peer support play in protecting the mental health of MOs, especially in response to psychological maltreatment experiences. The focus group also exposed a need for increased knowledge of psychological resiliency skills and available coping resources to ensure the prevention of future psychological maltreatment experiences threatening MO well-being and mental health stability.

Framework and intervention for delivery

The Trauma-Informed Practice Developmental Model, also referred to as the Missouri Model (Carter & Blanch, 2019) was adopted as a suitable means to address the MO scholars' needs in a systematic, evidenced informed, and meaningful way. The Missouri Model is a developmental framework for a Trauma-Informed Approach to mental health and well-being awareness, support, and change. The underlying principle is a presumption of a previous or existing psychological trauma experience in each of the MO scholars. Trauma-Informed Practice is a strengths-based approach that is aligned to Positive Psychology principles. The general framework adopted acknowledged the impact of trauma on MO lives. The approach emphasised psychological and emotional safety and empowered the MOs through skill-based task development and positive psychology informed coaching.

Using the Missouri Model, the intervention was broken down into four phases; phase one 'awareness' training of typical MO practice community prevalent trauma (e.g., well-being, mental health threats) and their impact on performance outcomes; phase two 'sensitivity' training explored processes involved in helping the MO scholars to understand trauma-informed principles, causes, expressions, and ways to overcome problems; the 'response' phase (three) implemented changes in MO scholars' team culture, routines, and processes to eliminate any organisational triggers of psychological distress or maltreatment; the final fourth phase assessed how 'informed' the MO scholars were in implementing trauma-informed practices.

The objectives of the intervention were to provide the match official scholars team with the basic principles of trauma-informed approaches and how to embed these into their practices and various match official settings; to develop a common language and framework for discussion of referee mental health challenges and well-being threats; and to help increase the effectiveness of early support, awareness of trauma, and promote early help seeking behaviour.

Intervention delivery

Phase 1. Trauma 'aware' intervention – Workshop (1)

The first phase involved the delivery of a workshop to raise awareness and to explore the referee scholars' attitudes to referee mental health and well-being. The workshop explored the susceptibility of MOs to chronic performance-related stress, the high organisational demands associated with their role, and what support resources are available in order to cope with the pressures of being a MO. Specifically, the groups' attention to typical triggers that may predispose match officials to two major common mental disorders (failure-based depression and existential neurotic anxiety) were highlighted. The vulnerability of MOs to distress associated with their role was discussed with reference to the typical major change events occurring through their development / performance pathway – these included: impact of poor performance coping; dealing with a match outcome critical decision error; coping with a major injury experience; de-selection; and social maltreatment from players / coaches and public abuse through social media. This first workshop ended with a discussion about the prevailing stigma around disclosing a referee mental health issue or well-being threat.

Phase 2. Trauma 'sensitive' intervention – Workshop (2)

The second workshop focused on knowledge acquisition, application practices, and skill development utilising positive psychology interventions (PPI). Its purpose was to introduce scholars to a 'toolkit' for protecting their referee mental health / well-being in response to a match officiating role trauma. The positive psychology vocabulary around flourishing versus languishing was discussed (Keyes, 2002), and the effects of PPI on role challenge enjoyment, increased awareness for signature strengths, performance satisfaction and role optimism were emphasised. Using the PERMA model of Well-being, the match officials explored how their involvement in the referee scholars programme and in the match officiating practice community more broadly promotes their well-being through; increased opportunities for sharing positive feeling states associated with their match officiating role, reminding each other of what makes match officiating interesting and worthwhile, increased access to actual and/or perceived peer referee social support, greater recognition of the importance of their role to the success of the scholars programme and the wider sport community, and finally the opportunity for sharing success stories with one's self and others in the referee scholars programme. This workshop also introduced the referee scholars' group to specific positive psychology intervention techniques.

First, the MOs were asked to write a gratitude letter – choosing someone in their refereeing life who has been helpful and kind and has made a positive impact on their refereeing success to date. The scholars were encouraged to present this story within the workshop and to send the letter post-workshop to the person to whom they were grateful.

Second, the scholars were asked to think about their favourite referee and write down what they considered to be the strengths of the chosen person's character and what they admired most in them. They were then asked to describe the 'match official' to the refereeing group. Each referee scholar was then asked to identify and share three signature strengths they identified with the 'referee' they chose as their role model.

Finally, as a group the scholars watched a clip of the 2015 Rugby World Cup final referee, Nigel Owens, talking about his referee journey and experience. The scholars were then asked to consider and list what items/memorabilia they might use to help trigger a pleasurable match officiating memory. In small groups, each scholar was then encouraged to tell a story about the significance of one identifying item and its positive influence on their match officiating journey.

Phase 3. Trauma 'responsive' intervention – Individual Referee Positive Psychology Coaching

The final delivery phase provided the scholars with one-on-one positive coaching psychology sessions. These were used to promote the integration of positive psychology intervention principles into each referee's self-care behaviours and practices and to support scholars to address any referee trauma experiences they were coping with. The positive coaching psychology approach provided each scholar a safe psychological space within which they were supported to activate their self-actualization tendency, working in collaboration with the Coaching Psychologist, the scholar was supported to move towards a mindset that accepts periods of vulnerability and encourages meaning and growth through challenge. Within the coaching sessions, the referees were encouraged to address any self-discrepancies between the actual, ideal, and feared selves from a referee identity context.

This coaching psychology approach emphasised to each Scholar a 'strength through adversity' model where vulnerability is seen as manageable, and not as a defining character flaw. The coaching process worked with each scholar to identify and practise ways to facilitate a shift in mindset away from one characterised by threat, instability, confusion, and contradiction to one that promotes and maintains optimism, emotional resilience, and ultimately life satisfaction in times of referee-based trauma. As such, each MO Scholar was coached to effectively negotiate key referee/life role transitions, major change events, and emotional upset. They were supported by the Coach to more effectively live through change positively and to cope, grow, develop, and/or maintain satisfaction in their performances by securing their mental health and well-being.

Intervention evaluation and lessons learned through self-reflection

A post-intervention critical reflective discussion was undertaken at the end of the academic year across the referee scholar's group. This activity was aligned to Phase 4 of the Trauma-Informed Practice Developmental Model (Missouri Model; Carter & Blanch, 2019). These reflective accounts of the workshops and individual support were used to evaluate referee mental health literacy, understanding of positive psychology and usefulness of positive psychology interventions in supporting their well-being and mental health. The focus group format was framed using four discussion themes. An 'insight' theme was discussed first. This explored any changes in awareness and acceptance of referee mental health issues as a result of the intervention and was used to gain a sense for improved personal and referee practice community understanding of mental health vulnerability and any changes in attitude around mental health discourse, disclosure, and help seeking behaviour. Essential facts, information, descriptions, and skills concerning the typical signs, symptoms, and risk factors associated with the more common referee mental health difficulties were explored through a 'knowledge' guided discussion. Selected case studies highlighting particular referee circumstances, conditions, surroundings, and factors were then used to scaffold a 'contextual' discussion on the use of positive psychology interventions to protect and support mental health and well-being in referees. Finally, the group discussed, developed, and rehearsed 'helping' referee peer support conversations and self-care practices.

The focus group discussion highlighted self-reported improvements in referee quality of life and well-being. A high level of participation within sessions and outside sessions in terms of increased referee 'trauma' based conversations and engagement with positive psychology activities was also highlighted. Indications suggested a referee scholars' group which felt more confident to openly discuss mental health challenges and to do so in an informed manner. The focus group seemed to further demonstrate that when a mental health challenge did emerge, the referee sought a fellow scholar to disclose to, and that the peer responded with understanding and with an increased awareness for match official 'trauma' triggers and appropriate coping skills suggestions with available support resources.

To summarise, these were the reported benefits of the intervention:

- The perceived frequency and quality of mental health / well-being support improved.
- There was a perceived ease and timely response when accessing 'trauma' informed support.
- The processes, usefulness, and frequency of the positive psychology one-on-one coaching was highly valued and felt beneficial to performance as well as in dealing with academic demands.
- The psychoeducation workshop content and delivery activities were deemed highly beneficial for establishing an early sense of belonging within the scholars' cohort.
- The referees felt better prepared to deal with referee 'trauma' experiences, and each other's experiences.

The intervention outlined provides a useful and worthwhile heuristic framework for Match Official Governing Bodies and sport more generally to address the mental health and well-being needs of their match officials. Adopting a developmental framework for a Trauma-Informed Approach to mental health and well-being awareness, support, and change provides referees with a strengths-based approach enabling them to better cope in a highly demanding and, at times, stressful and 'threatening' environment. With increasing match official reports of social maltreatment experiences, a spotlight is now on sport governing bodies/federations to explicitly acknowledge the duty of care owed to referees. Research into referee mental health and well-being has demonstrated to sport organisations just how prevalent referee mental ill-health is and how damaging it can be for the individual referee and for the referee practice community more widely. Sport and match official bodies/federations need to become 'trauma' sensitive and responsive to referees – better assuring a safe environment, and working with referees collaboratively and in an inclusive and trustworthy manner. The University of Gloucestershire Match Officials Scholars' approach demonstrated that when achieving this, MOs feel greater senses of empowerment, control, and resilience within their role leading to better assured mental health and well-being.

Future research recommendations

Given the dearth of evidence on sports officials' mental health and well-being, there is a need for research that reports mental health and illness prevalence and incidence (e.g., within a single sporting season) across sports. Further epidemiological data is required to determine the true scope of the understanding of mental health symptoms and disorders. Like the intervention described in this chapter, it is important to understand what is needed and, subsequently, how research can be used to design, deliver, and disseminate mental health interventions to governing bodies/federations and to sports officials themselves. Mental health assessments using valid and reliable tools could be undertaken with sports officials to detect which officials are at a greater risk of developing mental health issues. Doing so might help to enable appropriate and timely intervention to support the mental health needs of officials and improve their retention within our sports.

Mental health awareness raising is required across sports, perhaps building on the effective programmes designed for athletes and coaches (see Breslin et al., 2022) with the addition of integrating what is currently known about reports of verbal and physical abuse amongst sports officials (Brick et al., 2022; Mojtahedi et al., 2022; Webb et al., 2020b) and how this abuse cannot be tolerated. Examples from some sports, such as soccer and Gaelic games have adopted referee respect campaigns that aim to reduce or eliminate the prevalence of abuse through targeting players, coaches and spectators, key perpetrators of both verbal and physical abuse in sport (Brick et al., 2022; Webb et al., 2020b). Whether such top-down organisational campaigns can be effective to reduce or eliminate abuse is subject to debate, however, with mixed evidence to support their effectiveness to change cultural norms and attitudes toward referees, it is worth trialing different intervention approaches (Cleland, 2021; Webb et al., 2017). Underpinning such interventions with relevant psychological theory (e.g., Social Identity Theory; Tajfel & Turner, 1979) may help to improve the effectiveness of these campaigns. For example, based on Social Identity Theory, efforts to enhance positive intergroup contact between athletes, coaches, spectators (i.e., the 'ingroup') and sports officials (i.e., the 'outgroup') may help to develop more positive attitudes toward officials in sport by enhancing ingroup members' knowledge about the challenges of being a sports official (Webb et al., 2020a), increasing empathy and perspective taking, and decreasing unconscious bias toward sports officials (see Böhm et al., 2020). To date, no such theory-informed interventions with sports officials exist.

Finally, longitudinal studies that follow sports officials from initial qualification, through their first season and any matches, needs to be considered. To date, while informative, most of the extant literature on sport official mental health has employed a career-based, cross-sectional research design (Brick et al., 2022; Carson et al., 2020; Lima et al., 2022). Future longitudinal design studies could involve survey methods, interviews, focus groups and the co-production of suitable interventions like the one reported in this chapter. To overcome issues with career-based methods (e.g., memory decay, recall bias), event-focused interviews (Jackman et al., 2021) that ask participants to recount episodic details (e.g., behaviours, thoughts, feelings) in a chronological sequence soon after the event may be especially useful to determine the impact of abuse on mental health, to identify effective and maladaptive coping strategies used by sports officials, and to highlight mental health support needs. In other sporting contexts, previous longitudinal, survey-based research has successfully explored temporal relationships between athletes' psychological needs satisfaction/frustration and mental health outcomes over the course of a sporting season (Shannon et al., 2022). As such, future research adopting these approaches could provide much needed information to better inform officials' development and support needs during the formative stages of their careers. This is important both to support sports officials' mental health and to help retain more officials within our sports. As with other areas of research highlighted here, it is important that this work is underpinned by appropriate psychological models.

Practical implications

The practical implications of the intervention discussed in this chapter, and the subsequent learning points for those involved in officiating, governing bodies/federations, and officiating organisations, are important to emphasise. The positive impact of the intervention presents some insights into how to support MOs. These insights can be applied to different sports and different contexts with regard to mental health and well-being.

Referees involved in the intervention felt that the support around them improved, particularly related to the frequency and quality of the mental health support and the speed at which they could access this 'trauma' informed support. Nevertheless, sporting organisations (governing bodies/federations) have not routinely provided mental health support for sports officials and, if they do, this support is often sporadic or in pilot form in terms of its delivery (Gorczynski & Webb, 2020; 2021). As such and responding to the feedback from the scholars involved in the intervention, governing bodies/federations should consider the formal and informal support networks that exist for officials in their sports. Increased attention on training and the content of such training workshops should focus on raising awareness of mental health challenges in officiating, how to address these challenges and also understanding the benefits of having good mental health for sports officials, and what good mental health looks like.

Increased understanding of the different support networks and the mental health support required for referees/sports officials should also focus on the different requirements for officials depending on their progression and position in the officiating development pathway (Webb at al., 2021). For example, officials operating at elite levels require different support than those engaged at grassroots or mass participation levels. As such, any training and support should be tailored for the specific sport in which they officiate and the levels and requirements of the officials themselves. Sports often work in isolation, however, given the shared issues and trends across sports and countries that have been uncovered in recent research (see for example Webb et al., 2020b), sports should work together to address some of these issues. This would involve strategic approaches to the support and mental health provision for sports officials. It would also provide opportunities for the understanding of good practice and any initiatives/policies that have been successful.

Consideration should be given to the mentoring programmes available and the availability of mentors as well as the training provided. Training should be designed to provide mentors with understanding and experience in mental health support, particularly related to incidents of 'trauma'. Given that, following the intervention described in this chapter, referee scholars felt better prepared to deal with 'trauma' experiences, governing bodies/federations should identify how this information and training can be disseminated and implemented in order to provide increased support for officiating workforces. However, it is also important to reduce the number of traumatic incidents for officials wherever practicable, and therefore a concerted focus upon training around reductions in decision making errors, preventing injury, as well as dealing with abuse from players, coaches and the public should be a priority (Webb et al., 2020b).

Despite the success of the intervention identified in this chapter, there are also associated implications which should be addressed by governing bodies/ federations. Interventions with sports officials in and of themselves address some of the challenges that officials face, but they cannot reduce these sport-wide issues or alter the environment in which officials operate. As such, there should be internal conversations at governing bodies between managers and senior staff involved in officiating, playing and coaching to improve the environment in which officials, players, and coaches operate.

Finally, recent research has identified that mental health problems for referees were associated with a wide range of variables including younger age, being single, refereeing at lower-levels, performance concerns, and inadequate social support (Lima et al., 2022). As such, interventions can address some of these issues, such as the development of support and fixture selection for younger referees, concerns around the stressors and types of 'trauma' for sports officials at lower levels, and the wider support networks and mentoring available to these officials. All of these factors and the associated mental health challenges identified in this chapter mean that sports are not maximising the potential of their officiating workforce. With officiating numbers decreasing across sports and countries around the world, a focus on the mental health of sports officials and their increased recruitment and retention has never been so important.

References

Böhm, R., Rusch, H., & Baron, J. (2020). The psychology of intergroup conflict: A review of theories and measures. *Journal of Economic Behavior & Organization*, 178, 947–962. https://doi.org/10.1016/j.jebo.2018.01.020

Breslin, G., Shannon, S., Cummings, M., & Leavey, G. (2022). An updated systematic review of interventions to increase awareness of mental health and well-being in athletes, coaches, officials and parents. *Systematic Reviews*, 11(1), 1–29. https://doi.org/10.1186/s13643-022-01932-5

Brick, N. E., Breslin, G., Shevlin, M., & Shannon, S. (2022). The impact of verbal and physical abuse on distress, mental health, and intentions to quit in sports officials. *Psychology of Sport and Exercise*, 63, 102274. https://doi.org/10.1016/j.psychsport.2022.102274

Carson, F., Dynon, N., Santoro, J., & Kremer, P. (2020). Examining negative emotional symptoms and psychological wellbeing of australian sport officials. *International Journal of Environmental Research and Public Health*, 17(21), 8265. https://doi.org/10.3390/ijerph17218265

Carter, P. and Blanch, A. (2019). 'A trauma lens for systems change', *Stanford Social Innovation Review*, 17(3), 48–54.

Cleland, J. (2021). Respecting referees? An analysis of abuse, support, retention and policy. In E. C. K. Pike (Ed.), *Research Handbook on Sports and Society* (pp. 188–201). Cheltenham, UK: Edward Elgar Publishing.

Cunningham, I., Mergler, J., & Wattie, N. (2022). Training and development in sports officials: A systematic review. *Scandavian Journal of Medicine and Science in Sports*, 32, 654–671. https://doi.org/ 10.1111/sms.14128

Cuskelly, G., & Hoye, R. (2013). Sports officials' intention to continue. *Sport Management Review*, 16(4), 451–464. https://doi.org/10.1016/j.smr.2013.01.003

Du Preez, E. J., Graham, K. S., Gan, T. Y., Moses, B., Ball, C., & Kuah, D. E. (2017). Depression, anxiety, and alcohol use in elite rugby league players over a competitive season. *Clinical Journal of Sport Medicine*, 27(6), 530–535. https://doi.org/10.1097/JSM.0000000000000411

Eime, R. M., Young, J. A., Harvey, J. T., Charity, M. J., & Payne, W. R. (2013). A systematic review of the psychological and social benefits of participation in sport for children and adolescents: Informing development of a conceptual model of health through sport. *International Journal of Behav Nutrition and Physical Activity*, 10, 98. https://doi.org/10.1186/1479-5868-10-98

El Bakry, S. T. (2013). A survey on the significance of psychological and psychiatric assessment among qualified African football referees. *Egyptian Journal of Psychiatry*, 34(2), 85–92. https://doi.org/10.7123/01.EJP.0000418693.73007.54

García-Santos, D., Gómez-Ruano, M. A., Vaquera, A., G, & Ibáñez, S. J. (2020). Systematic review of basketball referees' performances. *International Journal of Performance Analysis in Sport*, 20(3), 495–533. https://doi.org/10.1080/24748668.2020.1758437

Gorczynski, P., & Webb, T. (2020). Call-to-action: The need for a mental health research agenda for sports match officials. *Managing Sport and Leisure*. https://doi.org/10.1080/23750472.2020.1792803

Gorczynski, P., & Webb, T. (2021). Developing a mental health research agenda for football referees, *Soccer & Society*, 22(6), 655–662. https://doi.org/10.1080/14660970.2021.1952695

Gorczynski, P. F., Coyle, M., & Gibson, K. (2017). Depressive symptoms in high-performance athletes and non-athletes: a comparative meta-analysis. *British Journal of Sports Medicine*, *51*(18), 1348–1354.

Gouttebarge, V., Johnson, U., Rochcongar, P., Rosier, P., & Gino Kerkhoffs, G. (2017). Symptoms of common mental disorders among professional football referees: A one-season prospective study across Europe. *The Physician and Sportsmedicine*, 45(1), 11–16. https://doi.org/10.1080/00913847.2017.1248796

Hancock, D., Bennett, S., Roaten, H., Chapman, K., & Stanley, C. (2021). An analysis of literature on sport officiating research. *Research Quarterly for Exercise and Sport*, 92(4), 607–617. https://doi.org/10.1080/02701367.2020.1756198

Henriksen, K., Schinke, R., Moesch, K., McCann, S., Parham, W. D., Larsen, C. H., & Peter Terry, P. (2020) Consensus statement on improving the mental health of high performance athletes. *International Journal of Sport and Exercise Psychology*, 18(5), 553–560. https://doi.org/10.1080/1612197X.2019.1570473

Hill, D. M., Matthews, N., & Senior, R. (2016). The psychological characteristics of performance under pressure in progssional rugby union referees. *The Sport Psychologist*, 30(4), 376–387. https://doi.org/10.1123/tsp.2015-0109

Jackman, P. C., Schweickle, M. J., Goddard, S. G., Vella, S. A., & Swann, C. (2021). The event-focused interview: What is it, why is it useful, and how is it used? *Qualitative Research in Sport, Exercise and Health*, 14(2), 167–180. https://doi.org/10.1080/2159676X.2021.1904442

Kellett, P., & Shilbury, D. (2007). Umpire participation: Is abuse really the issue? *Sport Management Review*, 10(3), 209–229. https://doi.org/10.1016/S1441-3523(07)70012-8

Keyes, C. L. M. (2002). The mental health continuum: From languishing to flourishing in life. *Journal of Health and Social Research*, 43, 207–222. https://doi.org/10.2307/3090197

Kilic, Ö., Johnson, U., Kerkhoffs, G. M. M. J., Rosier, P., & Gouttebarge, V. (2018). Exposure to physical and psychosocial stressors in relation to symptoms of common mental disorders among European professional football referees: A prospective cohort study. *BMJ Open Sport & Exercise Medicine*, 4, e000306. https://doi.org/10.1136/bmjsem-2017-000306

Lima, L., Devran, S., Öz, N. D., Webb, T., & Bayraktar, B. (2022): Examining the mental health status of referees in the Turkish professional football league. *Science and Medicine in Football*, https://doi.org/10.1080/24733938.2022.2084150

Meichenbaum, D. (1985). *Stress Inoculation Training*. Hoboken, NJ: Pergamon Press.

Mojtahedi, D., Webb, T., Leadley, C. B., & Jones, M. (2022). Match officials and abuse: A systematic review. *European Sport Management Quarterly*, https://doi.org/10.1080/16184742.2022.2099441

Oja, P., Titze, S., Kokko, S., Kujala, U. M., Heinonen, A., Kelly, P., Koski, P., & Foster, C. (2015). Health benefits of different sport disciplines for adults: Systematic review of observational and intervention studies with meta-analysis. *British Journal of Sports Medicine*, 49(7), 434–440.

Prior, E., Papathomas, A., & Rhind, D. (2022). A systematic scoping review of athlete mental health within competitive sport: Interventions, recommendations, and policy. *International Review of Sport and Exercise Psychology*, https://doi.org/10.1080/1750984X.2022.2095659

Reardon, C. L., Hainline, B., Aron, C. M., Baron, D., Baum, A. L., Bindra, A., … Engebretsen, L. (2019). Mental health in elite athletes: International Olympic Committee consensus statement. *British Journal of Sports Medicine*, 53(11), 667–699. http://dx.doi.org/10.1136/bjsports-2019-100715

Seligman, M. (2011). *Flourish: A Visionary New Understanding of Happiness and Well-being*. New York: Free Press.

Shannon, S., Prentice, G., Brick, N. Leavey, G., & Breslin, G. (2022). Longitudinal associations between athletes' psychological needs and burnout across a competitive season: A latent difference score analysis. *Journal of Sport and Exercise Psychology*, 44(4), 240–250. https://doi.org/10.1123/jsep.2021-0250

Slack, L. A., Maynard, I., Butt, J., & Olusoga, P. (2015). An evaluation of a mental toughness education and training program for early-career English football league referees. *Sports Psychologist*, 29 (3), 237–257. https://doi.org/10.1123/tsp.2014-0015

Tajfel, H., & Turner, J. (1979). An integrative theory of intergroup conflict. In W. G. Austin, & S. Worchel (Eds.), *The Social Psychology of Intergroup Relations* (pp. 33–47). Monterey, CA: Brooks/Cole.

Tingle, J. K., Jacobs, B. L., Ridinger, L. & Warner, S. (2021). Female sports officials and mental health: The overlooked problem. *Journal of Sport Management*, https://doi.org/10.1123/jsm.2020-0443

Webb, T., Cleland, J., & O'Gorman, J. (2017) The distribution of power through a media campaign: The respect program, referees, and abuse in association football. *Journal of Global Sport Management*, 2(3), 162–181. https://doi.org/10.1080/24704067.2017.1350591

Webb, T., Dicks, M., Thelwell, R., van der Kamp, J., & Rix-Lievre, G. (2020a). An analysis of soccer referee experiences in France and the Netherlands: Abuse, conflict, and level of support. *Sport Management Review*, 23 (1), 52–65. https://doi.org/10.1016/j.smr.2019.03.003

Webb, T., Rayner, M., Cleland, J., & O'Gorman, J. (2020b). *Referees, Match Officials and Abuse*. Routledge.

Webb, T., O'Gorman, J., & Markham, L. (2021). Striving for excellence: Talent identification and development in English football refereeing. *European Sport Management Quarterly*. https://doi.org/10.1080/16184742.2020.1864748

Further reading

Brick, N. E., Breslin, G., Shevlin, M., & Shannon, S. (2022). The impact of verbal and physical abuse on distress, mental health, and intentions to quit in sports officials. *Psychology of Sport and Exercise*, 63:102274.

This article provides figures on prevalence of verbal and physical abuse towards match officials. It highlights that abuse-induced distress can lead to poorer mental health and increased intentions to quit. The authors describe an urgent need to provide mental health support for sports officials. The measures used in the survey may also be of interest to those conducting research in this area of research.

Webb, T., Rayner, M., Cleland, J., & O'Gorman, J. (2020b). *Referees, Match Officials and Abuse*. Routledge.

Drawing on research evidence, this book explores issues related to the abuse of sports officials, why abuse occurs, and the impact of abuse on sport officials. The book provides policy recommendations to develop a more inclusive and facilitative environment for sports officials.

Carter, P. and Blanch, A. (2019) 'A Trauma Lens for Systems Change', *Stanford social innovation review*, 17(3), pp. 48–54.

This article provides insights into the changes that an organization needs to make to become trauma-informed. The developmental model of trauma-informed organizational change, such as the Missouri Model evidenced in this article can help guide sport officials' governing bodies/federations and communities toward the deeper, systemic change required to address sport officials' mental health and well-being appropriately.

SECTION 2

Engaging the wider community in mental health awareness through sport

9

TACKLING THE BLUES

A sport and arts-based mental health programme for children and young people

Andy Smith, Rachel Wilcock, Aston Monro, Helen O'Keeffe and Jon Jones

Learning objectives

After reading this chapter you should be able to:

1. Understand the relationship between mental health, education and social inequality.
2. Critically examine the features of a sport- and arts-based education programme which addresses mental health literacy in children and young people.
3. Appreciate and justify the benefits of using quantitative and qualitative methods with children and young people in mental health programmes.
4. Summarise the benefits of deploying a realist evaluation approach to understanding school-based mental health programmes.

Introduction to the theme

The mental health of children and young people (CYP) is a public health problem which is of increasing concern globally, especially following COVID-19 which exposed and accelerated the already widening and deep-seated inequalities in mental health and other health problems among this population group (Bambra, Lynch, & Smith, 2021; Centre for Mental Health, 2020; Marmot, Allen, Boyce, Goldblatt, & Morrison, 2020). The World Health Organization (WHO, 2020) has estimated that 10–20% of children and adolescents globally experience mental illness, though this varies between and within countries. In England, the latest data indicate that one-in-six (16.7% boys, 15.2% girls) 5–16-year-olds had a probable mental disorder, an increase from one-in-nine

DOI: 10.4324/9781003291695-11

(11.4% boys, 10.3% girls) in 2017 (NHS Digital, 2021; Newlove-Delgardo et al., 2021). Among primary aged children (5–10-year-olds), 14.4% had a probable mental disorder compared to 17.6% of secondary-aged children (11–16-year-olds) (NHS Digital, 2021). In the United Kingdom (UK), suicide is also the leading cause of death amongst the under 25s: in 2019, there were 601 suicide deaths among 10–24-year-olds, a 24% increase since 2017, with particular rises among young women (Office for National Statistics [ONS], 2020). Evidence also suggests that the prevalence of self-harm, as one of several antecedents to suicide in young people (others include family mental illness, bereavement, bullying, abuse, current/pending exam results, suicide-related online experience, Rodway, Ibrahim, Tham, Turnbull, Kapur, & Appleby, 2022; Rodway, Tham, Richards, Turnbull, Kapur, & Appleby, 2022), is increasing among young people and at a greater rate among young women than men (Uh, Dalmaijer, Slugzdaite, Ford, & Astle, 2021). Indeed, in England, it is estimated that 13–20% of adolescents engage in self-harm (Uh et al., 2021), while rising rates of non-suicidal self-harm, often as a means of coping with anxiety, depression, stress and tension, is an additional indicator of the mental health of children and young people (CYP) (McManus et al., 2019).

Considering these data, childhood and youth (including adolescence) are socially constructed life stages with important implications for mental health. Although the ages when youth (typically 16–25-year-olds) 'begins and ends have varied by time and place, and often between social groups in the same places and at the same time' (Roberts, 2016, p. 12), it is during this life stage during when many mental health problems (e.g. depression, anxiety, psychosis, eating problems, substance-use disorders) first appear and when the risks of suicide and self-harm behaviour progressively increase (Blakemore, 2019; McManus et al., 2019; Public Health England [PHE] 2021a; Yoon, Eisenstadt, Lereya, & Deighton, 2022). The development of adverse childhood experiences (e.g. abuse, neglect, parental mental illness, drug use) which can impact all CYP, but especially those living in low-income and under-served communities, also have their foundations in these life stages and compound the impacts of other social inequalities associated with mental health and illness (Blakemore, 2019; Marmot et al., 2020; Yoon et al., 2022). Consequently, much attention has been paid to the adequacy of mental health services – known in the UK as Child and Adolescent Mental Health Services (CAMHS) – in meeting the mental health needs of CYP and the potential of other settings, including schools, to act as important contexts for the prevention, early intervention and treatment of mental health problems (Weare, 2015; Weare and Nind, 2011).

In this chapter, we will discuss the design and delivery of an on-going sport- and arts-based mental health literacy programme – *Tackling the Blues* (TtB) – which was first introduced in January 2015 as a partnership between Edge Hill University and Everton in the Community (EitC), the official charity of

Everton Football Club (see Haycock, Jones, & Smith, 2020; Jones, O'Keeffe, & Smith, 2019). Since September 2020, Tate Liverpool (an art gallery) became a third partner of TtB which is intended for primary and secondary school-aged CYP who are experiencing, or are at risk of developing, mental illness. More specifically, for the period October 2020-July 2022, we examine (i) how participants were identified, recruited and engaged; (ii) features of the selected theoretical framework (i.e. realist evaluation) which underpinned the programme; (iii) the lessons learned from using the brands of a professional football club and nationally recognised art gallery to engage CYP and the training and use of university student peer mentors; and (iv) the inevitable limitations of the programme imposed by the various inequalities which beset the participants' lives.

Group targeted

Between October 2020 and July 2022, the target client group of TtB were 6–16-year-olds attending 20 junior (primary) schools and 9 secondary schools in three areas of north-west England (Merseyside and West Lancashire). These areas include some of the most deprived local authorities nationally, where approximately 10 per cent of CYP have a diagnosed mental illness (PHE, 2021b). For example, according to the 2019 Indices of Multiple Deprivation (IMD), Liverpool is the fourth most deprived local authority in England, with 32 per cent of CYP living in poverty and where mental illness is significantly higher than the national average (Ministry of Housing, Communities & Local Government [MHCLG], 2019). Data from PHE (2021a, b) also indicate the significant health problems experienced by CYP who lived in the target areas where TtB was delivered in 2020–22:

- Liverpool is ranked third lowest in England for child wellbeing (based on the child wellbeing index);
- 445 CYP in Liverpool were admitted to hospital for mental health conditions or self-harm;
- CYP in Liverpool are in the worst 25th percentile for, not in education, employment or training (NEET), low academic achievement (gaining fewer than 5 A*- C GCSEs), looked after in care, and for school pupils with social, emotional and mental health needs (primary school aged children);
- Lancashire is in the top 25th percentile nationally for the number of 15-year-olds who have been bullied recently.

While structurally similar, the schools varied in their socio-demographic profiles. The IMD (MHCLG, 2019) rank of the 20 primary schools (pupils aged 2–11) ranged from 25,846 (the least deprived) to 82 (the most deprived) with an average rank of 7641. The average proportion of pupils eligible for

TABLE 7.1 Mental health risk factors identified by schools

Child	*Family*	*School*
Behavioural disorders (e.g. ADHD)	Family disharmony or break-up	Bullying
Low self-esteem	Parent or parents with a mental illness	Discrimination
Physical illness	Parental criminality or alcohol and/or drug abuse	Deviant peer influences
Difficult temperament	Death and loss	Breakdown in or lack of positive friendships
Communication difficulties		Poor pupil-teacher relationship

Source: Based on PHE, 2016 and Department for Education, 2018.

free school meals (FSM, a common proxy school-level measure of deprivation) was 41.2 per cent (range 20.1 to 60.3), and the number of pupils attending the schools ranged from 43 to 594. In the 9 secondary schools (pupils aged 11–18), the average IMD rank was 12,008 (range 349 to 27,809) and the proportion of pupils eligible for FSM ranged from 11.6 to 56.8 per cent, with an average of 37.3 per cent. The number of pupils attending the schools ranged from 149 to 1670.

The target group of participants who engaged in TtB included CYP who were identified by their school as having a diagnosed mental illness (identified by their use of services such as CAMHS), or as displaying behaviours or symptoms which are associated with poor mental health and which might lead to the diagnosis of mental illness if the pupil was accessing specialist mental health services (PHE, 2016). Several risk factors associated with poor mental health or the existence of a mental illness were identified by the school, and are summarised in Table 7.1.

Initial needs assessment

Once identified, recruited to, and engaged in the programme, the participants' mental health needs and current status were assessed using a mixed-methods approach. The methods were: The Stirling Children's Wellbeing Scale (SCWBS) (Liddle & Carter, 2015) and The Student Life Satisfaction Scale (Heubner, 1991) to provide a baseline assessment of wellbeing, quality of life (QoL) and life satisfaction, and focus groups and write and draw techniques to help examine mental health literacy. These methods were also used regularly throughout the programme as part of a realist evaluation framework (explained in more detail later) to help us understand what worked, for whom, in what circumstances, in what respects, over what durations, with what outcomes, and why (Pawson, 2006, 2013; Pawson & Tilley, 1997).

Stirling Children's Wellbeing Scale and Student Life Satisfaction Scale

The SCWBS was developed by the Stirling Council Educational Psychology Service (UK) to be a measure of emotional and psychological wellbeing of children aged 8–15-years-old and is a positively worded and holistic measure. The scale is intended for use by educational and health professionals who work to promote the wellbeing and emotional development of children and maximise the impact of associated interventions (Liddle & Carter, 2015). It has been shown to be a reliable, valid, culturally sensitive and conceptually/linguistically appropriate measure, particularly as the scale does not include connotations of negativity or failure which makes it a more acceptable scale by children and their parents, guardians or carers (Liddle & Carter, 2015). SCWBS explores two wellbeing sub-components: Positive Emotional State and Positive Outlook. A global score is derived from responses given to questions answered on 5-point Likert type scales assessing the frequency or intensity of particular behaviours (Liddle & Carter, 2015).

The SLSS (Heubner, 1991) is a self-report questionnaire for children aged 8–18-years-old which measures global life satisfaction. A global score results from the responses provided to the seven-item questionnaire, answered on a 6-point Likert scale which includes 1 (strongly disagree), 2 (moderately disagree), 3 (mildly disagree), 4 (mildly agree), 5 (moderately agree), 6 (strongly agree), with items three and four reversed scored.

The participants were provided with a copy of the SCWBS and SLSS simultaneously and these took up to 30 minutes to complete. The questionnaires were distributed to CYP on a face-to-face basis in a school classroom prior to engaging in the programme (pre-measure) and then after 20 school weeks of delivery in primary schools and after 12 weeks of school delivery in secondary schools (post-measure) which reflected the nature of TtB delivery in those settings. Intended as a screening monitoring and evaluation tool during the initial needs assessment (Heubner, 1991; Liddle & Carter, 2015), the SCWBS and SLSS helped to assess changes in subjective health and wellbeing, and life satisfaction, during this period and within and between schools. The results of the questionnaire also enabled us to help contextualise the responses given in the supplementary focus groups and write, draw, show and tell technique (WDST) held with participants.

Focus groups

During the baseline assessments, group discussions were used with participants in each school to help identify key features of the mental health of individuals and the group, and then focus groups were held towards the end of each school year to explore their experiences of TtB and its impact on pupils' mental health literacy. All focus groups involved pre-existing groups of participants who were already known to each other from TtB and, in that regard, shared similar experiences, norms and goals associated with the programme (Haycock et al., 2020). Useful for unearthing reasons for crucial choices on the programme (Pawson & Tilley, 1997), the focus groups provided participants – individually and as a group – to share and compare relevant thoughts, actions and experiences (Morgan, 2010, 2017) about the programme and relevant topics. These included: their understanding and experiences of mental health and wellbeing, impacts on mental health (e.g. loneliness, social media use, bullying), experiences of TtB, relationships with significant others (e.g. parents, friends, teachers, programme mentors), and the social determinants of mental health and other sources of inequality. This was particularly important not only to the initial needs assessment, but especially to follow-up focus groups where we sought to understand the participants' experiences of the on-going development and delivery of TtB. Thus, maximising participants' engagement in the sharing and comparing of thoughts and experiences during the focus groups was essential for helping to ensure the research was as inclusive as possible of the voices of our participants (Mannay et al., 2019), and enabling participants to share and compare how and why they think the way they do about the topics discussed (Morgan, 2017).

Write, draw, show and tell techniques (WDST)

To generate further data on what the participants thought and felt about their mental health and TtB more broadly, and why this was so, we also incorporated WDST techniques into our research and as learning activities in the educational workshops (see Haycock et al., 2020). Driessnack (2006) advocates the use of this type of child-centred research technique, suggesting that the act of drawing helps take the focus away from the adult researcher, reduce the power imbalances involved, and instead provide a way for CYP to share their lived experiences of the topics in hand in their own terms. Noonan, Boddy, Fairclough, and Knowles (2016) have similarly claimed that compared to traditional (and hitherto dominant) write and draw approaches, the WDST method encourages children 'to articulate their own meaning embedded within their drawing' (Noonan et al., 2016, p. 3), assists in the formation of individual narrative commentary, and 'provides children with alternative ways of expression and enables a deeper exploration of children's thoughts and perceptions by not limiting children to verbal communication' (Noonan et al., 2016, p. 4).

Providing WDST opportunities via art and drawing activities enabled us to explore similar themes to those addressed in the focus groups (Haycock et al.,

2020). This also helped provide an assessment of the participants' knowledge and understanding of mental health which could then be tracked throughout their involvement in the programme, and was successful in making sense of the experiences recalled in ways that might not have been possible if focus groups had been the sole method used. In particular, this approach enabled participants to write, draw or otherwise illustrate their thoughts and feelings which they were unable, or less likely, to articulate verbally in front of others, and in so doing emphasised to pupils our concern with understanding their lifeworlds, perspectives and experiences (Mannay et al., 2019; Noonan et al., 2016).

Framework and intervention for delivery

TtB is a prevention and early intervention programme delivered in partnership by Edge Hill University, EitC and Tate Liverpool between October and July (i.e. during a standard school year). Since its launch, TtB has engaged 3650 young people in primary (n= 24) and secondary (n = 11) schools through a range of weekly interactive and engaging activities intended to improve mental health literacy, tackle experiences of mental illness, and promote good mental health. Like many public health programmes (Moore et al., 2014; Wong, Greenhalgh, Westhorp, & Pawson, 2012), the intention of TtB was to contribute towards the improvement of health of a particular population (school-aged CYP) or 'at-risk' group (those with a diagnosed/diagnosable mental illness). More specifically, TtB was introduced as a targeted school-based mental health literacy programme focusing on clinically diagnosed mental health problems (e.g. depression, anxiety and eating disorders), social and emotional challenges (e.g. behavioural problems) and other difficulties (e.g. stress, burnout and attainment difficulties) experienced by CYP (Haycock et al., 2020). The programme was also intended to become part of whole-school approaches to mental health which, when implemented effectively and embedded into schools' wider activities, have been shown to positively impact mental health (e.g. Barry, Clarke, & Dowling, 2017; O'Reilly et al., 2018; Weare, 2015; Weare and Nind, 2011).

Since the programme was introduced, however, we were acutely aware that delivering TtB into diverse and complex environments such as schools would present many challenges, and that the delivery of the programme was likely to result in the production of many outcomes, some intended, others unintended and unpredictable. The production of such unintended outcomes, it should be noted, is the *normal* result of (often very) large numbers of people acting in ways which may or may not have been anticipated (Elias, 1978). Thus, it is unlikely that the programme could be equally effective (if at all) in achieving the intended aims for all participants in all schools given, for example, the complex interactions between pupils' individual and family circumstances, experience of school and their engagement in the programme.

In light of these observations and experience of previous practice, we sought to combine our focus on outcomes with a concern to undertake a process evaluation of the programme within the framework of realist evaluation, which is a form of theory-driven evaluation (see Pawson, 2006, 2013; Pawson & Tilley, 1997). As Wong et al. (2012, p. 95) have noted, because

> realist approaches acknowledge and accommodate the messiness of real-world interventions, and because they ask different questions (not just 'whether' but 'how' and 'for whom'), they can inform the tailoring of interventions and policy for particular purposes (such as for particular kinds of learning), particular target groups and particular sets of circumstances.

Realist evaluation is thus centrally concerned with developing and refining theoretical explanations of programme effectiveness by focusing on a key proposition: 'what is it about a programme that works for whom, in what circumstances, in what respects, over which duration … and why' (Pawson, 2013, p. 15)? These are known as programme *conditionalities*, or caveats, which focus attention on the *necessary conditions* (i.e. participation is a necessary condition to obtain any of a programme's supposed benefits) and *sufficient conditions* (those under which potential programme impacts might be achieved) which help explain programme effectiveness (Pawson, 2006, 2013; Pawson & Tilley, 1997). The concern with understanding the necessary and sufficient conditions of a programme such as TtB reflects the focus of realist evaluation on *programme mechanisms* (i.e. the people) and *families of mechanisms* (i.e. the processes, experiences and relationships formed) which help make programmes work, and it reflects how these can be explained theoretically. More specifically, enabling participants to make different choices (expressing previous experiences, beliefs, attitudes) and use choice-related behaviours (or 'reasoning') and/or the resources (e.g. information, skills, material resources, support) available to them in particular contexts are what constitutes the mechanisms that make programmes more likely to work and produce the desired outcomes (Coalter, 2007, 2016; Pawson, 2006, 2013). A consideration of these issues helps realist evaluators to understand whether the original programme theory (i.e. how the programme was originally assumed to work) was met by the actualities of the programme mechanisms (Pawson, 2013), and how the outcomes produced can be explained.

Since explaining the context-mechanism-outcome configuration of programmes is central to any realist approach to theory-based evaluation (Pawson, 2006, 2013; Pawson & Tilley, 1997), it was essential that TtB was designed and delivered in ways that accounted for the inevitable contextual variations (e.g. in pupils' mental health needs and knowledge, school arrangements, pre-existing relationships) encountered in schools, rather than adopting a one-size-fits-all approach. Since the school setting is frequently identified as an important context for the promotion of emotional and social competence (Barry et al.,2017; O'Reilly et al., 2018; Weare, 2015; Weare and Nind, 2011) where the social interactions between CYP, teachers and other professionals are crucial, TtB was designed to consider the nature of these pre-existing relationships which shape much of the time participants spend at school. We also sought to develop an in-depth understanding of the characteristics of the specific groups of CYP regarded by schools as benefitting from the programme, especially their values, preferences, motivations and mental health challenges that they encountered (Haycock et al., 2020). These were in turn considered in relation to teachers' background knowledge of pupils' needs and engagement, existing curricular content and wider school activity in relation to (mental) health and wellbeing, availability of resources and leadership commitment to the aims of the programme (Askell-Williams, Dix, Lawson, & Slee, 2013), all of which varied across schools.

Other features of our formative evaluation work included the delivery of a series of mental health-themed sporting and art-based activities which were tailored to personal and group needs – within and between schools – based on the findings of the initial needs assessment. This was essential because too few school-based mental health programmes have incorporated the voices and experiences of children and young people (Brown and Dixon, 2020; Clarke et al., 2015; O'Reilly et al., 2018), even though these help 'provide greater insight into pupils' lived experiences than standardised measures often used in experimental designs' (Haycock et al., 2020, p. 667). Among other things, this exercise involved exploring what themes would best address the mental health needs of CYP, and the related challenges faced by teachers and schools, before the programme was delivered, but also throughout its delivery in response to extensive feedback from participants, facilitators and key stakeholders (e.g. teachers, senior school leaders). As well as the types of activities to be delivered, we also explored the participants' and stakeholders' preferences for other features of the programme, including the setting, time of day, mode of delivery, duration of activity and the 'dose' of activity. We also sought to use the brands of Everton Football Club and Tate Liverpool as a 'hook' to engage participants via the design and recruitment strategy of TtB. In particular, the brands were used: (i) to help deliver activities at local schools, a football club stadium, and exhibition spaces in an art gallery; (ii) as a basis for enabling participants to support the co-design and delivery of the programme; (iii) and to encourage the recruitment and retention of volunteer university student mentors by providing them with TtB branded kit and equipment.

The recruitment of student mentors was particularly important and central to the design and delivery of TtB for, as Pawson (2004) has noted, the development of positive mentoring relationships (in our case, between university and school students) can be critical for maximising the effectiveness of programmes. While the impact of mentoring relationships is of course conditional and circumstantial (rather than a given) (Pawson, 2004), we deliberately sought to recruit a mix of male and female student mentors (or 'coaches', as they were sometimes seen as by the participants) with diverse backgrounds who would deliver the activities in an empathetic manner, that is, with a sensitivity towards, and with an appreciation of, the diverse mental health needs and experiences of CYP, and with appropriate resources to support themselves and the participants. They were also encouraged to develop relationships with participants which were perceived to be less hierarchical and authoritarian than those which are common in many school-based pupil-teacher relationships, whilst retaining an important degree of respect, trust and mutual understanding (Pawson, 2004). These types of non-authoritarian and supportive relationships were considered crucial to facilitating engagement in the programme generally, and generating informal discussion about mental health and illness in particular.

To help build mentors' confidence in facilitating and supporting discussion around mental health, they were each required to undertake a variety of training courses related to mental health. These included the one-day Youth Mental Health First Aid (MHFA) course, Ambassador of Hope training with Chasing the Stigma, and Zero Suicide alliance. These were also complemented by a suite of sports coaching, art, education, safeguarding, Children's Rights, and health and safety training to assist with the practical delivery of the programme.

Informed by the theoretical premises and assumptions of our realist evaluation approach, and the lessons learned from its formative development, TtB was delivered as a targeted programme where sport and art activities which acted as a 'fly paper' to recruit participants were supplemented by other activities (such as mental health education workshops) through which much of the developmental work and learning took place. The programme incorporated a mixture of one-hour long sport, physical activity and art-based mental health literacy activities delivered to 6–16-year-olds in curricular or extra-curricular time between October and July of each school year. To encourage programme acceptability by the participants, TtB used engaging activities from the outset that, where appropriate, were different to their traditional school lessons.

The classroom-based educational workshop sessions (especially those involving art activities) were used to encourage CYP to talk informally about mental health, establish their understanding of the signs and symptoms of poor mental health, and how conditions associated with mental illness can be managed effectively. Some activities, including 'emoji bingo', where CYP choose emojis related to feelings and emotions they have experienced during that week, were developed in response to the ways in which CYP interacted with others daily and as a non-threatening means of discussing the importance of emotions and feelings to mental health. The sport and art activities provided in all sessions, self-selected or designed by the participants, were intended to be 'fun' while developing understanding of mental health. The developmental potential of these activities – which were deliberately responsive and sensitive to the changing nature of participants' needs and experiences – was greatly facilitated by the length (i.e. school year long) of the project, which was an important prerequisite for developing long-term opportunities for establishing trust and rapport with the same mentors allocated to their school (Pawson, 2004).

Intervention evaluation and lessons learned through self-reflection

As we noted earlier, TtB is an on-going programme which at the time of writing was nearing the end of its sixth year of delivery. The first year of delivery was supported by 12 months external funding received from a local Clinical Commissioning Group and the involvement of a young carers group, though in the second year the programme was delivered without external funding by Edge Hill University and EitC only. Thereafter, TtB has been funded by the Premier League Charitable Fund and, in 2020, the programme received additional funding from the Office for Students and Research England to extend university students' engagement in knowledge exchange activities involved in TtB. We shall focus on some of the lessons learned from the project delivery since 2020.

The brand of professional football and national art organisations: A necessary but insufficient condition

Since the introduction of TtB we, like several others before us, felt that the brand and attraction of a professional football club would be important to the recruitment of participants to the programme and to its effectiveness (see Hunt et al., 2014; Parnell, Stratton, Drust, & Richardson, 2013), and once Tate Liverpool joined the partnership, we anticipated this would be similarly important given the perceived mental health benefits of art and other cultural engagement in schools (O'Hanlon, Cochrane, & Evans, 2020). In practice, the appeal of working in collaboration with a local Premier League football club and prominent art gallery was most attractive to the head teachers and senior leaders of schools rather than to the CYP. It became clear that TtB represented an important marketing and commercial opportunity for schools (Ball, 2021; O'Hanlon et al., 2020; Smith, 2015). It also provided an important opportunity to engage in externally provided, and above all cost free, opportunities to promote pupil engagement in sport- and art-based activities which were expected to make a positive contribution to pupils' mental health, education and other school-level outcomes (PHE, 2015, 2016). This, together with the very real pressures on school budgets, resources, staff workload, pupil standards, curriculum activity and league table performance (Ball, 2021; O'Hanlon et al., 2020), proved very favourable in securing consent to work with schools in our target areas.

While initially powerful, the appeal of the brand of a professional football club and art gallery became progressively less important for pupils throughout the period of programme delivery. Other more important features of the programme design became much more significant, including: (i) the non-threatening, non-authoritarian relationships established between the mentors and mentees; (ii) the emphasis placed on fun, enjoyment and choice, especially in relation to the selection and ownership of non-stigmatising activities; (iii) the familiarity established between project staff, mentors and pupils via consistent and regular contact in each of the schools; (iv) the use of real world examples of others (including sportspeople, artists and high-profile celebrities) as a starting point for personalised discussions about mental health which were of most relevance to individual pupils; and (v) the use of modern technologies (such as mobile phones and emojis) and creative art activities to express thoughts, feelings and emotions associated with mental health. We shall focus on one of these – the relationships between mentors and mentees – next, but it was clear that involving a professional football club and nationally recognised art gallery is a necessary, but insufficient, condition for engaging pupils and their schools in TtB.

Relationships between mentors and their mentees

We noted earlier that attractiveness factors, such as the qualities of the peer leader or mentor, the activity setting and the relationships with other participants, often encourage people to remain engaged in programmes such as TtB and that these cannot be separated from the physical components of programmes, particularly when promoting mental health (Fox, 2000). Of particular importance to the success of TtB has been the investment of time and resources in fostering positive, supportive and mutually respectful relationships between the programme coordinators, mentors and mentees. The decision to recruit and prioritise the work of student mentors was driven by a concern with reducing the potential status differentials between CYP and adults which characterises traditional relationships in schools. As shown in many mentoring programmes (Pawson, 2004), downplaying the status distinctions between themselves and adults such as teachers enabled the mentors to be perceived by the mentees as being more similar, relevant and simply 'like them'. Bridging the status gap with CYP was critical for engaging them in the various activities provided and especially in discussions about personal circumstances, experiences of mental health, social relationships and other concerns – all crucially from the perspective of the CYP themselves, rather than adult-interpretations of the circumstances described.

One of the outcomes of reducing the status distinctions between the mentor and mentee was the emergence and development of affective, emotional bonds between the two groups (Pawson, 2004). This was an important ingredient in encouraging pupils to continue attending TtB and engaging with the activities delivered, though this was by no means guaranteed. Indeed, it is well established that 'the success of mentoring turns minutely on the mentee's appetite for change' (Pawson, 2004, p. 4) which is to a large extent mediated by the mentee's level of identification with their present status. This 'reference group affiliation' provided an important insight into 'determining whether, how and in what respects they might be persuaded or helped to change' (Pawson, 2004, p. 5) their thoughts and actions in relation to mental health and illness. The degree to which participants engaged in TtB was connected to their social identities, loyalties and ties (Pawson, 2004), and also to their association with the identities of the mentors. Indeed, the social identities of the student mentors, like those of the mentees, were located along a continuum between, at the one end, an active role model encouraging pupils to 'do as I do' and, at the other end, a more passively oriented mentor whose own status was not 'conceived as a goal for the protégé, but rather as an available resource' (Pawson, 2004, p. 5) to access, use and learn from as needed. Neither were privileged, and it appeared that a mixture of these approaches – and the many variants in between – were important to stimulating desired behavioural change among the participants.

Being realistic: social inequalities and programme effectiveness

All programmes have certain limitations and have only degrees of effectiveness. The reasons for this are many and diverse, some of which may be known, others of which may be more difficult to determine. Some of the clues to these can be understood by applying the principles of realist evaluation articulated here and elsewhere (Pawson, 2006, 2013; Pawson & Tilley, 1997), throughout all stages of programme design, delivery and evaluation; others might be gleaned from an understanding of the broader social contexts in which programmes like TtB are delivered. In our case, it is important to remind ourselves that there currently exists a significant public mental health challenge in relation to CYP, exacerbated by the impacts of COVID-19, and schools are frequently identified in policy as priority settings for tackling the rising rates of mental illness in this population (Haycock et al., 2020). The launch of TtB in 2015 coincided with the publication in the same year of *Future in Mind: Promoting, Protecting and Improving Our Children and Young People's Mental Health and Wellbeing* (DH, 2015), which made numerous recommendations, including the need to build resilience, promote good mental health and adopt school-based prevention and early intervention strategies during childhood (DH, 2015). The political and policy commitment to expanding the role of schools in supporting the mental health of CYP was also reinforced in the British Government's 2017 green paper, *Transforming Children and Young People's Mental Health Provision* (DH and DfE, 2017), and associated proposals (DH and DfE, 2018), as well as the 2019 Office for Standards in Education, Children's Services and Skills (Ofsted) inspection framework which now requires schools in England to be judged in relation to the support they give to pupils' mental health as part of a whole-school approach to (mental) health promotion (Ofsted, 2022).

The success of the aforementioned policy initiatives and action on the determinants of, and inequalities in, mental health provide the very social conditions under which TtB is delivered and are an important part of the context within which its effectiveness must be understood. Indeed, many of the participants in TtB were recruited from some of the types of low-income, under-resourced, communities where mental illness is especially prevalent, where it is experienced in family contexts characterised by clusters of adverse experiences which threaten mental health, and where the scale of material inequality has a fundamental impact on the quality of social relationships (Marmot, 2015; Marmot et al., 2020; Wilkinson & Pickett, 2010, 2018). The experience of these kinds of inequalities in early childhood is significant for, as Marmot (2015, p. 121) has noted, they have

> a powerful effect on health and disease in adult life … The long-term effects of early exposure and the accumulation of advantage and disadvantage through life, whereby childhood experiences determine education, employment, income and, more generally, empowerment in adult life, are responsible for determining inequalities in health.

Since the first symptoms of mental illness often present in childhood (as witnessed in our participants) and can contribute to the perpetuation of cycles of inequality through generations, the emphasis on prevention and early intervention in programmes such as TtB may assist the management and improvement of lifetime public mental health, reduce the costs associated with and help prevent mental illness, as well as enhance the capacity of people to parent so that their children also have reduced risk of mental illness and disadvantage (Marmot, 2015; Marmot et al., 2020). However, as in many other countries and particularly following the impacts of COVID-19, policy decisions that lead to reductions in investments in mental health services which focus on prevention and treatment (especially during childhood) is often something of a false economy, and may do more to increase than decrease the costs of mental health care and associated service costs (Centre for Mental Health, 2020). These policy decisions have also been shown to widen income and wealth inequalities in many countries around the world, with the result that the larger the income differences in a society are the higher the prevalence of many health and social problems that tend to occur most frequently lower down the social ladder (Bambra et al., 2021; Marmot et al., 2020; Wilkinson & Pickett, 2010, 2018). Considering the costs to individuals, communities and whole societies of inequality, it would be churlish to conclude individual programmes such as TtB will have a significant impact on breaking down deeply entrenched patterns of social and health inequality experienced by those in the communities it serves. This conclusion may appear rather defeatist, and is certainly not one which is likely to appeal to even the most open-minded of policy makers or funders, but it is a realistic one and certainly one that is fundamental to understanding the potential effectiveness of programmes such as TtB. As we have attempted to show in this chapter, there is, however, much potential in using approaches like realist evaluation to better understand the degree to which school-based programmes, such as TtB, can contribute meaningfully to collective efforts intended to improve the mental health of children and young people.

References

Askell-Williams, H., Dix, K., Lawson, M., & Slee, P. (2013). Quality of implementation of a school mental health initiative and changes over time in student's social and emotional competence. *School Effectiveness and School Improvement*, 24, 357–381.

Ball, S. (2021). *The Education Debate* (4th ed.). Bristol: Policy Press.

Bambra, C., Lynch, J., & Smith, K. (2021). *The Unequal Pandemic: COVID-19 and Health Inequalities*. Bristol: Policy Press.

Barry, M., Clarke, A., & Dowling, K. (2017). Promoting social and emotional well-being in schools. *Health Education*, 117, 434–451.

Blakemore, S. (2019). Adolescence and mental health. *The Lancet*, 393, 2030–2031.

Brown, C., & Dixon, J. (2020). 'Push on through': Children's perspectives on the narratives of resilience in schools identified for intensive mental health promotion. *British Educational Research Journal*, 46, 379–398.

Centre for Mental Health. (2020). *Covid-19: Understanding Inequalities in Mental Health During the Pandemic*. London: Centre for Mental Health.

Clarke, A., Sixsmith, J., & Barry, M. (2015), Evaluating the implementation of an emotional wellbeing programme for primary school children using participatory approaches. *Health Education Journal*, 74, 578–593.

Coalter, F. (2007). *A Wider Social Role for Sport*. London: Routledge.

Coalter, F. (2016). Youth and sport-for-change programmes: What can you expect? In K. Green & A. Smith (Eds.), *The Routledge Handbook of Youth Sport*. London: Routledge.

Department of Health (DH). (2015). *Future in Mind: Promoting, Protecting and Improving Our Children and Young People's Mental Health and Wellbeing*. London: DH.

Department of Health (DH) & Department for Education (DfE). (2017). *Transforming children and young people's mental health provision: a green paper*. London: DH/DfE.

Department of Health (DH) & Department for Education (DfE). (2018). *Government Response to the Consultation on Transforming Children and Young People's Mental Health Provision: A Green Paper and Next Steps*. London: DH/DfE.

Driessnack, M. (2006). Draw-and-tell conversations with children about fear. *Qualitative Health Research*, 16, 1414–1435.

Elias, N. (1978). *What is Sociology?* London: Hutchinson.

Fox, K. (2000). The influence of exercise on self-perceptions and self-esteem. In S. J. H. Biddle, K. R. Fox, & S. H. Boucher (Eds.), *Physical Activity and Psychological Well-being*. London: Routledge, 89–117.

Haycock, D., Jones, J., & Smith, A. (2020). Developing young people's mental health awareness through education and sport: Insights from the Tackling the Blues programme. *European Physical Education Review*, 26, 644–681.

Huebner, E. S. (1991). Initial development of the students' life satisfaction scale. *School Psychology International*, 12, 231–243.

Hunt, K., Gray, C., Maclean, A., Smillie, S., Bunn, C., & Wyke, S. (2014). Do weight management programmes delivered at professional football clubs attract and engage high risk men? *BMC Public Health*, 28, 690–701.

Jones, J., O'Keeffe, H., & Smith, A. (2019). Tackling the blues: A sport and education based mental health programme for children and young people. In G. Breslin & G. Leavey (eds) *Mental Health and Well-being Interventions in Sport: A Case Study Analysis* (1st ed.). London: Routledge, 91–106.

Liddle, L., & Carter, G. F. A. (2015). Emotional and psychological well-being in children: The development and validation of the Stirling children's well-being Scale. *Educational Psychology in Practice*, 31, 174–185.

McManus, S., Gunnell, D., Cooper, C., Bebington, P. … Appley, L. (2019). Prevalence of non-suicidal self-harm and service contact in England, 2000–14: repeated cross-sectional surveys of the general population. *The Lancet Psychiatry*, 6 (7), 573–581.

Mannay, D., Staples, E., Hallett, S., Roberts, L., Rees, A., Evans, R., & Andrews, D. (2019). Enabling talk and reframing messages: Working creatively with care experienced children and young people to recount and re-represent their everyday experiences. *Child Care in Practice*, 25, 51–63.

Marmot, M. (2015). *The Health Gap: The Challenge of an Unequal World*. London: Bloomsbury.

Marmot, M., Allen, J., Boyce, T., Goldblatt, P., & Morrison, J. (2020) .*Health Equity in England: The Marmot Review 10 Years on*. London: Institute of Health Equity.

Ministry of Housing, Communities, & Local Government. (2019). *The English Indices of Deprivation 2019*. London: HM Government.

Moore, G., Audrey, A., Barker, M., Bond, L., Bonnell, C., Cooper, C., … Baird, J. (2014). Process evaluation in complex public health intervention studies: The need for guidance. *Journal of Epidemiology and Community Health*, 68, 101–102.

Morgan, D. L. (2010). Reconsidering the role of interaction in analysing and reporting focus groups. *Qualitative Health Research*, 20, 718–722.

Morgan, D. L. (2017). Conclusions: A call for further innovations in focus groups. In: R. Barbour & D. Morgan (eds) *A New Era in Focus Group Research*. London: Palgrave Macmillan, 411–420.

Newlove-Delgado, T., McManus, S., Sadler, K., Thandi, S., Vizard, T., Cartwright, C., & Ford, T. (2021). Child mental health in England before and during the COVID-19 lockdown. *The Lancet Psychiatry*, *8*(5), 353–354.

NHS Digital. (2021). *The Mental Health of Children and Young People in England, 2020*. London: Crown Copyright.

Noonan, R., Boddy, L., Fairclough, S., & Knowles, Z . (2016). Write, draw, show, and tell: A child-centred dual methodology to explore perceptions of out-of-school physical activity, *BMC Public Health*, 16, 326.

O'Hanlon, J., Cochrane, P., & Evans, M. (2020). *Arts and Cultural Education in Outstanding Schools*. London: Arts Council England.

O'Reilly, M., Svirydzenka, N., Adams, S. .... (2018). Review of mental health promotion interventions in schools. *Social Psychiatry and Psychiatric Epidemiology*, 53, 647–662.

Office for National Statistics. (2020). *Suicides in the UK: 2019 Registrations*. London: Office for National Statistics.

Office for Standards in Education, Children's Services and Skills (Ofsted). (2022). *School Inspection Framework*. London: Ofsted.

Parnell, D., Stratton, G., Drust, B., & Richardson, D. (2013). Football in the community schemes: Exploring the effectiveness of an intervention in promoting healthful behaviour change. *Soccer & Society*, 14, 35–51.

Pawson, R. (2004). *Mentoring Relationships: An Explanatory Review*. Leeds: University of Leeds.

Pawson, R. (2006). *Evidence-Based Policy: A Realist Perspective*. London: Sage.

Pawson, R. (2013). *The Science of Evaluation*. London: Sage.

Pawson, R., & Tilley, N. (1997). *Realistic Evaluation*. London: Sage.

Public Health England (PHE). (2015). *Promoting Children and Young People's Emotional Health and Wellbeing: A Whole School and College Approach*. London: PHE.

Public Health England (PHE). (2016). *The Mental Health of Children and Young People in England*. London: PHE.

Public Health England (PHE). (2021a). *Child and Maternal Health*. London: PHE.

Public Health England (PHE) (2021b). *Children's and Young People's Mental Hhealth and Wellbeing Profiling Tool*. London: PHE.

Roberts, K. (2016). Young people and social change. In K. Green & A. Smith (eds.), *The Routledge Handbook of Youth Sport*. London: Routledge, 10–17.

Rodway, C., Ibrahim, S., Tham, S-G., Turnbull, P., Kapur, N., &. Appleby, L. (2022). Bereavement and suicide bereavement as an antecedent of suicide in children and young people: Prevalence and characteristics. *Journal of Affective Disorders*, 300, 280–288.

Rodway, C., Tham, S. G., Richards, S., Turnbull, P., Kapur, N., & Appleby, L. (2022). Online harms? Suicide-related online experience: A UK-wide case series study of young people who die by suicide. *Psychological Medicine*, *53*(10), 1–12. doi:10.1017/S0033291722001258

Smith, A. (2015). Primary school physical education and sports coaches: Evidence from a study of school sport partnerships in north-west England. *Sport, Education and Society*, 20, 872–888.

Uh, S., Dalmaijer, E., Slugzdaite, R., Ford, T., & Astle, D. (2021). Two pathways to self-harm in adolescence. *Journal of the American Academy of Child & Adolescent Psychiatry*, 60, 1491–1500.

Weare, K. (2015). *What Works in Promoting Social and Emotional Well-being and Responding to Mental Health Problems in Schools?* London: National Children's Bureau.

Weare, K., & Nind, M. (2011). Mental health promotion and problem prevention in schools: What does the evidence say? *Health Promotion International*, 26(S1), i29–i61.

Wilkinson, R., & Pickett, K. (2010). *The Spirit Level.* London: Penguin.

Wilkinson, R., & Pickett, K. (2018). *The Inner Level.* London: Allen Lane.

Wong, G., Greenhalgh, T., Westhorp, G., & Pawson, R. (2012). Realist methods in medical education research: What are they and what can they contribute? *Medical Education*, 46, 89–96.

World Health Organization (WHO). (2020). *Child and Adolescent Mental Health.* Available at: www.who.int/mental_health/maternal-child/child_adolescent/en/

Yoon, Y., Eisenstadt, M., Lereya, S. T., & Deighton, J. (2022). Gender differences in the change of adolescents' mental health and subjective wellbeing trajectories. *European Child and Adolescent Psychiatry*, https://doi.org/10.1007/s00787-022-01961-4

Further reading

Haycock, D., Jones, J., & Smith, A. (2020). Developing young people's mental health awareness through education and sport: Insights from the Tackling the Blues programme. *European Physical Education Review*, 26, 644–681.

This article outlines the use of pupil-centred learning activities to explore pupils' awareness of, and learning about, mental health as part of the Tackling the Blues programme.

Noonan, R., Boddy, L., Fairclough, S., & Knowles, Z. (2016). Write, draw, show, and tell: A child-centred dual methodology to explore perceptions of out-of-school physical activity. *BMC Public Health*, 16, 326.

This article outlines the write, draw, show and tell method which can be effective in generating data on mental health and illness among children and young people.

Wilkinson, R., & Pickett, K. (2018). *The Inner Level.* London: Allen Lane.

This book explores the links between income inequality and various social and health problems which need to be considered in any evaluation of programmes intended to address mental health and illness.

10

APPLYING SELF DETERMINATION THEORY TO MOTIVATE PRISONERS TO EXERCISE

The Cell Workout Workshops

Hannah Hammond and Rosie Meek

Learning objectives

After reading this chapter you should be able to:

1 Describe and evaluate the principles of Self-Determination Theory and how these can be applied to support prisoners' exercise motivation and well-being.
2 Critically examine the challenges faced to deliver and evaluate sport-based interventions in a prison setting.
3 Summarise the mental health needs of prisoners and consider how exercise can support these.

Introduction to the theme

This chapter presents an evaluation and observation of the *Cell Workout Workshops*, an innovative prison-based physical activity intervention for prisoners run by ex-prisoner, L. J. Flanders, inside a Category B adult male prison in England.

The mental well-being of offenders is of concern from the moment they encounter the criminal justice system, with high prevalence and comorbidity of mental health needs (Tyler et al., 2019) at a far greater extent than reflected in the general population (Bebbington et al., 2017; Fazel et al., 2016; Rebbapragada et al., 2021). Moreover, releasing offenders into the community without engaging them in any health rehabilitation processes during their incarceration has worsening effects on their physical and mental well-being (De Viggiani, 2007; Fazel & Danesh, 2002; Gatherer, Moller, & Hayton,

DOI: 10.4324/9781003291695-12

2005). Prisons have become a holding place for individuals with a wide range of mental and emotional disorders that the prison service is not sufficiently equipped to deal with. In responding to this prominent contemporary public health matter, it is argued that those with responsibility for prison regimes need greater support to facilitate health rehabilitation through the treatment of offenders' physical and psychological needs. The prison setting, all too often, fails to adopt a proactive approach to improving health (Gatherer, Enggist, & Moller, 2014; Jakab, 2014), and efforts to introduce 'health promoting prisons' by the World Health Organisation (WHO) in 1995 have fallen short (Ismail, 2023; WHO, 1995; Woodall, 2016).

Alternative strategies to promote prisoners' well-being are clearly required, and research demonstrates that sport and exercise can play a key role in this. Researchers have established the benefits of sport in prisons on rehabilitation and health behavioural change (Buckaloo, Krug, & Nelson, 2009; Parker et al., 2014; Woods et al., 2020), particularly in promoting desistance, positive social relationships, identity transformation and education and employment opportunities (Meek, 2014; Meek et al., 2022). The relevance of the research discussed in this chapter lies in its potential to expand a currently limited field of academic research by promoting the use of sport and exercise to improve physical and mental well-being in the prison setting.

Description of the group being targeted

Those participating in the *Cell Workout Workshops* were serving a prison sentence at a category B local male prison (housing prisoners not in need of the highest security conditions that are either awaiting trial or taken directly from court post-conviction, most commonly for violent offences). The Service Specification for Physical Education (for application in prisons), published by HM Prison and Probation Service (HMPPS) specifies that, where reasonably permitted, prisoners over the age of 21 should be allowed to participate in an average of one hours' worth of physical education (PE) a week (National Offender Management Service (now known as HMPPS), 2011). In contrast, the recommended weekly level of physical activity from the Department of Health (DoH) is 150 minutes of moderate intensity activity (DoH, 2011), whilst healthcare campaigns increasingly focus on 'lifestyle exercise' – the incorporation of exercise into one's daily routine, with guidelines measuring the recommended amount of physical activity as 10,000 steps per day (Spilner & Robertson, 2000). These figures and recommendations are contentious in the context of prisons when offenders are spending much of their day in their cells, unable to maintain an active lifestyle and accrue physical activity through alternative means.

At present, there are approximately 120 male prisons across all categories in England and Wales, with a male prisoner population of 80,659 as of 30 June 2022 (Ministry of Justice, 2022). The most recent annual report released by Her Majesty's Chief Inspector of Prisons (2022) included findings from inspections of 20 establishments covering adult male prisons and young offender institutions holding young adult men, as well as a survey of male prisoners. This report revealed that pandemic restrictions have had a substantial negative impact on prisoners' purposeful physical activity, with an average of 53% of prisoners reporting that they usually spend less than two hours out of their cell on a typical weekday, rising to 69% of prisoners at weekends. Perhaps of greatest concern is that purposeful activity outcomes for 15 of the 20 establishments were rated as either not sufficiently good or poor, and none were rated as good. One way of meeting the recommended physical activity guidelines is through prison gym use. However, access to gyms has been heavily curtailed and PE staff are frequently redeployed to cover staff shortages elsewhere, with just 20% of prisoners in the report saying they went to the gym at least twice a week. It should be noted that these accessibility problems are not solely attributable to the restrictions of the pandemic however, with prior research revealing that all categories of English prisons provided infrequent or non-existent access to gyms, with no apparent reasons for the variation (Condon, Hek, & Harris, 2008).

Leon & Norstrom's (1995) physical activity pyramid suggests that a complete exercise programme essential to receiving preventative health benefits should aim to encourage active daily lifestyles alongside recreational, resistance and leisurely forms of structured physical activity. However, an exercise prescription that reflects the preference of each individual whilst spanning such a variety of physical activity types is just not possible within the current confines and restrictions of the prison environment. Injuries are a strong influence on maintenance or dropout rates of physical activity in the community (Sallis et al., 1990), and injured prisoners may suffer even further, as those who are injured in the community generally report more time spent walking as a form of exercise (Hofstetter et al., 1991), whereas opportunities for walking are limited for prisoners. Although remedial gym sessions are available for people referred by the prison healthcare team, these are limited in frequency and duration; depending on the injury and related exercise intensity they may not provide sufficient time and resource as an alternative to walking.

Research has found the success of physical activity interventions within secure mental health units to be negatively impacted by a lack of resources, such as staff capacity issues (Mateo-Urdiales et al., 2020). Although comparative studies in the wider secure estate are limited, it is widely known that prisons are experiencing rising populations and an increasing lack of resource. Taking these factors into account, the challenge that prisons face is the provision of a varied physical activity programme delivered with limited time and resources.

Structural barriers to exercise engagement in prisons are evident. It is widely known that difficulties in recruiting and retaining staff has led to a forced change in regime across some UK prisons which sees prisoners behind their cell doors for much of the day (Independent Monitoring Board, 2013). However, reasons for the varying levels of participation in physical activity across prisons are more diverse than this and include cultural and individual barriers. Researchers, therefore, must look to identify the attitudes and beliefs surrounding such barriers so that they can be transformed to increase prisoners' motivation to engage in physical activity, and in turn, promote healthy lifestyle behaviours.

Initial needs assessment

Due to the constraints of the prison regime the amount of contact time available with participants during the two-week *Cell Workout Workshops* was limited. There was only one opportunity for a brief individual consultation at the outset of the workshops which was used to obtain physiological measurements (weight; body fat; water levels; muscle mass; bone density; basic metabolic rate (BMR); heart rate; pulse rate; blood oxygen; and lung capacity) and answer any questions, the remaining contact time between the trainer and the participants was delivered in time-limited group sessions of 3 hours in the morning (including a 40 minute workout and post-workout shower) and 1 hour 45 minutes in the afternoon. Consequently, providing sufficient support to cater for individual needs whilst maximising impact by engaging a sizeable group of prisoners in each workshop was not possible. Therefore, it was decided that a formal individual needs assessment was not appropriate, and instead the design of the workshops was informed by academic literature on the specific healthcare needs of the prison population and a review of prison-based physical activity interventions.

Prisoners' health needs

Although little information exists on the true extent of mental illness in UK prisons (Ministry of Justice, 2021), research estimates that 70% of prisoners meet the criteria for two or more mental illness diagnoses (Centre for Mental Health, 2021). An investigation by the Prisons and Probation Ombudsman (PPO) discovered that nearly one in five prisoners diagnosed with a mental health problem had not received any care from a mental health professional (PPO, 2016). Whilst high attrition rates for prisoners who do engage in psychological therapies are one of the most commonly identified problems in prison-based randomised clinical trials (Yoon et al., 2017).

In addition to these complications, there are many more prisoners living with mental health issues that remain undiagnosed, as well as prisoners who, although perhaps without a clinical disorder, nevertheless are vulnerable to mental illness due to overcrowding, violence, inadequate health services, isolation and a lack of purposeful activity (Durcan & Zwemstra, 2014). Thus, a comprehensive approach to improving psychological well-being is needed to engage the diverse prisoner population and support the existing provision of mental health services in prisons.

Introducing sport and exercise programmes into prisons as a means of improving psychological well-being creates an opportunity to address unmet needs as well as supporting existing healthcare pathways. Despite claims to the contrary, people from so-called 'hard to reach' socially and economically deprived communities, similar to the backgrounds of many prisoners, respond very well when encouraged to engage in leisure-time physical activity of at least moderate intensity, with long-term adherence amongst sedentary individuals from such communities (Lowther, Mutrie, & Scott, 2002), and interest in participating in sport and physical activity of all kinds is often high in prisons (Buckaloo et al., 2009; Meek & Lewis, 2012). Additionally, it could be argued that sport and exercise has a broader reach than more traditional means of prison-based psychological interventions such as pharmacology or psychotherapy, as there are likely to be high numbers of prisoners with mental health illnesses who remain undiagnosed and therefore do not seek or qualify for treatment, whereas inclusion in physical activity should aim to be all-inclusive. Furthermore, the experience of incarceration is likely to have a negative psychological impact on all prisoners to some extent, and formal psychological treatment is not always necessary. Sport and exercise can provide an informal, less stigmatizing means of support to promote well-being on a larger scale and perhaps ease the pressure on existing prison-based healthcare providers.

Previous research into the mental health needs of service users in a high secure setting[1] led to the development of the domains of need model (Glorney et al., 2010) which, given the prevalence of poor psychological well-being in the general prisoner population, was considered a suitable reference point for the development of the *Cell Workout Workshops*.

The domains of need model identifies eight domains: Therapeutic Engagement, Risk Reduction, Education, Occupational, Mental Health Recovery, Management and Promotion of Physical Healthcare, Diversity and Spirituality, and Care Pathway Management. Although the *Cell Workout Workshops* aim to improve prisoners' mental well-being, they do not form part of a formal treatment plan, and as such, the domains of risk reduction, mental health recovery and care pathway management were not explicitly considered in their development. However, needs across the remaining five domains have been addressed along with their sub-needs and proposed interventions, as outlined in Table 10.1.

It can often be the case in forensic settings that academia and practice act in relative isolation. Conducting empirical research can be problematic in forensic settings due to constraints around accessibility, whilst practitioners are often guided by experience rather than academic scholarship. Nonetheless,

TABLE 10.1 Domains of need, sub-needs and proposed interventions considered in the development in the workshops, as outlined in Glorney et al.'s (2010) domains of need model

Domain of need	*Sub-need(s)*	*Intervention(s)*
Therapeutic Engagement	• Develop relationships with others • Enhance treatment engagement	• Group psycho-educational work • Motivational work • Contact with family
Education	• Improve mental/ physical health and risk awareness • Language, literacy, numeracy skills	• Educational groups/ courses • Discussion groups
Occupational	• Achieve a balanced lifestyle • Develop interpersonal skills • Promote social inclusion	• Provide opportunities for inclusion • Assess and provide means to develop independent functioning • Facilitate roles of responsibility
Management and promotion of physical healthcare	• Address physical health problems • Promote physical health	• Medical screening/ consultation • Health information and discussion • Sports activities
Diversity and spirituality	• Recognise, understand and support needs within and beyond the prison	• Work with families • Facilitate cultural practice needs and (external) support

a recent example of academics and practitioners collaborating on an evidence-based physical activity toolkit for adults with depression (Glowacki et al., 2019) demonstrates how effective this partnership can be. It is imperative that these two groups can inform one another to create a more comprehensive understanding of 'what works' in prisons, and this is particularly true of a field such as sport and exercise which has received relatively little attention to date.

In recognition of this, the workshops' development also drew on good practice and experience across the various practitioners and organisations in community settings that use sport and exercise for rehabilitation by engaging those at risk of offending in healthy behaviours and alternatives to crime. In 2016 the UK umbrella organisation, the Alliance of Sport in Criminal Justice (AoS), consulted with 69 organisations across England and Wales delivering sports interventions and a further 202 service users across the criminal justice system in order to develop their own 'theory of change' (ToC), a sector-wide framework to support the development of effective programmes using sports and physical activity to promote desistance from crime (AoS, 2016). In 2018, tangible examples for each strand of the ToC framework were created from sport and physical activity provision audits across 21 establishments in the justice estate and 13 community organisations in England and Wales. This led to a refined ToC framework, for which an academic review was published in 2020 (Morgan et al., 2020). The framework outlines four measurable outcomes which were considered in the development of the *Cell Workout Workshops* as a means of highlighting their importance in the justice system, namely: physical and mental wellbeing; individual development; education and training; and social and community development.

Promoting diversity

If the workshops are to be considered an effective means of increasing well-being in the context of prisons, then it is crucial that the chosen sample reflect the diverse nature of the prisoner population. The prison in which the workshops are delivered is divided into six wings which accommodate prisoners based on several factors including sentence length and vulnerability. To promote participation from a diverse range of prisoners five wings were given the opportunity to engage in the workshops. These wings included prisoners who were on remand (awaiting sentencing), convicted, engaged in integrated drug treatment services (IDTS), vulnerable, employed, unemployed and those on the resettlement unit designed to prepare prisoners for release. The workshops were promoted on the wings using posters and word of mouth, with the only criteria for application being English literacy at a basic level which was crucial for engagement in the workshops' theory sessions, although limited literacy support was provided when requested.

Sport and exercise interventions in prisons tend to favour participation from those who are responsibly behaved and well-disciplined, with selection criteria often including consideration of the prisoners' current level within the Incentives and Earned Privileges (IEP) scheme.[2] The Prison Reform Trust recognise that rewards for good behaviour should be distinct from the support and information prisoners need to prepare for resettlement, and selection and engagement with only those who are most compliant undermines the principles of the scheme (Prison Reform Trust, 2014). The *Cell Workout Workshops* are not a leisure activity; they have been designed to promote well-being in a population who are most at need, and as such participation should not be viewed as a luxury only afforded to those whose behaviour conforms to the expectations of the prison. Arguably, such an intervention is likely to have the greatest impact on those who are *not* conforming and therefore need additional support to engage them in their sentence planning.

The broad demographic of those participating in the workshops mean that the exercises must be adaptable to suit a range of diverse abilities whilst also addressing the pertinent issue of accessibility within prisons. As such, the workshops focused on body weight training exercises designed for safe and effective use in a prison cell. The premise of this approach to exercise is that it can be adapted to suit individuals of any age, ability or fitness level, and importantly, that it can be performed inside a prison cell without the need for any equipment.

Key outcome variables

An examination of the relationship between motivation, fitness and health is crucial in maximising mental well-being from sport and exercise participation (Power, Ullrich-French, Steele, Daratha, & Bindler, 2011), and to align with HM Prison and Probation Service's (HMPPS) priority to reduce reoffending, prison-based programmes such as the *Cell Workout Workshops* must promote long-term behavioural change in its participants. Therefore, to measure the potential long-term impact of the workshops, participants' level of motivation to engage in physical activity is considered as a key outcome variable, alongside measures of psychological well-being and physical fitness. The relationship between these variables to promote behavioural change is discussed in greater detail in the following section.

Framework and intervention for delivery

Researchers are becoming increasingly aware of the importance of applying theoretical frameworks to inform the development of sport and exercise interventions, and recommendations have been made to incorporate a theory of change approach into the Medical Research Councils' framework for complex interventions (De Silva et al., 2014). Meek and Lewis' (2014) review of a sports initiative for young men in prison highlights the need for future initiatives to draw upon behaviour change theories to assist in our understanding of the specific role that sport has to play in sport-based interventions with prison populations. This is supported by Woods, Breslin and Hassan's (2017) review which proposes that testing behaviour change theories within the design and evaluation of interventions leads to a clearer understanding of what works and why, facilitating the development of practical guidelines for prisons to use in sport and exercise service provisions that explicitly target psychological well-being.

Self-Determination Theory and Alliance of Sport Theory of Change

The measures used to evaluate the *Cell Workout Workshops* are underpinned by Self-Determination Theory (SDT; Deci & Ryan, 1985), a clear and testable theory of behavioural change that has been used in previous physical activity research (Chatzisarantis, Hagger, Biddle, & Karageorghis, 2002; Daley & Duda, 2006; Power et al., 2011; Ullrich-French & Cox, 2009; Wang, Chatzisarantis, Spray, & Biddle, 2002) and more recently, research in prisons (Bunce, 2019; van der Helm, 2018). Self-Determination Theory proposes that internal motivation can predict behaviour regardless of self-efficacy, unlike more traditional behaviour change theories such as Social Cognitive Theory (Bandura, 1986) and the Transtheoretical Model (TTM; Prochaska & DiClemente, 1983), which place self-efficacy at the heart of behavioural change. According to Chatzisarantis, Biddle, and Meek (1997), cognitive theories such as the TTM analyse behaviours in terms of cognitive representations of desired outcomes, whilst failing to recognise the conditions within which these desires are formed and the significant impact this has on the strength of intentions. In response to this, SDT identifies three innate psychological needs that influence the strength of intentions when behavioural desires are formed: competence (Harter, 1978; White, 1963); relatedness (Baumeister & Leary, 1995; Reis et al., 2000) and autonomy (deCharms, 1968; Deci, 1975). These basic psychological needs (BPNs) are central to SDT, proposing that satisfaction of these needs is a requirement for self-motivation, social functioning and well-being. The application of SDT to promote long-term adherence to exercise behaviours is centred on the basic needs of autonomy and relatedness.

Support for the application of SDT in the context of sport and exercise in prisons is provided by the ToC which informed the development of the workshops (AoS, 2016). The four measurable outcomes at the heart of the ToC are underpinned by a series of psychosocial processes and stages of development, for which the model proposes corresponding supportive activities based on consultation with 13 sport for development organisations across England and Wales. Several of these processes and stages align with the BPNs proposed by SDT, namely; the stages of self and collective efficacy, and self-esteem (competence); and the psychosocial processes of respect and trust, and intimacy (relatedness); and autonomy.

Proposed activities to support progression through the stages of self and collective efficacy and self-esteem include supporting and encouraging the ownership of realistic goals/ manageable SMART (specific, measurable, agreed, realistic and time-based: Doran, 1981) targets; enabling a safe space to fail; aspirational statements from staff around learning from failure; and sharing achievements with families. Activities to support the psychosocial processes of respect and trust, and intimacy, include sport sessions that cater for all abilities; role models leading by example, joining in, encouraging and being alongside the participants; the offer of informative, purposeful and aspirational qualifications, workshops and healthy lifestyle messages; and opportunities to be heard and valued by staff advocating for participants. Activities to support the process of autonomy include opportunities for self-reflection; providing enough space to be physically active and to reach their limits; and promoting the use of sport to relieve stress and promote fun.

According to the ToC, sports organisations who can support the proposed psychosocial processes and enable progression through the corresponding stages for their participants are better able to maximise the use of sport to tackle crime and anti-social behaviour. Thus, the *Cell Workout Workshops* apply the principles of SDT and the ToC alongside the domains of need as a comprehensive framework to promote prisoners' well-being and engagement by promoting internalisation of motivations to exercise through support of the three basic psychological needs in relation to exercise.

The workshop content

The *Cell Workout Workshops* were delivered by a qualified personal trainer and ex-prisoner Lewis Flanders (L.J.). Whilst serving his prison sentence, and in response to a lack of gym access, L.J. wrote a book based on safe and effective body weight exercises which can be performed in a prison cell. L.J.'s book, 'Cell Workout' (Flanders, 2016) is available in prison libraries across the UK. The primary aim of the book was to improve the health and well-being of prisoners through exercise, education and self-achievement.

A total of ten workshops were delivered inside the prison, each workshop running for two consecutive weeks with 15 prisoners attending a three-hour morning and a one hour 45-minute afternoon session from Monday to Friday. There is a fortnightly lockdown of all cells due to staff training, so each cohort attended nine days' worth of sessions across the duration of the workshop. The morning sessions were exercise based and aimed to introduce the principles of cell workouts as outlined in the book, whilst the afternoon sessions were theory-based and focused on topics such as goal setting and nutrition. The workshops culminated in a graduation day centred around an awards ceremony with a certificate of achievement, a chance to reflect on experiences of the workshop, and an opportunity for participants to lead their own workout.

The workshops were advertised on posters in five different wings across the prison. The poster explained what the workshops offered in terms of an 'Intense Cell Workout bodyweight training session' and 'Group discussions including self-achievement.' The poster also highlighted that the workshops were available to 'All ages, abilities and fitness levels.' Participation requirements included English literacy at key stage 2, a positive reference from a wing officer and to be available to participate in all sessions. It was also made clear that all those accepted onto the course would be required to undertake a health check and gym induction prior to commencement. A total of 86 prisoners expressed an interest in participating in the first workshop. Wing officers reviewed these applications and excluded applications from prisoners who had caused trouble

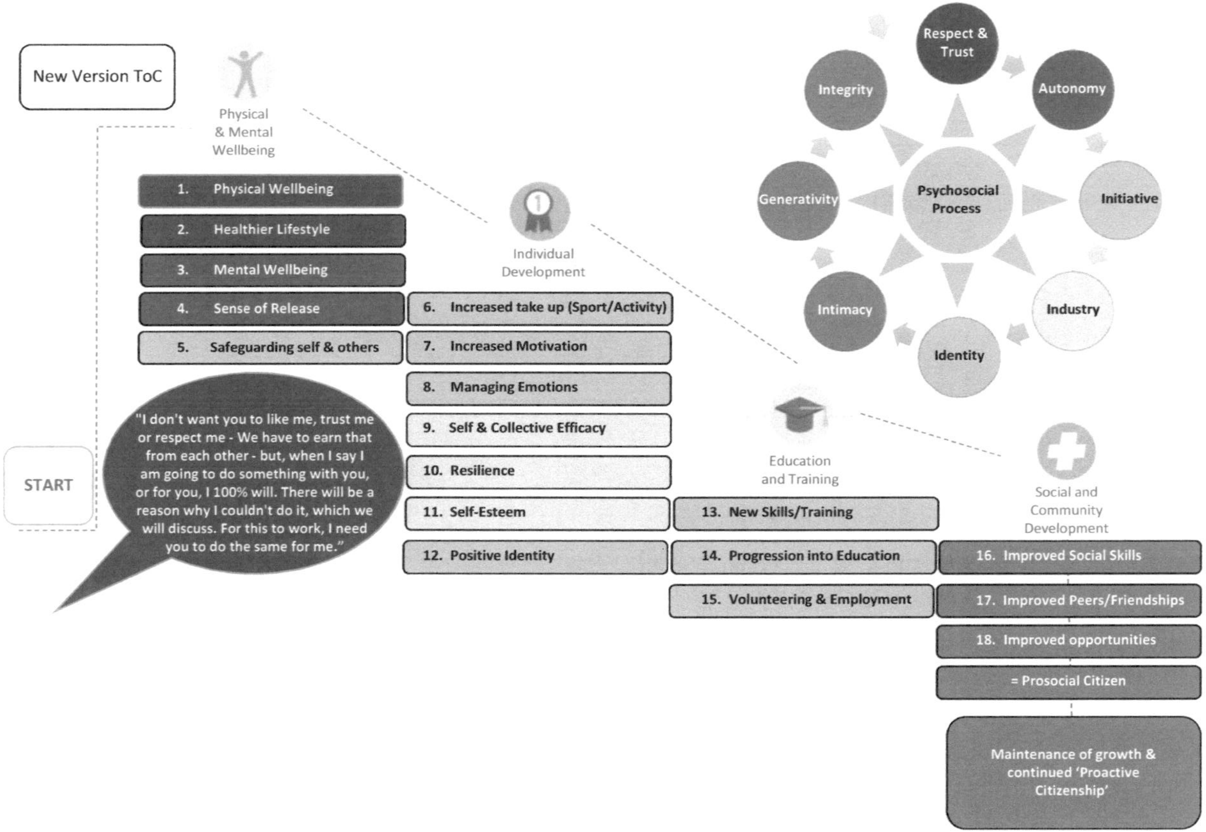

FIGURE 10.1 Alliance of Sport in Criminal Justice Theory of Change.

in recent weeks, and highlighted any prisoners who they felt would engage positively. Prisoners on each wing had an opportunity to apply for at least two workshops, and those who were unsuccessful in their initial application were given priority to participate in the following workshop, providing it was being delivered on their wing.

Workouts

The first Monday of the workshop was used to gather participants' physiological data in assigned individual slots referred to as full body health MOTs, where data was recorded across 10 measures including resting heart rate, body weight, lung capacity and body fat. In line with the domain of ***management and promotion of physical healthcare*** from the domains of need model, these sessions included a consultation with L.J. to discuss physical fitness and general well-being prior to the start of the workshops, answering any specific queries and providing advice on how to achieve health goals. The first time the participants met as a group was on the morning of the second day of the workshop where they all participated in a physical workout. The workouts lasted for 40 minutes and were based on the body weight exercises outlined in the Cell Workout book including aerobic exercises such as running on the spot and strength building exercises such as press-ups. Each 40-minute session focused on a muscle group, including chest, back, arms, legs and abdominals. To support participants' sense of autonomy and competence there was an emphasis on choice with regards to the intensity and style of the workouts, and so each exercise was demonstrated with both a beginners' and an advanced option. For example, conventional press-ups with just toes and hands meeting the floor were offered as the advanced version, whilst the beginners' version encouraged the individual to bring their knees into contact with floor for additional support. Exercises were performed for 30 seconds in total with 15 seconds' rest. Flanders (2016) provides more details on the exercises and guidance on how they are performed.

Initially, the morning workouts were led by the trainer, allowing attendees to become familiar with the principles of the exercises in the book and to build on their fitness and strength. As the workshop progressed and the attendees' competence grew there was a shift of responsibility to the participants as they were encouraged to think of their own exercise routines. To address occupational needs to develop interpersonal skills and promote social inclusion the final group session on the second Friday of the workshop consisted of a series of five-minute group workouts led by each of the participants individually, thus promoting independent functioning across the whole group.

The latter part of the first morning session began with L.J. telling his own story, explaining how and why his personal experience of prison inspired him to write the Cell Workout book and eventually devise these workshops, highlighting barriers encountered and how these were managed. This introduced the participants to the key themes of motivation and resilience which were highlighted throughout the workshop, as well as created a genuine sense of relatedness between the trainer and the participants, which was central to their continued engagement.

Upon commencing the workshop each participant was given a copy of the Cell Workout book which formed the focus of the late-morning sessions. The book introduces the reader to static body weight exercises, high-intensity interval training (HIIT) and relaxation techniques. Each exercise performed in the morning workout was studied in-depth, helping to develop a better understanding of how they can be performed safely and effectively, as well as how they can be utilised to improve both mental and physical well-being. This included highlighting the differences between active versus passive stretching and aerobic versus anaerobic training to identify when these are most useful, explaining the importance of balancing exercise intensity and duration in different measures depending on the desired outcome, and teaching basic relaxation techniques to promote positive thoughts and boost energy levels. Providing participants with this level of detail promoted competence and enabled them to engage in autonomous exercise, whether this be in their cell, the landing or the prison gym.

Soft skills sessions

The workshops' afternoon sessions were an opportunity to address the needs of therapeutic engagement and education in greater depth. These theory-based sessions include group discussions, motivational work and talks from organisations running educational courses in the prison. The first week's sessions addressed behavioural change and how to achieve it, exploring the difference between a fixed and growth mindset, the importance of setting SMART targets, the ToC, motivation and the power of resilience. Participants were encouraged to set themselves a target or targets at the start of the workshop which they were asked to write down and either share with the group or with a chosen 'supporter,' either in or outside the prison. Although it was stipulated that the targets should be measurable and achievable they did not have to relate to exercise, for example they might be to smoke one less cigarette a day (at this point the prison smoking ban in England and Wales had not come into force), or to write to an estranged friend or family member. The session on resilience encouraged participants to identify any potential barriers to achieving their targets and how they might go about managing these, and in the final session of the workshop everyone revisited their targets and were invited to share their progress, either with the group or their supporter. By introducing the idea of setting personal, achievable targets that can be measured and shared with significant others, these sessions aimed to help prisoners identify the aspects of their lives which they have control over, supporting a sense of autonomy and competence which is often lacking in the prison environment.

The second week's afternoon sessions aligned with existing educational programmes within the prison including the Prisoners' Education Trust's 'Fit for Release' report, focusing on how sports-based learning can help prisoners engage in education, gain employment and desist from crime (Meek & Champion, 2012); two organisations looking to improve healthy eating inside prisons; and the Centre for Entrepreneurs Ltd., promoting the role of entrepreneurship in breaking the cycle of offending (centreforentrepreneurs.org). Participants were encouraged to engage with these organisations and programmes to seek opportunities for further education and employment opportunities following completion of the workshop.

'Supporters' day

To promote therapeutic engagement further and to support spiritual needs it was considered crucial to engage individuals from outside of the prison who were close to the participants. As well as encouraging prisoners to identify a 'supporter' with whom to share their goals and achievements, a 'supporters' day' was also held on the day of the final workshop session. Unfortunately, due to time and resource constraints, not all participants were able to take part in this family day; instead the trainer chose a selection of participants who he felt would benefit most from participating. These included those who improved most on their measures of well-being, those who engaged most with the workshops and those who saw the greatest increase in their fitness. The supporters' day provided the prisoners with an opportunity to demonstrate what they had learnt to friends and family by delivering a short workout to their fellow participants. This also provided a valuable opportunity to gather data from friends and family about their thoughts and perspectives on the workshops, along with contact details to increase the chances of obtaining follow-up data post-release, which is notoriously difficult to obtain.

Intervention evaluation and lessons learned through self-reflection

The present evaluation adopted a mixed-methods design across physiological and psychological variables to identify any changes in participants' exercise motivation, fitness levels or physical and emotional well-being, whilst seeking to provide tangible explanations for these changes.

The life of a prisoner differs dramatically from those on the 'outside'; many experience mental health problems which are often undiagnosed, and the isolation, risk and uncertainty which they continuously experience is likely to have an ongoing impact on their well-being. Therefore, psychological or behaviour measures which are appropriate for the general population, or even the clinical population, may not be suitable for those in prison and it is important to consider the construct validity of any measure being used on prisoners.

Contemporary research advocates for the use of stronger research designs in prison settings (Hassan et al., 2022). A systematic review of the impact of sport-based interventions on the psychological well-being of people in prison by Woods et al. (2017) proposed that future research of this kind should make clear and balanced choices in relation to measurement scales, using a broad range of robust measures focusing on both increases in well-being and decreases in ill-being, with a specific definition of psychological well-being as well as utilisation of pre-post designs and follow-up data. In response to Woods et al.'s (2017) review, the present research employed a broad range of qualitative and quantitative measures at three time points with a focus on increasing well-being, as well as considering decreases in ill-being.

Health outcome measures

Physiological data across 10 variables was collected through full body health MOTs with as many participants as possible at two time points: the first Monday of the workshops (start: $n = 89$) and the second Thursday (end: $n = 78$). Seven of the measures saw significantly positive changes from the start to the end, namely, body weight ($Z = -1.932$, $p < .053$), body fat percentage ($Z = -3.832$, $p < .000$), basal metabolic rate ($Z = -2.183$, $p < .029$), bone density ($Z = -2.250$, $p < .024$), water level percentage ($Z = -2.351$, $p < .019$), muscle mass ($Z = -2.881$, $p < .004$) and lung capacity ($Z = 6.654$, $p < .000$), whilst the remaining three (heart rate, pulse rate and blood oxygen) moved in a positive direction.

All psychological measures were reviewed for suitability on the prison population, and questions were rephrased if possible, or removed if they were deemed entirely unsuitable. Surveys were completed by prisoners prior to beginning the workshop (start: $n = 105$), on the final day of the workshop (end: $n = 70$) and again at between two to six months following completion of the workshop (follow up: $n = 34$). Due to the nature of the prison environment and the frequency with which prisoners can move within and between prisons, obtaining follow-up data can be particularly challenging, and studies often fail to provide any longitudinal data at all (Woods et al., 2017). However, in light of the potential adverse effect caused by a lack of purposeful activities to engage with following prison-based interventions (as demonstrated by Leberman, 2007) it is crucial to obtain as much follow-up data as possible, and the present evaluation managed to obtain data from all 34 participants who remained in the prison 10 months following the start of the first workshop.

To avoid ambiguity, the surveys provide a clear definition of exercise at the outset, followed by a visual-analogue stages of change ladder as developed by Beiner and Abrams (1991), measuring participants' motivation to engage in physical activity. The stages of change, as developed by Prochaska and DiClemente (1983), are of relevance in relation to increasing motivation to exercise through the principles of Self-Determination Theory by helping to identify the type of regulatory style required. Readiness to exercise increased significantly for participants from the start to the end of the workshops ($Z = -5.648$, $p < 0.000$), and was still significantly higher at follow up compared to the start ($Z = -3.559$, $p < 0.000$), suggesting that engagement with exercise was being maintained to some extent.

Previous research has highlighted the importance of clearly defining what is meant by 'well-being' when reviewing sport-based interventions in prison (Woods et al., 2017), whilst Pollard and Lee (2003) emphasise the importance of assessing more than one domain of well-being. In response to this, prisoners' well-being was measured in terms of their health-related quality of life (HRQL) using a revised version of the Medical Outcomes Survey Short Form-36 (MOS SF-36) questionnaire (Ware & Sherbourne, 1992) outlining five domains of well-being:[3] physical functioning, general health, social functioning, emotional well-being and vitality. Physical and social functioning outcomes remained consistently high with median scores of 100 at all three time points: the maximum score possible. Measures of vitality, emotional well-being and general health increased significantly from the start to the end of the workshops ($Z = -3.426$, $p = 0.001$; $Z = -5.230$, $p = 0.001$; and $Z = -5.936$, $p = 0.001$, respectively), and general health continued to increase significantly at follow up compared with the end ($Z = -2.584$, $p = 0.010$). Unfortunately, follow-up measures in the other two domains were not as positive, in fact, vitality and emotional well-being had both significantly *decreased* at follow up compared with the end of the workshops ($Z = -4.215$, $p < 0.000$; and $Z = -4.468$, $p < 0.000$, respectively). These findings suggest that a lack of long-term support has had a detrimental effect on some aspects of the participants' lives in prison. Research in line with SDT has shown that vitality and well-being are outcomes of autonomous behaviour (Ryan & Deci, 2000; and Nix et al., 1999), which indicates that prisoners' health outcomes at follow-up are reflective of a lack of engagement in autonomous behaviours.

The three basic psychological needs were assessed using a scale adapted for use in relation to exercise (Basic Psychological Needs in Exercise Scale; BPNES; Vlachopoulos & Michailidou, 2006). Measures of competence, relatedness and autonomy had all increased significantly from the start to the end of the workshops ($Z = -3.135$, $p = 0.002$; $Z = -3.634$, $p < 0.000$; and $Z = -3.796$, $p < 0.000$, respectively). Relatedness and competence remained significantly higher at follow than at the start ($Z = -3.044$, $p = 0.002$; and $Z = -3.177$, $p = 0.001$, respectively). Perceived autonomy support was also measured at the end of the workshops using The Sport Climate Questionnaire, revealing a mean score of 6.85 out of a maximum 7. However, measures of autonomy on the BPNES had begun to decrease at follow up and were lower than they had been at the start, although this was not significant.

Analysis of qualitative responses provided in the end and follow-up surveys as well as interviews with 15 participants revealed tremendously positive outcomes. There was an overwhelming sense that the workshops and L.J.'s story had 'reignited' something within participants, encouraging them to use their time proactively. Participants who did not exercise prior to the workshops had grown in competence, and many reported that they were now engaging in exercise on the wing or getting to the gym when possible, whilst those who were already regular exercisers had relished the opportunity to learn more about exercise and nutrition. Just over a third of participants had signed up to or were already engaged in an educational course within the prison as a direct result of participating in the workshops, either because it had motivated them to do so or provided them with information they had not previously known about. The importance of a supportive environment which promotes autonomy to increase motivation for exercise is recognised throughout the literature (Andrews & Andrews, 2003; Biddle, Fox, Boutcher, & Faulkner, 2000; Hassan et al., 2022; Meek and Lewis, 2012, 2014; Sloan, Gough & Conner, 2010), whilst Morgan et al.'s (2020) rationale for developing positive interpersonal relationships in sport to promote desistance from crime emphasises leaders as role models who understand and appreciate the everyday challenges that participants encounter. Two of the key themes in prisoners' discourse about the workshops were relatedness and comradery; L.J.'s position as an ex-prisoner and the element of relatedness that this provided became crucial in the promotion of prisoners' motivations to engage in the workouts as well as the soft skills sessions, and participants were able to exercise and engage positively and freely with other prisoners in the workshops in a way which can be tough in other areas of the prison where they are often negotiating risk.

The decrease in follow-up measures of emotional well-being, vitality and autonomy for exercise are reflective of the impact that can be had when a positive intervention such as this is complete, and prisoners are then left without any purposeful activity to engage in. With more time and resource, the workshops would seek to employ serving prisoners to act as supporters within the prison, engaging with participants of the workshops following completion, providing them with new exercise and nutrition plans, delivering regular group workouts and acting as a figure of relatedness. Such an approach is in line with Meek's (2018) recommendation for sport provision in prisons to be responsive to individual needs, advocating for the employment of prisoners to assist PE staff, take classes and provide personal training, and act as peer supporters, whilst being mindful that for engagement across the diverse prison population, these prisoners should represent the wider demographic of the establishment.

Evaluations of prison-based interventions such as the *Cell Workout Workshops* in the form of carefully designed natural experiments are crucial in informing practitioners, funders and the prison and probation service about 'what works' in relation to motivating prisoners to engage in healthy behaviours, particularly given the current lack of robustly evaluated sports-based interventions to support prisoners' well-being (Meek, 2022). The present evaluation has highlighted the importance of continued support and engagement with prisoners following an intervention such as this one, as well as the potential for sport and exercise-based interventions to engage prisoners in other positive behaviours such as education and employment.

Notes

1 A high secure setting is a hospital that detains individuals under the Mental Health Act 1983 as amended in 2007 (c. 20) who are deemed to require treatment in conditions of high security due to dangerous, violent or criminal propensities as outlined by the National Health Service Act, 2006 (c. 41).

2 The IEP scheme is a tool used by prison management to incentivise conforming behaviour by offering prisoners the chance to earn benefits such as increased gym access in exchange for responsible behaviour. The scheme consists of three levels; basic, standard and enhanced.

3 Domains measuring role limitations due to physical and emotional problems and bodily pain were removed as they referred to engaging in daily activities which were not applicable to all prisoners.

References

Alliance of Sport in Criminal Justice. (2016). Our theory of change: Exploring the role of sport for development in the prevention and desistance from crime. Retrieved from www.nasdc.org/power-of-sport/theory-of-change/

Andrews, J. P., & Andrews, G. J. (2003). Life in a secure unit: The rehabilitation of young people through the use of sport. *Social Science & Medicine*, *56*, 531–550.

Bandura, A. (1986). *Social Foundations of thought and Action: A Social Cognitive Theory*. Englewood Cliffs, NJ: Prentice-Hall.

Baumeister, R., & Leary, M. R. (1995). The need to belong: Desire for interpersonal attachments as a fundamental human motivation. *Psychological Bulletin*, *117*, 497–529.

Bebbington, P., Jakobowitz, S., McKenzie, N., Killaspy, H., Iveson, R., Duffield, G., & Kerr, M. (2017). Assessing needs for psychiatric treatment in prisoners: 1. Prevalence of disorder. *Soc Psychiatry Psychiatr Epidemiol*, *52*, 221–229. http://10.1007/s00127-016-1311-7

Beiner, L., & Abrams, D. B. (1991). The contemplation ladder: Validation of a measure of readiness to consider smoking cessation. *Health Psychology*, *10*, 360–365.

Biddle, S. J. H., Fox, K. R., Boutcher, S. H., & Faulkner, G. (2000). The way forward for physical activity and the promotion of psychological well-being. In S. J. H.

Biddle, K. R. Fox, & S. H. Boutcher (Eds.), *Physical Activity and Psychological Well-being* (pp. 154–168). London: Routledge.

Buckaloo, B. J., Krug, K. S., & Nelson, K. B. (2009). Exercise and the low-security inmate: Changes in depression, stress, and anxiety. *The Prison Journal*, *89*(*3*), 328–343.

Bunce, A. E. (2019). *'What We're Saying Makes Sense So I've Subscribed to It and I Try to Live by It.' A Qualitative Exploration of Prisoners' Motivation to Participate in an Innovative Rehabilitation Programme through the Lens of Self-Determination Theory* [Doctoral dissertation, University of Surrey]. ProQuest Dissertations Publishing. https://doi.org/10.15126/thesis.00852929

Centre for Mental Health. (2021). *The Future of Prison Mental Health Care in England.* www.centreformentalhealth.org.uk/sites/default/files/publication/download/CentreforMentalHealth_TheFutureofPrisonMentalHealthCare_0.pdf

Chatzisarantis, N. L. D., Biddle, S. J. H., & Meek, G. A. (1997). A self-determination theory approach to the study of intentions and the intention-behaviour relationship in children's physical activity. *British Journal of Health Psychology*, *2*, 343–360.

Chatzisarantis, N. L. D., Hagger, M. S., Biddle, S. J. H., & Karageorghis, C. (2002). The cognitive processes by which perceived locus of causality predicts participation in physical activity. *Journal of Health Psychology*, *7*, 685–699.

Condon, L., Hek, G., & Harris, F. (2008). Choosing health in prison: Prisoners' views on making healthy choices in English prisons. *Health Education Journal*, *67*(*3*), 155–166. doi:10.1177/0017896908094633

Daley, A. J., & Duda, J. L. (2006). Self-determination, stage of readiness to change for exercise, and frequency of physical activity in young people. *European Journal of Sport Science*, *6*(*4*), 231–243. https://doi.org/10.1080/17461390601012637

deCharms, R. (1968). *Personal Causation.* New York, NY: Academic Press.

Deci, E. L. (1975). *Intrinsic Motivation.* New York, NY: Plenum.

Deci, E. L., & Ryan, R. M. (1985). *Intrinsic Motivation and Self-Determination in Human Behavior.* New York, NY: Plenum.

Department of Health. (2011). Physical activity guidelines for adults (19–64 years). Retrieved from www.gov.uk/government/uploads/system/uploads/attachment_data/file/213740/dh_128145.pdf

De Silva, M. J., Breuer, E., Lee, L., Asher, L., Chowdhary, N., Lund, C., & Patel, V. (2014). Theory of change: A theory-driven approach to enhance the medical research council's framework for complex interventions. *Trials*, *15*, 267. doi:10.1186/1745-6215-15-267

de Viggiani, N. (2007). Unhealthy prisons: Exploring structural determinants of prison health. *Sociology of Health & Illness*, *29*, 115–135.

Doran, G. T. (1981). *There's a S. M. A. R. T. way to write a management's goals and objectives. Management Review: AMA Forum*, *70*(*11*), 35–36.

Durcan, G., & Zwemstra, J. C. (2014). Mental health in prison. In World Health Organisation (Ed.), *Prisons and Health* (pp. 87–85). Copenhagen: World Health Organisation.

Fazel, S., & Danesh, J. (2002). Serious mental disorder in 23000 prisoners: A systematic review of 62 surveys. *The Lancet*, *359*(9306), 545–550.

Fazel, S., Hayes, A. J., Bartellas, K., Clerici, M., & Trestman, R. (2016). Mental health of prisoners: Prevalence, adverse outcomes, and interventions. *Lancet Psychiatry*, *3*(9), 871–881. http://10.1016/S2215-0366(16)30142-0

Flanders, L. J. (2016). *Cell Workout*. England: Hodder & Stoughton.
Gatherer, A., Enggist, S., & Moller, L. (2014). The essential about prisons and health. In S. Enggist, L. Moller, G. Galea et al. (Eds.), *Prisons and Health* (pp. 1–5). Copenhagen: World Health Organization.
Gatherer, A., Moller, L., & Hayton, P. (2005). The world health organization European health in prisons project after 10 years: Persistent barriers and achievements. *American Journal of Public Health, 95*(10), 1696–1700.
Glorney, E., Perkins, D., Adshead, G., McGauley, G., Murray, K., Noak, J., & Sichau, G. (2010). Domains of need in a high secure hospital setting: A model for streamlining care and reducing length of stay. *International Journal of Forensic Mental Health, 9*(2), 138–148.
Glowacki, K. Arbour-Nicitopoulos, K., Burrows, M. Chesick, L., Heinemann, L., Irving, S., Lam, R. W., Macridis, S., Michalak, E., Scott, A., Taylor, A., & Faulkner, G. (2019). It's more than just a referral: Development of an evidence-informed exercise and depression toolkit. *Mental Health and Physical Activity, 17*, 1–12. https://doi.org/10.1016/j.mhpa.2019.100297
Harter, S. (1978). Effectance motivation reconsidered: Toward a developmental model. *Human Development, 1*, 661–669.
Hassan, J., Shannon, S., Tully, M. A., McCartan, C., Davidson, G., Bunn, R., & Breslin, G. (2022). Systematic review of physical activity interventions assessing physical and mental health outcomes on patients with severe mental illness (SMI) within secure forensic settings. *Journal of Psychiatric and Mental Health Nursing, 29*(5), 630–646. http:// https://onlinelibrary.wiley.com/doi/10.1111/jpm.12832
Her Majesty's Chief Inspector of Prisons. (2022). *HM Chief Inspector of Prisons for England and Wales Annual Report 2021–22*. www.justiceinspectorates.gov.uk/hmiprisons/wp-content/uploads/sites/4/2022/07/HMIP-Annual-Report-web-2021-22.pdf
Hofstetter, C. R., Hovell, M. F., Macera, C., Sallis, J. F., Spry, V., Barrington, E., … Rauh, M. (1991). Illness, injury, and correlates of aerobic exercise and walking: A community study. *Research Quarterly for Exercise and Sport Journals, 62*(1), 1–9.
Independent Monitoring Boards. (2013). *HMP/YOI ISIS: Report of the Independent Monitoring Board*. Retrieved from www.imb.org.uk/wp-content/uploads/2015/01/isis-2013.pdf
Ismail, N. (2023). *The English Prison Health System after a Decade of Austerity, 2010-2020: The Failed Political Experiment*. London: Routledge.
Jakab, Z. (2014). Foreword. In S. Enggist, L. Moller, G. Galea et al. (Eds.), *Prisons and Health*. Copenhagen: World Health Organization.
Leberman, S. (2007). Voices behind the walls: Female offenders and experiential learning. *Journal of Adventure Education & Outdoor Learning, 7*, 113–120.
Leon, A. S., & Norstrom, J. (1995). Evidence of the role of physical activity and cardiorespiratory fitness in the prevention of coronary heart disease. *Quest, 47*, 311–319.
Lowther, M., Mutrie, N., & Scott, E. M. (2002). Promoting physical activity in a socially and economically deprived community: A 12 month randomized control trial of fitness assessment and exercise consultation. *Journal of Sports Sciences, 20*(7), 577–588. doi:10.1080/026404102760000071
Mateo-Urdiales, A., Michael, M., Simpson, C., & Beenstock, J. (2020). Evaluation of a participatory approach to improve healthy eating and physical activity in a secure mental health setting. *Journal of Public Mental Health, 19*(4), 301–309.

Meek, R. (2014). *Sport in Prison: Exploring the Role of Physical Activity in Correctional Settings*. Oxon: Routledge.
Meek, R. (2018). A Sporting Chance: An Independent Review of Sport in Youth and Adult Prisons. Ministry of Justice. www.gov.uk/government/publications/a-sporting-chance-an-independent-review-of-sport-in-justice
Meek, R. (2022). Measuring and demonstrating the impact of prison-based sporting initiatives. In D. Silva & L. Kennedy (Eds.), *Power Played: A Critical Criminology of Sport*. Vancouver: UBC.
Meek, R., & Champion, N. (2012). Fit for Release: How Sports-Based Learning Can Help Prisoners Engage in Education, Gain Employment and Desist from Crime. Prisoners Education Trust. Retrieved May 26, 2017, from www.prisonerseducation.org.uk/resources/fit-for-release-how-sports-based-learning-can-help-prisoners-engage-in-education-gain-employment-and-desist-from-crime
Meek, R., & Lewis, G. (2012). The role of sport in promoting prisoner health. *International Journal of Prisoner Health, 8(3–4)*, 117–130. doi:10.1108/17449201211284996
Meek, R., & Lewis, G. (2014). The impact of a sports initiative for young men in prison: Staff and participant perspectives. *Journal of Sport and Social Issues, 38*(2), 95–123. doi: 10.1177/0193723512472896
Meek, R., Morgan, H. & Parker, A. (2022). The history and development of policy for sport andphysical activity in youth and adult prisons. In H. Morgan & A. Parker (Eds.), *Sport, Physical Activity and Criminal Justice*. London: Taylor & Francis.
Ministry of Justice. (2021). The Scale of Mental Health Issues Within Prisons in England and Wales and Whether Enough *is* in Place to Determine the Scale of the Problem (Mhp0044). https://committees.parliament.uk/writtenevidence/36355/html/
Ministry of Justice. (2022, July 28). Offender Management Statistics Quarterly: January to March 2022. www.gov.uk/government/statistics/offender-management-statistics-quarterly-january-to-march-2022/offender-management-statistics-quarterly-january-to-march-2022
Morgan, H., Parker, A., Meek, R. & Cryer, J. (2020). Participation in sport as a mechanism to transform the lives of young people within the criminal justice system: an academic exploration of a theory of change. *Sport, Education and Society, 25*(8), 917–930. http://doi.org/10.1080/13573322.2019.1674274
National Health Service Act. (2006). *ch.41*. Retrieved from www.legislation.gov.uk/ukpga/2006/41/pdfs/ukpga_20060041_en.pdf
National Offender Management Service. (2011). *Service Specification for Physical Education*.
Nix, G. A., Ryan, R. M., Manly, J. B. & Deci, E. L. (1999). Revitalization through Self-Regulation: The Effects of Autonomous and Controlled Motivation on Happiness and Vitality. *Journal of Experimental Social Psychology, 35*, 266–284.
Parker, A., Meek, R., & Lewis, G. (2014). Sport in a youth prison: Male young offenders' experiences of a sporting intervention, *Journal of Youth Studies, 17*(3), 381–396.
Pollard, E. L., & Lee, P. D. (2003). Child well-being: A systematic review of the literature. *Social Indicators Research, 61(1)*, 59–78.
Power, T. G., Ullrich-French, S. C., Steele, M. M., Daratha, K. B., & Bindler, R. C. (2011). Obesity, cardiovascular fitness, and physically active adolescents' motivations

for activity: A self-determination theory approach. *Psychology of Sport and Exercise, 12*, 593–598.

Prison Reform Trust. (2014). Punishment without Purpose: What is the Incentives and Earned Privileges (IEP) Scheme? Prison Reform Trust. London. Retrieved April 12, from www.prisonreformtrust.org.uk/Portals/0/Documents/punishment%20without%20purpose%20FINAL2941007.pdf

Prisons and Probation Ombudsman. (2016). *Prisoner Mental Health.* London: Prisons and Probation Ombudsman. Retrieved from www.ppo.gov.uk/wp-content/uploads/2016/01/PPO-thematic-prisoners-mental-health-web-final.pdf

Prochaska, J., & DiClemente, C. (1983). Stages and processes of self-change of smoking: Toward an integrative model of change. *Journal of Consulting and Clinical Psychology, 51*(3), 390–395.

Rebbapragada, N., Furtado, V. & Hawker-Bond, G. W. (2021). Prevalence of mental disorders in prisons in the UK: A systematic review and meta-analysis. *BJPsych Open,* 7(1), 283–284. http://10.1192/bjo.2021.755

Reis, H. T., Sheldon, K. M., Gable, S. L., Roscoe, J., & Ryan, R. M. (2000). Daily well-being: The role of autonomy, competence, and relatedness. *Personality and Social Psychology Bulletin, 26*, 419–435.

Ryan, R. M. & Deci, E. L. (2000). Self-determination theory and the facilitation of intrinsic motivation, social development, and well-being. *American Psychologist, 55*(1), 68–78. https://doi.org/10.1037/0003-066X.55.1.68

Sallis, J. F., Hovell, M. F., Hofstetter, C. R., Elder, J. P., Hackley, M., Caspersen, C. J., & Powell, K. E. (1990). Distance between homes and exercise facilities related to frequency of exercise among San Diego residents. *Public Heath Reports, 105*(2), 179–185.

Sloan, C., Gough, B., & Conner, M. (2010). Healthy masculinities? How ostensibly healthy men talk about lifestyle, health and gender. *Psychology & Health, 25*(7), 783–803. doi:10.1080/08870440902883204

Spilner, M., & Robertson, S. (2000). Take 10,000 steps a day! Prevention 2000, 90.

Tyler, N., Miles, H. L., Karadag, B. & Rogers, G. (2019). An updated picture of the mental health needs of male and female prisoners in the UK: Prevalence, comorbidity, and gender differences. *Social Psychiatry and Psychiatric Epidemiology, 54*, 1143–1152. https://doi.org/10.1007/s00127-019-01690-1

Ullrich-French, S., & Cox, A. (2009). Using cluster analysis to examine the combinations of motivation regulations of physical education students. *Journal of Sport and Exercise Psychology, 31*, 358–379.

van der Helm, G. H. P., Kuiper, C. H. Z., & Stams, G. J. J. M. (2018). Group climate and treatment motivation in secure residential and forensic youth care from the perspective of self determination theory. *Children and Youth Services Review, 93*, 339–344. https://doi.org/10.1016/j.childyouth.2018.07.028

Vlachopoulos, S. P., & Michailidou, S. (2006). Development and initial validation of a measure of autonomy, competence, and relatedness in exercise: The basic psychological needs in exercise scale. *Measurement in Physical Education and Exercise Science, 10*, 179–201.

Wang, C. K. J., Chatzisarantis, N. L. D., Spray, C. M., & Biddle, S. J. H. (2002). Achievement goal profiles in school physical education: Differences in self-determination, sport ability beliefs, and physical activity. *British Journal of Educational Psychology, 72*, 433–445.

Ware, J. E., & Sherbourne, C. D. (1992). The MOS 36-item short-form health survey (SF-36). I. Conceptual framework and item selection. *Medical Care, 30*(6), 473–483.

White, R. W. (1963). *Ego and Reality in Psychoanalytic Theory*. New York, NY: International Universities Press.

Woodall, J. (2016). A critical examination of the health promoting prison two decades on. *Critical Public Health*. doi:10.1080/09581596.2016.1156649

Woods, D., Breslin, G., & Hassan, D. (2017). A systematic review of the impact of sport-based interventions on the psychological well-being of people in prison. *Mental Health and Physical Activity, 12*, 50–61.

Woods, D., Leavey, G., Meek, R. & Breslin, G. (2020). Developing mental health awareness and help seeking in prison: A feasibility study of the State of Mind Sport programme. *International Journal of Prisoner Health, 16*(4), 403–416. https://doi-org.bham-ezproxy.idm.oclc.org/10.1108/IJPH-10-2019-0057

World Health Organisation. (1995) *Health in Prisons. Health Promotion in the Prison Setting*. Summary Report on a WHO meeting, London, 15–17, October 1995. Copenhagen: Author.

Yoon, I. A., Slade, K., & Fazel, S. (2017). Outcomes of psychological therapies for prisoners with mental health problems: A systematic review and meta-analysis. *Journal of Consulting and Clinical Psychology, 85*(8), 783–802. https://doi.org/10.1037/ccp0000214

Further reading

Meek, R. (2014). *Sport in Prison: Exploring the Role of Physical Activity in Correctional Settings*. Oxon: Routledge.

This book is the first of its kind to explore the role of sport in prisons and its subsequent impact on rehabilitation and behavioural change.

Woods, D., Breslin, G., & Hassan, D. (2017). A systematic review of the impact of sport-based interventions on the psychological well-being of people in prison. *Mental Health and Physical Activity, 12*, 50–61.

This article presents a contemporary overview of sports-based interventions in prisons with a comprehensive set of guidelines that future interventions should adhere to when targeting prisoners' well-being.

11

MENTAL HEALTH AND WELL-BEING OF MEN IN PRISON

Evidence from the Active Choices Rugby and State of Mind Sport Programmes

David Woods and Gavin Breslin

Learning objectives

After reading this chapter you should be able to:

1. Describe the risks to mental health of men in prison.
2. Critically examine how two different sport-based programmes can be incorporated into mental health interventions in prison.
3. Identify merits for including behaviour change theory in programme development and evaluation design.
4. Consider the factors required to implement and evaluate a mental health awareness programme in prison.

Introduction to the theme

In this chapter two programmes, the Active Choices Rugby Programme and State of Mind Sport will be described. Both were aimed at enhancing mental well-being of prisoners through either physical activity participation in rugby or via mental health awareness educational content. The aims of the chapter are: to provide an insight into the specific challenges to mental well-being faced within the prison environment; to outline how sporting interventions can be used to help tackle these challenges; to present a reflexive account of implementing and evaluating sport based interventions within the unique prison environment; and to provide researchers and practitioners alike with what lessons have been learned, with the hope that it will help shape future research, theory and practice in this growing area.

DOI: 10.4324/9781003291695-13

Included programmes targeted both the hedonic and eudaimonic aspects of mental well-being of men in prison. Hedonic well-being is concerned with experiencing positive affect, carefreeness and subjective life satisfaction, and eudaimonic well-being is concerned with feelings of meaning, value, accomplishment, self-realisation and good relationships (Huta, 2016; Stewart-Brown & Janmohamed, 2008). Steger and Shin (2012), succinctly surmise that hedonia equates to pleasure and eudaimonia equates to mattering. Specific factors of interest were also improvements in perceived autonomy, competence and relatedness, the three elements of Basic Psychological needs Theory (Ryan & Deci, 2001).

Within the prison population, researchers have reported a myriad of perceived benefits to mental well-being from sport based interventions (Amtmann & Kukay, 2016; Gallant et al., 2015; Woods & Breslin, 2022). Positive effects have been shown for life-skills, self-esteem, self-efficacy, confidence, hopelessness, depression, mood and resilience. Despite these positive reports, there has been a consistent absence of incorporating health behaviour change theories across sporting interventions (Meek & Lewis, 2014a; Morgan et al., 2020). In essence, a greater understanding of 'how and why' sporting interventions achieve their outcomes within prison contexts is required. This mirrors a criticism of the broader youth-sport development literature that "while there is a wealth of knowledge on the youth development outcomes sport can influence, there is much less on how or why this development occurs" (Jones et al., 2017, p. 163). The programmes detailed in this chapter and the associated research conducted aimed to assess whether benefits to multiple constructs such as mental well-being, autonomy support, resilience, and help-seeking could be achieved in an effort to strengthen future research and practice.

Describe the client or group being targeted

The most recent UK Justice Committee "Mental health in prison" report (House of Commons, 2021) noted that there are issues with trying to accurately report the overall prevalence of mental health diagnoses, with all data summarised by the Centre for Mental Health being at least five years old. Taking that data as a baseline, it is estimated that within the United Kingdom up to 90% of prisoners aged over 16 years are mentally unwell (Durcan, 2016), whilst Leigh-Hunt and Perry (2015) presented estimates of prisoners suffering from depression and anxiety ranging from 30% to 75%, depending on data collection technique and definitions of mental health and disorders used. In a limited prevalence study by Tyler et al (2019), conducted in 13 prisons in the south of England, two-thirds of participants screened positive for clinical symptoms of at least one type of mental disorder (66.7%, n = 313), while 54.8% screened positive for personality disorder (54.8%, n = 257), with depression being most prevalent (28.1%, n = 132), followed by masochistic

(22.4%, n = 105), and schizoid disorder (21.3%, n = 100). In a recent scoping review of mental health of prisoners during COVID-19, social restrictions and their effects on mental health were highlighted as a concern (Johnson et al, 2021).

Although definitive figures are difficult to ascertain, the research consistently demonstrates a high prevalence of poor mental health and well-being of prisoners, coupled with an absence of targeted and consistent mental health promotion training (Durcan, 2021; Lewis & Meek, 2012). This is particularly concerning when you consider that criminal justice systems gather people with pre-existing, serious health problems and exacerbate them (Fazel at al., 2022). Conditions such as over-crowding, interpersonal distrust, bullying, marginalisation, social withdrawal, a decreased sense of self-worth, mental health stigma, discrimination and a lack of purposeful activity or lack of privacy can have a detrimental effect (Butler et al, 2022; Wildeman & Wang, 2017).

Prisoners with comparatively lower mental health are also at greater risk of suicide, self-harm, violence and victimisation (Fazel et al., 2016). This is critical to address when you consider recent figures from HM Prison and Probation Service in the UK which show that in the year 2020–21, 86 deaths were self-inflicted, a 28% increase from the 67 self-inflicted deaths in the previous 12 months. There were 52,726 self-harm incidents in the 12 months to September 2021, down 11% from the previous 12 months.

Initial needs assessment

Despite being faced with such startling statistics related to the prevalence of mental ill-health and the hostile environment and social conditions outlined within prisons, there remains scope for optimism in relation to meeting the mental health needs of prisoners. A unique opportunity exists to implement targeted health promotion activities to those with limited experience of accessing similar activities prior to incarceration (Wildeman & Wang, 2017; MacNamara & Mannix-McNamara, 2014). Dumont et al. (2012), reported that within the United States of America (USA), contact with prison health care for some individuals represents the first experience of accessing preventative and chronic medical care. A targeted example of this was the establishment by the World Health Organisation (WHO) of the Health in Prisons Project (HIPP) in 1995. Although over two decades ago HIPP advocated the promotion of a whole-prison approach to the successful implementation of health promotion and reforming interventions (WHO, 1999). Regarding mental health and well-being specifically, the Trenčín Statement highlighted that "promoting mental health and well-being should be central to a prison's health care policy" (WHO, 2007, p. 6). While the realisation of health promoting prisons has been criticised for lack of pace and weakening commitment over the last decade (Woodall, 2016), the principle of the policy highlighted in the statement remains critical and should be further implemented. A rationale for its implementation is that improved mental well-being is of benefit not only to those imprisoned, but wider society, given its centrality to successful prisoner rehabilitation and reintegration into the community following release (Durcan, 2021; Hayton, 2007).

A multitude of key services, partnerships and actions exist within the criminal justice system to potentially meet the mental health needs of prisoners and improve their mental well-being (Forester et al, 2018; Morgan & Parker, 2022). However, many prisoners who stand to benefit from those services do not wish to engage with traditional treatment pathways (Stewart, 2008), or for those that do there are many barriers in place to prevent the delivery of adequate services from initial Screening, Triage, Assessment, Intervention and Reintegration (STAIR) post release (Forester et al, 2018). Access to sport and exercise facilities are judged to have potential to meet these health needs and positively impact prisoners' mental well-being (WHO, 1999; Morgan & Parker, 2022; Woods et al., 2017b). Researchers have demonstrated that sport can offer a more acceptable means to engage prisoners in health and well-being activity beyond traditional public health approaches (Meek, 2018; Meek & Lewis, 2014b). In line with these recommendations, both programmes detailed in this chapter, Active Choices Rugby and State of Mind Sport were offered within two different prisons as interventions designed in part, to use the context of sport to engage participants and improve their mental well-being. The Active Choices Rugby programme targeted young men aged between 18–24 years, serving time at a young offenders prison in Northern Ireland, whilst the State of Mind Sport Programme was available to all ages 18+ within a category C prison in England.

Framework and intervention for delivery

Active Choices Rugby

The Active Choices Rugby (ACR) programme was a sport-based initiative delivered by a sports governing body in partnership with local city councils. The main objective of the initiative was to encourage individuals to be more active through sport more often, and in turn benefit from improved physical and mental well-being. The local council delivery team worked in partnership with the young men's prison located within their council boundary, to facilitate a six-week rugby coaching programme. Each week the sessions would introduce new core rugby skills (e.g., passing, safe tackling, kicking), raise awareness of the rules and etiquette of the game, and facilitate a short match. Alongside the game skill improvement aims, additional aims of the programme were to improve teamwork, self-confidence, self-esteem and mental well-being, via the fostering of a positive mental outlook for the future. The coach had extensive experience of coaching rugby across all age groups and levels, and the programme was specifically designed to provide an induction into contact rugby (previously unavailable within the young men's prison), with an aim of coaching participants to a sufficient standard whereby they are match ready and can continue to play the sport in prison and in the community upon release.

The ACR programme was not created with a psychological theory of behaviour change incorporated. However, the coach felt improvements in well-being could be achieved informally throughout the progression of the programme as he gained participants' trust. This reflected the assumption of positive impact on mental well-being from sporting interventions, without theoretical foundations or subsequent testing of the supporting conditions, common in many sport-based intervention programmes (Jones et al., 2017; Woods et al., 2017a). We therefore, retrospectively assessed perceived benefit to mental well-being, through a mixed-methods approach incorporating one-to-one semi-structured interviews and quantitative measures of well-being with 14 prisoners aged 18–24, assessed at the start of the programme, after three weeks (the mid-point), six weeks and finally eight weeks.

Participants completed the Short Warwick Edinburgh Mental Well-being Scale (Stewart-Brown & Janmohamed, 2008) and the Basic Psychological Needs Scale (Deci & Ryan, 2000). The presence of an autonomy supportive environment within the Active Choices Rugby programme was also assessed through the Sport's Climate Questionnaire (Deci, 2001). Autonomy supportive environments have been shown to have a positive impact on mental well-being, basic psychological need satisfaction and self-determined motivation (Amorose, 2007; Gillet, 2010; Mageau & Vallerand, 2003; Meek & Lewis, 2014a). Questions included in the semi-structured interviews were piloted through the prison's education services to ensure understanding of the areas to be covered. Interview topics included previous experience of participation in sport, motivation for participation, expectations and benefits of the rugby programme, views on the programme delivery and challenges experienced. Interviews with the prisoners lasted up to 30 minutes, were recorded, transcribed and subjected to thematic analysis.

State of Mind Sport Programme

The State of Mind Sport (SOMS) programme was delivered as a 75 minute face to face group session. SOMS aimed to raise awareness of, and promote, mental well-being and resilience, tackle stigma towards mental health and help seeking, and highlight the importance of signposting prisoners to appropriate mental health services, with the overall aim of preventing suicide. The programme was delivered by a mental health and substance misuse nurse, and two former elite level rugby players who had lived experience of mental illness.

Therefore, although ACR and SOMS programmes explicitly incorporated sport within their design, these were implemented in two very different ways, the ACR was about participating physically in rugby, while SOMS was an educational programme with no rugby participation.

Through collaborative working with the Suicide and Self Harm project group within the National Offender Management Service, the SOMS programme was tailored from a community based mental health awareness programme to include a mixture of the original content (delivered to over 25,000 people in sports clubs, universities, construction and office workplaces), alongside specific contextual information relevant to the prison environment. Topics included in the programme were: (a) risks men face in relation to mental health and psychological well-being; (b) risk factors as a result of mental health stigma, macho-cultures, avoidance of help-seeking behaviours and negative coping strategies; (c) markers of stress and positive coping strategies; and (d) descriptions of well-being and resilience and practical steps to improve these. Two case-studies were presented by the former elite rugby league players who suffered from poor mental health and considered taking their own lives, prior to seeking help. Key messages they aimed to deliver included: (a) seek help/advice from someone you trust; (b) it is a strength, not a weakness to seek help; (c) respond to a mate who may be feeling down; (d) setting achievable goals for yourself and celebrating upon achievement; and (e) we are all part of a team that can support each other (www.stateofmindsport.org).

A total of 75 male prisoners agreed to participate (M age = 37.30, S.D. = 11.01) in an evaluation of the SOMS programme. A total of 47 prisoners (Mage = 38.3, S.D. = 11.4) volunteered to form the intervention group attending SOMS, with 28 prisoners (Mage = 35.3, S.D. = 10.2) volunteering as a waiting list control group, allowing for a mixed 2 x 2 factorial design. The intervention group received the SOMS mental health awareness programme. The waiting list control group completed the baseline and post questionnaires at the beginning and end of an education class, not related to mental health and matched for SOMS intervention duration. The participants completed the Short Warwick Edinburgh Mental Well-being Scale (SWEMWBS) (Stewart-Brown et al., 2009); The Brief Resilience Scale (Smith et al., 2008); The Mental Health Knowledge Schedule (MAKS) (Evans-Lacko et al., 2010); and the Reported and Intended Behaviour Scale (RIBS) (Evans-Lacko et al., 2011). Two focus groups were also held immediately following the SOMS sessions (Group A, n = 8; Group B, n = 7). A topic guide was developed exploring (a) perceived impact of participating in a sports-based mental health programme; (b) acceptability of the programme; and (c) potential challenges and improvements to the programme. A General Inductive Analysis (GIA) approach was adopted to interpret focus group data (Thomas, 2006).

Intervention evaluation and lessons learned through self-reflection

Active Choices Rugby – evaluation and lessons learned

Participants' mean SWEMWBS scores across all time-points remained stable with no large increase or decrease and were relatively positive. This indicated a more positive state of mental well-being within the young men's prison than has been reported across the prison population more generally (Durcan, 2021; Fazel et al., 2022). The positive SWEMWBS scores observed highlighted the dangers of assuming a 'deficit model' (Coalter, 2013), whereby poor mental well-being, and/or related constructs are assumed within all at-risk populations. However, it is also important to note that all participants reported previous consistent attendance at the gym up to five times a week, citing the positive impacts on their mental well-being as a key motivation. This view resonates with findings that those who engage with aerobic and gym activities are associated with a lower mental health burden (compared with those not engaging), in particular when they engage for durations of 45 minutes and frequencies of three to five times per week (Chekroud et al., 2018; Teychenne, 2020). Qualitative findings revealed a short-term perceived benefit to mental well-being, particularly the hedonic perspective of subjective happiness and satisfaction, as a result of the intervention. Short-term positive affect was demonstrated through reported improvements in mood, mental escapism and having an event to look forward to, similar to previous studies (Amtmann & Kukay, 2016; Bilderbeck et al,. 2013; Gallant et al., 2015). Participants also reported a short-term reduction in related deficit measures, specifically reduced feelings of anger and stress.

In contrast to the short-term positive benefits reported, an emergent theme was the absence of any lasting benefit to mental well-being, in contrast to findings from two previous prison-based studies incorporating intervention follow-up. These previous studies reported medium to long-term well-being benefits at two months (Leberman, 2007) and up to two years (Meek & Lewis, 2014a). However, intervention contact time was considerably less in the Active Choices Rugby Programme (one hour a week, over six weeks) in comparison to the Leberman study (20-day residential outdoor activity course) and the Meek and Lewis study (12 to 15 weeks, 5 days a week intensive contact course). Reflecting these comparative differences in intervention contact time, participants and the coach on the ACR programme cited course duration and frequency as reasons for the lack of lasting benefit, alongside inconsistent programme attendance by the participants. These findings, relating to programme efficacy and feasibility, highlighted the importance of facilitating programmes of sufficient duration and frequency within the prisons if the potential for a lasting benefit to mental well-being is to be realised (Woods et al., 2017b).

When examining if basic psychological needs (Ryan & Deci, 2001) mediated the relationship between the ACR intervention and any resultant perceived benefits to mental well-being, quantitative results suggested that autonomy, competence and relatedness were consistently perceived as being met for those who participated across each of the four data collection time-points, with no large increase or decrease observed. However, emergent themes reported from the qualitative analyses demonstrated increased feelings of relatedness for participants, during the programme and at follow-up, particularly with new or vulnerable prisoners. Increased feelings of relatedness are linked to improved mental well-being (Reis et al., 2000), both the hedonic perspective through an immediate positive affect, and the eudaimonic perspective, which partly focuses on developing and maintaining positive relationships. This supports previous researchers who reported improved prisoner relationships and pro-social behaviours following involvement in sport-based interventions (Morgan et al, 2020) alongside findings that sport provides a coping mechanism for new prisoners during their transition into prison life (Gallant et al., 2015). Results also revealed that the short duration of the ACR programme and a lack of opportunity to play rugby upon its conclusion within the prison prevented any on-going feelings of increased competence, resulting in limited short-term benefit to hedonic mental well-being.

In contrast to a perceived increase in the basic needs satisfaction of relatedness, there was qualitative evidence to support the thwarting of perceived autonomy due to participants being denied access to the course without prior notice, on occasions of acute security or staffing issues. Results also highlighted frustration at the lack of sign-posting to continue playing rugby upon release. This is not surprising as the programme offered no instruction on "through the gate" assistance in facilitating this, in contrast to programmes detailed within other studies (Meek & Lewis, 2014a; Parker et al., 2014; Williams et al., 2015). In contrast, quantitative results obtained from the Sport Climate Questionnaire (Deci, 2001) indicated the positive facilitation of an autonomy supportive environment during the programme. This would suggest that although participants experienced increased autonomy when having input into decisions during the training sessions, this did not translate outside of the sporting environment. Two key points emerge from this observation, it cannot be assumed that mental well-being benefits will transfer beyond the sporting environment within prisons. This mirrors the findings of non-prison-based research into the transferability of human-orientated functions in youth-sport development (Jones et al., 2017; Edwards, 2015), which highlight the importance of intentional design and well managed practices to achieve effective transfer beyond sport contexts. Leading on from this, the lack of transfer from the programme can potentially be linked to the lack of health behaviour change theory during design, and/or the lack of transitional support (Meek & Lewis, 2014a; Woods & Breslin, 2022).

The role of assets such as the influence of the coach, parents, peers and the contextual factors such as the environment in which the programme is delivered are influential in improving mental well-being (Amorose, 2007; Atkins et al., 2015; Gillet et al., 2010; Lerner et al., 2003). The results from the Active Choices Rugby Programme demonstrated both the positive and negative impact that assets and contextual influences can have. The relationship fostered between the coach and participants, which centred around values of positive reinforcement, respect and equality, emerged as a key influence on the positive affect reported by participants. In line with Basic Psychological Needs Theory (Deci & Ryan, 2000), participants reported that the programme allowed them to relate better to other prisoners, increased their competence and improved their sense of autonomy. They attributed these changes to the supportive coaching sessions. However, the impacts of the prison environment on programme efficacy and feasibility were consistent sources of frustration for participants and the coach, with programme duration, frequency and attendance all acting as limiters to the potential for longer-term perceived benefit to mental well-being that could have been accrued. An example of this was the cancellation of a scheduled session at the last minute due to a lack of staff resource available to walk participants from their cells to the sports facility. This was only communicated to participants as they were waiting to be escorted with their gear packed and moods high at the expectation of playing. This led to both frustration and low mood at the time, alongside lowered expectations of the programme being delivered and an associated drop in engagement.

Barriers to programme success such as low commitment, irregular attendance and poor scheduling, of which the latter two are under greater control of the prison, have been reported in previous studies (Harner et al., 2010; Gallant et al., 2015). Our findings expand on these, by highlighting the negative impact these factors can also have on programme efficacy, as fluctuating attendance led to an unachieved programme goal – to coach the team to a standard sufficient enough to compete against a visiting team, which the coach believed would have facilitated increased benefit to mental well-being. Therefore, if similar team-orientated sporting interventions within prison, dependent on attendance numbers, are to realise the potential benefit to mental well-being, they must actively seek to maximise prisoner engagement and aspirations in areas under their control. Flexibility in timetabling is one area, alongside continued facilitation of greater access to the sporting activities introduced, albeit dependent on sport specific expertise available and resource implications.

Programme feasibility and efficacy also had a direct impact on the fidelity of the research protocol, with the impact of fluctuating attendance numbers and lack of consistent participants from baseline to follow-up, negatively impacting the scope for longitudinal quantitative analysis. As one participant [P1] who declined to be involved at time-point three commented, "there's no point, nothing's changed". Although such a comment in itself represents a telling qualitative insight, the temporary withdrawal (he participated at time-point 4), alongside the broader changeable make-up of programme participants, was of detriment to the planned quantitative analysis. As a result, there was only limited realisation of one of the research aims, to provide a robust longitudinal measure of perceived benefit to mental well-being rather than ill-being, with the latter over-represented in sport-based intervention studies, both in prisons (Woods et al., 2017a) and in non-prison youth development studies (Jones et al., 2017). This therefore remains a requirement for future research in the area of sport and prisons.

State of Mind Sport – evaluation and lessons learned

As highlighted above in the evaluation of the ACR programme, there are multiple barriers to overcome when implementing sport-based interventions within prisons. For example, accessibility and availability of when these interventions take place over multiple weeks, and the limiting operational restrictions of the prison environment. While these findings should not mean that similar programmes are not pursued with careful planning, the complexity of co-existing factors within the prison environment, including operations level restrictions (e.g. sufficient staff resource, timetabling clashes forcing a choice of having dinner or attending interventions scheduled providing equality of opportunity to all categories of prisoner), through to individual barriers to help-seeking, demand that multiple innovative mental health awareness activities and research approaches are explored. Within the Ministry of Justice policy paper entitled 'Preventing Suicide in England' (Balogan, 2018), SOMS was highlighted as an innovative community based mental health and well-being initiative which could be trialled in prisons. As highlighted earlier, the programme is aimed at raising awareness and tackling stigma, as well as encouraging individuals to seek help when needed. The evaluation of a pilot SOMS intervention within the prison population was therefore a logical next step from the research on ACR to: (a) examine the feasibility of adopting the SOMS programme in a prison setting where a longer programme may not be feasible; and (b) test for effects of SOMS on participants' knowledge of mental health, intentions to seek help, well-being and resilience in comparison to a waiting list control group.

The results from the evaluation showed no significant differences between those who received the SOMS intervention compared to the control group at baseline for SWEMWBS, BRS, MAKS and RIBS. Mean scores and standard deviations for all measures across time-points 1 and 2 are presented in Table 11.1

TABLE 11.1 Mean outcome scores and standard deviations for SOMS intervention and waitlist control groups

Outcome Measures	*Time-point 1 (baseline)*		*Time-point 2 (post SOMS intervention)*	
	Intervention	*Control*	*Intervention*	*Control*
	M (SD)	*M (SD)*	*M (SD)*	*M (SD)*
SWEMWBS (0–35)	21.73 *(4.79)*	23.44 *(4.88)*	21.94 *(5.62)*	23.85 *(4.78)*
BRS (1–5)	3.07 *(0.96)*	3.35 *(0.88)*	3.11 *(0.90)*	3.38 *(0.89)*
MAKS (0–30)	21.21 *(3.12)*	20.71 *(2.88)*	23.09 *(2.79)*	20.89 *(3.06)*
RIBS (0–20)	16.13 *(3.29)*	15.68 *(3.22)*	16.91 *(2.56)*	16.04 *(2.80)*

Quantitative results

There was a significant interaction effect demonstrating a significant improvement in questions 1–6 of the Mental Health Knowledge Schedule (MAKS) scores from baseline to post-programme for the SOMS intervention group compared with the control ($F(1, 72) = 4.92$, $p = 0.03$, $\eta p2 = 0.06$). Furthermore, questions 7–12 of the MAKS relate to knowledge of different types of mental illness. Separate Wilcoxon Z tests were calculated to examine whether any change in knowledge was significant between pre and immediately-post intervention testing. Participants who received the SOMS training were more knowledgeable that stress ($Z = -3.30$, $p < 0.01$) was not a mental illness. There were no significant knowledge changes for grief, bipolar disorder, schizophrenia or depression for the intervention group, and no significant knowledge changes for the control group on any of the mental illnesses presented.

Within the RIBS results, higher scores were indicative of a greater willingness to engage with someone with a mental illness, directly related to stigma experienced within prisons. Although both the intervention and control groups increased their RIBS mean scores over time (see Table 11.1), neither were significant. For both the BRS and SWEMWBS, there was no significant interaction effects for the SOMS programme.

Focus group results

Four distinct themes emerged from the focus groups, these were Perceived Impacts, Sports Appeal, Potential Barriers to Impact and Suggested Improvements, with 12 associated sub-categories (see Table 11.2). A brief description of these themes are provided, for a more full description of the results see Woods et al. (2020).

TABLE 11.2 Emergent focus group themes and associated categories

	Theme	*Categories*
1	Perceived Impacts	a) Sense of Hope b) Sense of Perspective and Coping Efficacy c) Positive Social Networks
2	Sports Appeal	a) Attraction of Sport b) Sense of Legitimacy
3	Potential Barriers to Impact	a) Wary of Trusting Others b) Mental Health Stigma c) Lack of Appropriate Meeting Space d) Lack of Follow-up Support
4	Suggested Improvements	a) Handouts b) Prisoner Involvement

Theme: Perceived impacts

Participants felt they had a renewed sense of hope; that with a positive attitude, willingness to open up to others, and support from others, negative thoughts and feelings could be better dealt with. Participants also agreed that the SOMS programme offered a sense of perspective on their own personal problems. The prevailing view was that if the SOMS speakers could deal with the problems they faced (e.g., loss of identity, depression, disability, suicidal thoughts) and continue to be positive and succeed, then prisoners could also re-frame their problems more positively. As a result, there was also a sense of improved coping efficacy among the prisoners. Reflecting on the benefit the presenters received from opening up to their friends and family, prisoners commented on the potential for benefit to be gained from confiding in their own positive social networks within prison. Similarly, there was an increased awareness of their own potential to act as a 'positive sounding board' for prisoners at risk of poor mental well-being. However, this was tempered by a wariness of taking on other people's problems as they had enough to deal with; whilst others took the opposite view, that listening to other people's problems helped put theirs into a more positive perspective.

Theme: Sports appeal

Both the sporting context and the mental well-being theme of the session were equally attractive to participants, as voiced by Participant A1: "I think that makes it more appealing [the session theme], that it was ex-professional rugby players [presenting]". However, other participants commented they had no over-riding interest in sport or awareness of the presenters, their primary reason for attending was purely an interest in the topic: Participant A3 – "I'd never seen him before in my life, professional rugby player and that, but because they said they'd opened up, you're thinking yes alright I can relate to that, I can listen to that… that's what you need in here, something like that". There was also a connection made with the prisoners in terms of the macho culture within sports, particularly in Rugby League, and experiences within the prison of a culture which stigmatised help-seeking behaviour. Prisoners felt the life stories presented and the personal impacts described afforded them a sense of legitimacy when experiencing similar feelings of depression or anxiety for example, and that it was acceptable to open up and discuss these feelings with others.

Theme: Potential barriers to longer-term impact

Participants highlighted the crucial importance of trust and confidence within prison life and the need to ensure that other prisoners are genuinely interested in mutual helping. The low levels of trust made participants unwilling to open up and talk freely about these issues. Thus within prison, one had to be guarded as others will take advantage. This was particularly poignant, as having fellow prisoners to trust in was considered important in the absence of family members or friends, sources of support who were perceived as critical in positive outcomes with the SOMS presenters.

Although the personal stories presented by the ex-elite rugby league players had presented an alternative narrative to a toxic macho culture, concerns remained of the potential for stigmatisation upon revealing a mental health concern/issue. Participants highlighted that concerns regarding stigmatisation were applicable both within prison and on release, and could have a negative impact on how you were perceived by the prison regime, for example, in relation to parole. A lack of appropriate space for people to informally meet and discuss their issues or concerns in confidence was identified as an environmental barrier within the prison. Finally, questions were raised regarding what follow-up services might be provided within the prison in terms of support for well-being specifically in connection with the information presented. This was described by Participant A3: "You talk to us today, and you're not here tomorrow, is anything going to happen to us in here tomorrow to help us? Is there anything going to happen [as a result] of us talking today now?"

Theme: Suggested improvements

The first suggestion was the provision of related materials, both as paper handouts for those attending and those who were not ready to openly attend a programme related to mental health awareness. Participants recommended that information handouts capturing the key learning points and tools discussed would serve as a useful aid. Participant B6 commented "I took notes as fast as I could, but if you had a handout that would be better". The second suggestion for improvement was that alongside the stories of the ex-sportsmen, similar sessions could be run with current or ex-offenders who had experiences of successfully coping with mental health issues, as this would be very relatable to the prisoners.

The findings from the SOMS study presented a number of useful recommendations for future sport-based interventions, whilst also providing some mixed results, resonating with the findings from the ACR programme. The SOMS study demonstrated that a short mental health awareness programme using sport can successfully engage and elevate knowledge of mental health issues within the prison population. In contrast to the increase in knowledge of mental health, there was no associated significant increase in intentions to engage and offer support to those with mental health concerns. However, focus group results indicated that prisoners intended to act more readily as a 'sounding board' or source of support for others following the SOMS programme, alongside an increased willingness to open up to others, reflecting findings from a different mental health wellness programme (Keogh et al, 2017). It should be noted however that positive prisoner intentions to help others as expressed within the focus groups, were tempered by the concern of other prisoners that they may have enough to deal with themselves before acting as a confidant for fellow prisoners, which may have impacted responses to the items on the RIBS.

A second possible cause of the mixed results regarding intentions to support others relates to the suitability of RIBS as a measure within the prison setting. Items enquire about the respondent's intentions to: "live with", "work with", "work nearby" and "continue a relationship" with someone suffering from a mental illness. Within prison, there is minimum autonomy in relation to these variables (De Viggiani, 2012). Also, the point at which prisoners might be able to make such choices upon release can be many years in the future and may be viewed as abstract and hard to fully imagine. These two factors may have combined to impact the validity of the RIBS questionnaire in its current format, as despite reporting robust psychometric properties they are not widely tested in prisoner populations. Future studies, prison based or otherwise, should therefore consider an altered version of the RIBS, presenting scenarios better reflecting probable personal interactions within the chosen research environment.

No significant differences were recorded between the intervention and control groups for prisoner scores on psychological well-being and resilience immediately post-programme. Psychological well-being, as measured by SWEMWBS, reflects self-perceptions of positive 'functioning' more than 'feeling' (Tennant et al., 2007). Therefore, the absence of significantly enhanced levels of psychological functioning, which relate to personal feelings of value and meaning in life (Huta, 2016), is perhaps not surprising immediately following a 75-minute programme. Building resilience is an interactive evolving process (Herrman et al., 2011), which develops when provided with new adaptive coping strategies. Therefore, the messages and coping strategies delivered within SOMS, targeting increased well-being and resilience, would require increased time to become embedded and potentially reflected in the outcome measures used.

An emergent theme from the focus groups was prisoners' increased willingness to confide in fellow inmates and discuss their vulnerabilities as a positive coping mechanism. This is in contrast to the stereotypical male response of stoicism when faced with emotional distress within prisons (Ricciardelli et al., 2015). However, the translation of any increase in intentions to discuss mental health concerns into actions appeared to be restricted by an opposing theme, i.e., the perceived likelihood of being stigmatised for doing so. Fellow prisoners and the prison system were both identified as sources of stigmatisation. This view persisted despite the programme addressing issues regarding mental health stigma, and could act as a barrier to improved mental well-being. Lack of trust in other prisoners, prison staff, and the potential for low mental well-being to negatively impact parole hearings, were perceived as barriers to adopting a more transparent approach to discussing well-being. Fear of stigmatisation, lack of trust in other prisoners and the prison system all replicate findings from previous research examining help-seeking behaviour within prisons (De Viggiani, 2012; Howerton et al., 2007; Ricciardelli et al., 2015). Avoidance of help-seeking behaviours is also linked to the maintenance of prison masculinities and a weighing up of the risks associated with such disclosures (Ricciardelli et al., 2015).

Considering feasibility, future programmes that are designed as community-based programmes then transferred into a prison, must therefore ensure they gain a deep understanding of the nuances and specific challenges prisoners face when attempting to adopt coping strategies presented to them. Failure to recognise and cater for these contextual factors may open the potential for negative impacts rather than benefits within prison, similar to the access issues encountered within the Active Choices Rugby programme, negatively impacting upon autonomy. Results from the SOMS study show that providing safe spaces for developing trusted relationships with other prisoners, potentially on a sports field as was the case with the ACR programme, providing on-going support following workshops to develop and implement new coping skills, and the inclusion of prisoner testimonies could help mitigate these risks, increase coping-efficacy and overall programme feasibility.

An emergent theme from the focus groups was that SOMS, as a mental health awareness programme with its origins in the hyper masculine sport of rugby league, was effective in at least triggering a small shift in the restrictive toxic masculinities present within the prison environment (Kupers, 2005). The use of sport as a catalyst, specifically ex-professional rugby league players, was perceived to afford a legitimacy to the vulnerabilities of the prisoners and offer an alternative empowering narrative to that usually encountered prior to and within prison. This is an important finding regarding programme feasibility, as although several focus group participants reported motivation to attend due to the sport-based nature of the programme, many others had no overriding interest in sport and were attending due to the focus on mental health. Importantly, those with no sporting interest still felt the messages delivered by the ex-professional rugby players resonated with their current situation.

Combined with an increased willingness to seek help from others and a sense of perspective on their own problems, prisoners reported an increased sense of hope immediately following the SOMS programme. Prisoners referred to increased hoped they could overcome personal difficulties and transition through the gate a better person. This is an important outcome as a sense of hopelessness has been consistently linked with self-harm and suicide (Fazel et al., 2008; Gooding et al., 2017; Konrad et al., 2007).

Conclusion

From the evaluations of both programmes with regard to their impact on mental health and well-being, and their feasibility in prison environments, a number of key points emerge. The ACR programme for prisoners led to a reported benefit on short-term hedonic mental well-being, through increased positive affect and reduced stress and anger. However, quantitative results did not demonstrate a similar perceived benefit to eudaimonic mental well-being, and overall results did not evidence lasting benefits. Similar, The SOMS programme succeeded in increasing knowledge of mental health with the intervention group, however there was limited impact on the remaining measures of mental well-being, resilience and willingness to help others, and participants questioned the longer term benefits without associated programme materials or embedded programme support within the prison.

Within the ACR programme, short-term perceived benefits to the basic psychological needs of relatedness and competence were also reported in participant interviews, suggesting a link between these benefits and observed improvements in hedonic well-being. However, direction of causality could not be confirmed. The importance of contextual factors was evident in both programmes. Within the ACR programme, the coach-participant relationship was key in creating an autonomy supportive environment to the benefit of short-term mental well-being. Similarly within the SOMS programme, the delivery of key messages by ex-professional athletes from a macho culture of rugby league resonated well with participants in the prison environment.

Quantitative results did not reveal any substantial change in participant satisfaction of basic psychological needs within daily prison environment over the duration of the ACR programme. This demonstrates that benefits experienced within sporting interventions will not automatically transfer outside of the sporting environment to living in prison, and highlights the need for deliberate programme design and explicit facilitation in order to encourage wider positive benefits.

Although ACR and SOMS adopted differing models of delivery, programme duration, frequency and/ or follow-up were all cited as limitations to realising longer-term benefits to mental well-being, as well as sources of participant frustration. Providers of similar programmes and prison management therefore need to work collaboratively to ensure that sporting interventions are afforded appropriate time and space alongside other purposeful activities to increase the much needed realisation of positive impacts to prisoner mental health.

References

Amorose, A. J. (2007). Coaching effectiveness. In M. S. Hagger, & N. L. D. Chatzisarantis (Eds.), *Intrinsic Motivation and Self-Determination in Exercise and Sport* (pp. 209–227). Leeds: Human Kinetics.

Amtmann, J., & Kukay, J. (2016). Fitness changes after an 8-week fitness coaching program at a regional youth detention facility. *Journal of Correctional Health Care, 22*(1), 75–83.

Atkins, M. R., Johnson, D. M., Force, E. C., & Petrie, T. A. (2015). Peers, parents, and coaches, oh my! The relation of the motivational climate to boys' intention to continue in sport. *Psychology of Sport and Exercise, 16*, 170–180.

Balogan, F. (2018). Suicide Prevention in England: An Evaluation of Fifteen Years of Action. *Journal of Psychiatry, 21*(441), 2.

Bilderbeck, A. C., Farias, M., Brazil, I. A., Jakobowitz, S., & Wikholm, C. (2013). Participation in a 10-week course of yoga improves behavioural control and decreases psychological distress in a prison population. *Journal of Psychiatric Research, 47*(10), 1438–1445.

Butler, A., Nicholls, T., Samji, H., Fabian, S., & Lavergne, M. R. (2022). Prevalence of mental health needs, substance use, and co-occurring disorders among people admitted to prison. *Psychiatric Services, 73*(7), 737–744.

Chekroud, S. R., Gueorguieva, R., Zheutlin, A. B., Paulus, M., Krumholz, H. M., Krystal, J. H., & Chekroud, A. M. (2018). Association between physical exercise and mental health in 1·2 million individuals in the USA between 2011 and 2015: A cross-sectional study. *The Lancet, 5*, 739–746. https://doi.org/10.1016/S2215-0366(18)30227-X

Coalter, F. (2013). *Sport for Development: What Game Are We Playing?* London: Routledge.

De Viggiani, N. (2012). Trying to be something you are not: Masculine performances within a prison setting. *Men and Masculinities, 15*(3), 271–291.

Deci, E. L. (2001). The sport climate questionnaire. Retrieved January 2, 2016, from SelfDeterminationTheory.org website http://selfdeterminationtheory.org/pas-sport-climate/

Deci, E. L., & Ryan, R. M. (2000). The "what" and "why" of goal pursuits: Human needs and the self-determination of behavior. *Psychological Inquiry, 11*, 227–268.

Dumont, D. M., Brockmann, B., Dickman, S., Alexander, N., & Rich, J. D. (2012). Public health and the epidemic of incarceration. *Annual Review of Public Health, 33(1)*, 325–339.

Durcan, G. (2021). *The Future of Prison Mental Health Care in England: A National Consultation and Review*. London: Centre for Mental Health.

Durcan, G. (2016). *Mental Health and Criminal Justice: Views from Consultations across England & Wales*. London: Centre for Mental Health.

Edwards, M. B. (2015). The role of sport in community capacity building: An examination of sport for development research and practice. *Sport Management Review, 18*(1), 6–19.

Evans-Lacko, S., Little, K., Meltzer, H., Rose, D., Rhydderch, D., Henderson, C., & Thornicroft, G. (2010). Development and psychometric properties of the mental health knowledge schedule. *The Canadian Journal of Psychiatry, 55*(7), 440–448.

Evans-Lacko, S., Rose, D., Little, K., Flach, C., Rhydderch, D., Henderson, C., & Thornicroft, G. (2011). Development and psychometric properties of the reported and intended behaviour scale (RIBS): A stigma-related behaviour measure. *Epidemiology and Psychiatric Sciences, 20*(3), 263–271.

Fazel, S., Bromberg, D. J., & Altice, F. L. (2022). HIV, substance use, and mental health care in prisons. *The Lancet Psychiatry, 9*(9), 694–695.

Fazel, S., Hayes, A. J., Bartellas, K., Clerici, M., & Trestman, R. (2016). Mental health of prisoners: Prevalence, adverse outcomes, and interventions. *The Lancet Psychiatry, 3(9)*, 871–881.

Fazel, S., Cartwright, J., Norman-Nott, A., & Hawton, K. (2008). Suicide in prisoners: A systematic review of risk factors. *Journal of Clinical Psychiatry, 69*(11), 1721–31.

Forrester, A., Till, A., Simpson, A., & Shaw, J. (2018). Mental illness and the provision of mental health services in prisons. *British Medical Bulletin, 127*(1), 101–109.

Gallant, D., Sherry, E., & Nicholson, M. (2015). Recreation or rehabilitation? Managing sport for development programs with prison populations. *Sport Management Review, 18*(1), 45–56.

Gillet, N., Vallerand, R. J., Amoura, S., & Baldes, B. (2010). Influence of coaches' autonomy support on athletes' motivation and sport performance: A test of the hierarchical model of intrinsic and extrinsic motivation. *Psychology of Sport and Exercise, 11*, 155–156.

Gooding, P. A., Tarrier, N., Dunn, G., Awenat, Y., Shaw, J., Ulph, F., & Pratt, D. (2017). Psychological characteristics and predictors of suicide probability in high-risk prisoners. *Criminal Justice and Behavior, 44*(3), 321–335.

Harner, H., Hanlon, A. L., & Garfinkel, M. (2010). Effect of Iyengar yoga on mental health of incarcerated women: A feasibility study. *Nursing Research, 59(6)*, 389–399.

Hayton, P. (2007). Protecting and promoting health in prisons: A settings approach. In L. Møller, H. Stöver, R. Jürgens, A. Gatherer, & H. Nikogosian (Eds.), *Health in Prisons: A WHO Guide to the Essentials in Prison Health* (pp. 15–20). Copenhagen: WHO Regional Office for Europe.

Herrman, H., Stewart, D. E., Diaz-Granados, N., Berger, E. L., Jackson, B., & Yuen, T. (2011). What is resilience? *The Canadian Journal of Psychiatry, 56*(5), 258–265.

House of Commons. (2021). House of commons, justice committee. Mental health in prison. Fifth Report of Session 2021–22. Retrieved at https://committees.parliament.uk/publications/7455/documents/78054/default/

Howerton, A., Byng, R., Campbell, J., Hess, D., Owens, C., & Aitken, P. (2007). Understanding help seeking behaviour among male offenders: qualitative interview study. *BMJ*, *334*(7588), 303.

Huta, V. (2016). Eudaimonic and hedonic orientations: Theoretical considerations and research findings. In *Handbook of Eudaimonic Well-Being* (pp. 215–231). Chambersburg, PA: Springer International Publishing.

Johnson, L., Gutridge, K., Parkes, J., Roy, A., & Plugge, E. (2021). Scoping review of mental health in prisons through the COVID-19 pandemic. *BMJ Open, 11*(5), e046547.

Jones, G. J., Edwards, M. B., Bocarro, J. N., Bunds, K. S., & Smith, J. W. (2017). An integrative review of sport-based youth development literature. *Sport in Society*, *20*(1), 161–179.

Keogh, B., McBennett, P., deVries, J., Higgans, A., O'Shea, M., & Doyle, L. (2017). Prisoners perceptions of a mental health wellness workshop. *International Journal of Prisoner Health*, *13*(2), 81–90.

Konrad, N., Daigle, M. S., Daniel, A. E., Dear, G. E., Frottier, P., Hayes, L. M., ... & Sarchiapone, M. (2007). Preventing suicide in prisons, Part I: Recommendations from the international association for suicide prevention task force on suicide in prisons. *Crisis: The Journal of Crisis Intervention and Suicide Prevention, 28*(3), 113.

Kupers, T. A. (2005). Toxic masculinity as a barrier to mental health treatment in prison. *Journal of Clinical Psychology*, *61*(6), 713–724.

Leberman, S. (2007). Voices behind the walls: Female offenders and experiential learning. *Journal of Adventure Education & Outdoor Learning*, *7*, 113–120.

Leigh-Hunt, N., & Perry, A. (2015). A systematic review of interventions for anxiety, depression, and PTSD in adult offenders. *International Journal of Offender Therapy and Comparative Criminology*, *59*(7), 701–725.

Lerner, R. M., Dowling, E. M., & Anderson, P. M. (2003). Positive youth development: Thriving as the basis of personhood and civil society. *Applied Developmental Science*, *7*(3), 172–180.

Lewis, G., & Meek, R. (2012). Sport and physical education across the secure estate: An exploration of policy and practice. *Criminal Justice Matters*, *90*(1), 32–34.

MacNamara, C., & Mannix-McNamara, P. (2014). Placing the promotion of health and wellbeing on the Irish prison agenda – the complexity of health promotion in Irish prisons. *Irish Journal of Applied Social Studies*, *14*(1), 49–59.

Mageau, G. A., & Vallerand, R. J. (2003). The coach-athlete relationship: A motivational model. *Journal of Sports Sciences*, *21*, 883–904.

Meek, R. (2018). A Sporting Chance: An Independent Review of Sport in Youth and Adult Prisons. Ministry of Justice, London. Retrieved from https://assets.publishing.service.gov.uk/government/uploads/system/uploads/attachment_data/file/733184/a-sporting-chance-an-independent-review-sport-in-justice.pdf

Meek, R., & Lewis, G. E. (2014a). The impact of a sports initiative for young men in prison: Staff and participant perspectives. *Journal of Sport & Social Issues*, *38*(2), 95–123.

Meek, R., & Lewis, G. E. (2014b). Promoting well-being and desistance through sport and physical activity: The opportunities and barriers experienced by women in English prisons. *Women & Criminal Justice*, *24*(2), 151–172.

Morgan, H., & Parker, A. (2022). *Sport, Physical Activity and Criminal Justice: Politics,* Policy and Practice. London: Taylor & Francis.

Morgan, H., Parker, A., Meek, R., & Cryer, J. (2020). Participation in sport as a mechanism to transform the lives of young people within the criminal justice system: an academic exploration of a theory of change. *Sport, Education and Society, 25*(8), 917–930.

Parker, A., Meek, R., & Lewis, G. (2014). Sport in a youth prison: Male young offenders' experiences of a sporting intervention. *Journal of Youth Studies, 17*(3), 381–396.

Reis, H. T., Sheldon, K. M., Gable, S. L., Roscoe, J., & Ryan, R. M. (2000). Daily well-being: The role of autonomy, competence and relatedness. *Personality and Social Psychology Bulletin, 26*, 419–435.

Ricciardelli, R., Maier, K., & Hannah-Moffat, K. (2015). Strategic masculinities: Vulnerabilities, risk and the production of prison masculinities. *Theoretical Criminology, 19*(4), 491–513.

Ryan, R. M., & Deci, E. L. (2001). On happiness and human potentials: A review of research on hedonic and eudaimonic well-being. *Annual Review of Psychology, 52*(1), 141–166.

Smith, B. W., Dalen, J., Wiggins, K., Tooley, E., Christopher, P., & Bernard, J. (2008). The brief resilience scale: Assessing the ability to bounce back. *International Journal of Behavioral Medicine, 15*(3), 194–200.

Steger, M. F., & Shin, J. Y. (2012). Happiness and meaning in a technological age: A psychological approach. In P. Brey, A. Briggle, & E. Spence (Eds.), *The Good Life in a Technological Age* (pp. 92–108). New York, NY: Routledge.

Stewart, D. (2008). *The Problems and Needs of Newly Sentenced Prisoners: Results from a National Survey.* London: Ministry of Justice.

Stewart-Brown, S., & Janmohamed, K. (2008). Warwick-Edinburgh *M*ental *W*ell-being *S*cale. User guide. Version 1. Retrieved from www.healthscotland.com/documents/2702.aspx

Stewart-Brown, S., Tennant, A., Tennant, R., Platt, S., Parkison, J., & Weich, S. (2009). Internal construct validity of the Warwick-Edinburgh Mental Well-being Scale (WEMWBS): A Rasch analysis using data from the Scottish Health Education Population Survey. *Health and Quality of Life Outcomes, 9*, 7–15.

Tennant, R., Hiller, L., Fishwick, R., Platt, S., Joseph, S., Weich, S., … & Stewart-Brown, S. (2007). The Warwick-Edinburgh mental well-being scale (WEMWBS): development and UK validation. *Health and Quality of life Outcomes, 5*(1), 1–13.

Teychenne, M., White, R. L., Richards, J., Schuch, F. B., Rosenbaum, S., & Bennie, J. A. (2020). Do we need physical activity guidelines for mental health: What does the evidence tell us? *Mental Health and Physical Activity, 18*, 100315.

Thomas, D. R. (2006). A General Inductive Approach for Analyzing Qualitative Evaluation Data. *American Journal of Evaluation, 27*(2), 237-246. https://doi.org/10.1177/1098214005283748

Tyler, N., Miles, H. L., Karadag, B., & Rogers, G. (2019). An updated picture of the mental health needs of male and female prisoners in the UK: Prevalence, comorbidity, and gender differences. *Social psychiatry and Psychiatric Epidemiology, 54*(9), 1143–1152.

Wildeman, C., & Wang, E. A. (2017). Mass incarceration, public health, and widening inequality in the USA. *The Lancet, 389*(*10077*), 1464–1474.

Williams, D., Collingwood, L., Coles, J., & Schmeer, S. (2015). Evaluating a rugby sport intervention programme for young offenders. *Journal of Criminal Psychology*, *5*(*1*), 51–64.

Woodall, J. (2016). A critical examination of the health promoting prison two decades on. *Critical Public Health*, *26*(*5*), 615–621.

Woods, D., & Breslin, G. (2022) Using sport-based interventions to benefit the Mental Well-Being of people in prison. In H. Morgan, & A. Parker (Eds.). (2022). *Sport, Physical Activity and Criminal Justice: Politics, Policy and Practice*. London: Taylor & Francis.

Woods, D., Breslin, G., & Hassan, D. (2017a). A systematic review of the impact of sport-based interventions on the psychological well-being of people in prison. *Mental Health and Physical Activity*, *12*, 50–61.

Woods, D., Breslin, G., & Hassan, D. (2017b). Positive collateral damage or purposeful design: How sport-based interventions impact the psychological well-being of people in prison. *Mental Health and Physical Activity*, *13*, 152–162.

Woods, D., Leavey, G., Meek, R., & Breslin, G. (2020). Developing mental health awareness and help seeking in prison: A feasibility study of the State of Mind Sport programme. *International journal of prisoner health*, *16*(4), 403–416.

World Health Organisation. (1999). *Mental Health Promotion in Prison: Report on a WHO Meeting*. Copenhagen: World Health Organisation, Regional Office for Europe.

Further reading

Hassan, J., Shannon, S., Tully, M. A., McCartan, C., Davidson, G., Bunn, R., & Breslin, G. (2022). Systematic review of physical activity interventions assessing physical and mental health outcomes on patients with severe mental illness (SMI) within secure forensic settings. *Journal of Psychiatric and Mental Health Nursing*, *29*(5), 630–646.

This article provides the most up to date evidence from a systematic review on physical activity interventions in forensic settings.

Meek, R. (2018). A *Sporting Chance: An Independent Review of Sport in Youth and Adult Prisons*. London: Ministry of Justice.

This report gives a list of recommendations for the inclusion of sport-based interventions in prisons and demonstrates what is required in the UK for successful implementation.

Woods, D. and Breslin, G. (2022). Using sport-based interventions to benefit the mental well-being of people in prison. In H. Morgan, & A. Parker (Eds.). (2022). *Sport, Physical Activity and Criminal Justice: Politics, Policy and Practice*. London: Taylor & Francis.

This article provides the most up to take evidence summarising the benefits of sport based interventions on mental health and well-being. There is also a case made for the use of psychological theory informed interventions for them to be successful.

12

'STAY ONSIDE'

Exploring the impact of an academically accredited sport-based intervention on psychosocial well-being in prison

Conor Murray, Gavin Breslin and Brendan Coyle

Learning objectives

After reading this chapter you should be able to:

1. Understand the threats to the mental well-being of prisoners[1].
2. Critically examine the benefits and limitations of providing academically accredited sport-based interventions on general physical health, well-being and resilience.
3. Critically assess the benefits and limitations of using quantitative and qualitative methods when evaluating combined education and sport-based interventions with prisoners.
4. Appreciate the benefits of reflecting on the development, delivery, and evaluation of sport-based intervention in prison.

Introduction to the theme

The research conducted on the 'Stay Onside: Applied Football Studies' programme sought to explore the impact of the programme on the hedonic and eudaimonic well-being of participants on the separated regime in Maghaberry Prison. In this chapter we will focus on benefits and limitations of academically accredited sport-based interventions, with a view to achieving the following: highlighting the challenges involved in delivering sports-based Interventions (SBIs) to unique cohorts of prisoners; outlining how academically accredited SBIs can address the limited opportunities provided to these groups; offering a reflexive account of the development, delivery and evaluation of the Stay Onside: Applied Football Studies programme; and

DOI: 10.4324/9781003291695-14

providing insights into lessons learned from the project, to help shape future research, theory, policy and practice concerning academically accredited SBIs.

The Stay Onside: Applied Football Studies programme is an academically accredited sport-based intervention delivered in Maghaberry Prison[2] in Northern Ireland to politically affiliated prisoners[3] that are housed separately from the general or integrated prison population. The programme aims to improve both hedonic and eudaimonic well-being by engaging prisoners in classroom-based educational learning, and football (soccer). Hedonic and eudaimonic well-being are theoretically distinguishable (Delle Fave, 2014). Hedonic well-being refers to the maximisation of participants pleasurable moments, life satisfaction, and the absence of negative emotions (Delle Fave et al., 2011; Diener et al., 2018) while eudaimonic well-being relates to optimal psychosocial functioning by increasing personal and social skills and abilities, and subsequently providing individuals with a sense of life meaning, personal growth, and social connectedness (Ryff, 2018). An individual that has hedonic and eudaimonic well-being is considered to be 'flourishing': "a state where people experience positive emotions, positive psychological functioning and positive social functioning, most of the time" (Mental Health Foundation of New Zealand, 2010).

Research has consistently demonstrated the capacity of physical activity and sport to promote psychological well-being and improved cognitive skills and resilience (Contreras-Osorio et al., 2021; Luna et al., 2020; Ozkara et al, 2016; Taliaferro et al., 2011; Vella et al., 2018). The number of SBIs being delivered in prisons has been rising, which coincides with public health and political interest in the use of sport to promote social, psychological, and physical well-being (Schulenkorf et al., 2016; Whitley et al., 2019). In particular, there has been a focus on using football as the 'hook' to increase engagement for such interventions (Spaaij, 2013; Ekholm, 2019). Within the prison context, research has identified a range of perceived improvements to hedonic and eudaimonic well-being from SBIs, including improving confidence, self-efficacy, self-esteem and life skills, and reducing feelings of hopelessness, depression and mood (Martin et al., 2013; Battaglia et al., 2014; Parker et al., 2014; Gallant et al., 2015; Amtmann and Kukay, 2016; Woods et al., 2017; Woods and Breslin, 2019; Woods and Breslin, 2021).

Notwithstanding the positive findings from existing studies, research to date has indicated that prison-based SBIs have been conceived, designed, measured, delivered, theorised, and evaluated in different ways (Woods et al., 2017; Meek, 2018), and that SBIs being delivered in prisons consistently fail to incorporate psychologically informed health behaviour change theories with well-designed study protocols (Meek and Lewis, 2014; Woods et al., 2017). Despite these deficiencies, there is a growing international consensus on how these programmes should be better designed, delivered (e.g., minimal training requirements for facilitators), theoretically underpinned, monitored and evaluated (Murray et al., 2024).

Prisoners on the separated regime in Maghaberry prison

Following the Government of Ireland Act (1920), the island of Ireland was partitioned into two jurisdictions – the southern jurisdiction, which became the Republic of Ireland, and the northern jurisdiction, Northern Ireland (NI) which is part of the United Kingdom. Upon formation, NI was inhabited by a predominantly Protestant population (65 percent, compared to 35 percent Catholic). There was an under-representation of Catholics/Nationalists at all levels of government, and in the late-1960s Catholics/Nationalists commenced a civil rights campaign against political and economic discrimination. The civil rights movement faced violent opposition, culminating in the deployment of the British Army in August 1969 as a means of attempting to address the ensuing civil disturbances. Unrest continued to escalate, resulting in a sustained period of civil conflict known as 'The Troubles', involving Loyalist and Republican 'paramilitaries'[4] as well as state institutions. This period of conflict lasted for over 30 years, resulting in over 3,500 deaths, 40,000 casualties, and a fundamentally altered social and political landscape in NI (McKittrick and McVea, 2002).

Criminal justice was closely intertwined with the conflict. In attempts to quash civil unrest, Emergency legislation was introduced to allow internment without trial[5], juryless 'Diplock' courts[6], and increased police and army powers (Dwyer and McAlinden, 2015). Throughout the period of conflict, politically affiliated prisoners resisted[7] state attempts to categorise them as 'criminal' prisoners. They instead campaigned for 'special category status', asserting that their incarceration stemmed from politically motivated acts, rather than criminality (Bryson et al., 2021). Following guidance from the Steele Report (2003) the Northern Ireland Prison Service introduced a separated regime for politically affiliated prisoners in Maghaberry, which remains in place today. Those that took part in the Stay Onside: Applied Football Studies modules are imprisoned on the separated regime in two self-contained houses in Maghaberry Prison. Separated male republican prisoners are housed on two landings in Roe House, while separated male loyalist prisoners are housed on two landings in Bush House. They are separated from both the integrated prison population and from each other.

Initial needs assessment

In June 2016, the 'Fresh Start Panel report on the Disbandment of Paramilitary Groups in NI' published a series of recommendations to be actioned by the NI Executive. In response, the Executive published a 'Tackling Paramilitary

Activity, Criminality, and Organised Crime Action Plan', outlining the actions they intended to take in response to the Fresh Start Panel's recommendations. Of particular relevance to the prison context was Recommendation B9 that, "the Department of Justice should ensure that appropriate learning and training opportunities are provided to prisoners in the separated regime". In response, the Executive's Action Plan stated that, "The Department of Justice will commission a consultative evaluation of constructive activity in separated prison accommodation leading to the development and delivery of a new model of constructive activity for separated prisoners focused upon positive educational and wellbeing outcomes".

Given the characteristics of this group of prisoners, who predominately face charges under the Terrorism Act NI (2000), and their vehement opposition to being regarded as criminal offenders, it is not appropriate to draw comparisons between them and prisoners on integrated regimes. Prisoners on the separated regime have also been reluctant to participate in academic research, making conducting a needs assessment aligned with the recommendation above quite difficult. However, one of the only studies conducted with the prisoners over the last 20-years does provide some insight into potential opportunities for improving hedonic and eudaimonic well-being. Bell et al.'s (2019) study on Education and Training Opportunities for Prisoners on the Separated Regime (commonly known as the B9 report) involved questionnaires and interviews with prisoners held in Bush House. However, due to their resistance to the study's origins, which stemmed from the recommendations of the Fresh Start Panel, the prisoners in Roe House declined to either meet with or complete questionnaires provided by the B9 Review Team. The prisoners in Roe did submit a written document to the B9 team, which outlined their experiences and frustrations with educational provision within the separated regime. Bell et al. (2019) identified the significantly limited opportunities provided to prisoners on the separated regime. They suggested that maintaining and improving the well-being of separated prisoners could be challenging without offering a broader range of constructive activities. Further, they argued that the delivery of well-designed interventions could improve, "self-knowledge, develop self-confidence… [improve] health, including mental health, encourage self-esteem and improve communication skills" (p.16).

Bell et al. (2019) published a series of recommendations seeking to address the limited educational and recreational opportunities provided to those on the separated regime. In particular, they recommended that separated prisoners should be offered increased opportunities to "reduce prisoners' boredom and isolation including life skills and arts, music and sport activities" (p.27); and should be provided with the opportunity to "gain skills and qualifications… [that] build confidence and self-esteem" (p.24). These recommendations echo findings from Criminal Justice Inspection NI (CJINI) (2018) who suggested that"it remained unsatisfactory that the separated prisoners did not receive appropriate prisoner development and resettlement services" (p.55).

Although the Stay Onside: Applied Football Studies programme was not designed in relation to the 'Fresh Start Panel report on the Disbandment of Paramilitary Groups in Northern Ireland', or the B9 report's recommendations, we include these findings to contextualise the lack of academic research with this cohort of prisoners and to provide a context for the development of the content of the intervention.

Framework and intervention for delivery

In 2021, Ulster University (UU) partnered with the Irish Football Association (IFA) Foundation to develop the IFA's sport-based intervention, the 'Stay Onside' programme, into a series of UU accredited Personal and Professional Development (PDD) academic modules, under the series title Stay Onside: Applied Football Studies[8]. These modules continue to be delivered to individuals on the separated regime in the high-security Maghaberry prison. As the two groups cannot be mixed for safety reasons, UU and IFA deliver two identical sessions (a morning session and an afternoon session) on each occasion they are in the prison, one to the participants in Bush House and one to the participants in Roe House. The sessions are delivered in a two-hour block. The first hour includes the academic theory led element, consisting of one-hour of taught material and classroom-based discussion. Sessions are delivered by UU academics, IFA coaches, and expert guest speakers. The classroom-based sessions are followed by one-hour of football practice and coaching on an outside artificial football pitch, which concludes with a small-sided, high-intensity game.

Upon completion of any one of the modules included in the series[9], participants are awarded 10 credits towards an undergraduate Honours Degree at UU. These modules are unique, as they are a combined ***education and sport-based practical intervention***. This chapter focuses on the empirical findings and benefits to those in prison from two of the modules in the series: 'Introduction to the Sociology of Football' (PPD385) (see Murray et al. 2022a) and 'Football and Society' (PPD386) (see Murray et al. 2022b)[10].

Programme content

The "Introduction to the Sociology of Football" (PPD385) module took place over six separate days between November 2021 and March 2022[11]. The teaching element of the module focused on the sociology of sport, and topics included: an introduction to sociology and key definitions; violence, aggression, and football fan behaviour; identity, bias, and inclusivity in football; and girls and women in football (see Table 12.1). Assessment of the

TABLE 12.1 Example session taken from Stay Onside: Applied Football Studies, Module PPD385: Introduction to the Sociology of Football

Title of session:	*Girls and women in football*
Learning outcomes:	• Discuss girls and women's experiences of football. • Examine the evolution of girls and women's participation in football. • Consider how football can be more inclusive.
Presession reading:	Required reading: • Cleland, J. (2015). 'Gender: Football Culture in Transition?', The Sociology of Football. London: Routledge. Recommended reading: • Caudwell, J. (2017). 'Football and Misogyny', In Hughson, J., Moore, K., Spaaij, R., and Maguire, J. (Eds.). Routledge Handbook of Football Studies. Abingdon: Taylor and Francis. • Dunn, C. and Welford, J. (2017). 'Women's Elite Football', In Hughson, J., Moore, K., Spaaij, R., and Maguire, J. (Eds.). Routledge Handbook of Football Studies. Abingdon: Taylor and Francis. • Williams, J. (2017). 'The Hidden History of Women's Football', In Hughson, J., Moore, K., Spaaij, R., and Maguire, J. (Eds.). Routledge Handbook of Football Studies. Abingdon: Taylor and Francis.
Educational format:	Expert guest speaker: former women's football international team player, and Sports Community Engagement Officer. Short presentation followed by facilitated discussion.
Practical session format:	Lead by expert guest speaker: warm-up, 1x coaching session on passing, 1x participant-led coaching led session on passing, small-sided game.
Learning outcomes:	• Develop awareness of which part of the foot should be used for different passes. • Understanding the correct body shape (opening up) to receive a pass. • Exercising receiving the ball with foot furthest away from the ball (back foot).
Intensity of activity:	Moderate activity (warm-up and coaching sessions), progressing to vigorous (small-sided game).
Session debrief:	At side of the pitch: review how the session went; consider if learning objectives were met; reflect upon what could have been done better; and discuss the plan for the following week and what activities need to be completed before then.

module was conducted through learners giving an oral presentation in the final week of the module. The Football and Society (PPD386) module was similarly delivered over six days between March and May 2022. The teaching element of the module focused upon the role football plays in society, with topics including: sport psychology; physical fitness, well-being, and nutrition; leadership; and coaching principles and practice. For their module assessment, participants were tasked with working as a group to develop and deliver a one-hour football coaching session during the penultimate week. In the practical, session topics included, passing, shooting, defending, warm-ups and cool downs. In addition to seeking to improve participants' fitness, as well as their coaching and football skills, through the practical aspect of the programme, the modules also sought to promote leadership, teamwork, self-confidence, and self-esteem. From an educational and sport perspective the modules aimed to promote a positive outlook for the future, and where possible, encourage participants to think about continuing with education, coaching, and playing football upon their release from prison.

As part of the academic component of both modules, participants were expected to conduct 14.5 hours per week of independent study using assigned textbooks. As part of their commitment to widening access to higher education, UU waived any academic registration fees for participants and provided two textbooks to every participant that enrolled on the modules[12]. Due to the high-security restrictions[13] placed on prisoners on the separated regime, the participants had limited access to any forms of learning resource (research articles, or online content), therefore the weekly essential and suggested readings were primarily derived from the two textbooks provided.

Intervention evaluation and findings

The primary methods utilised for evaluating each module were qualitative, semi-structured interviews. In the "Introduction to the Sociology of Football" (PPD385) module, 10 interviews were conducted at the end of module (n= 7 prisoners, n=3 facilitators/organisers). The same number of interviews were conducted at the end of the delivery of the Football and Society (PPD386) module. Both sets of interviews consisted largely of the same cohort of prisoners (n=8 unique participants) and facilitators/organisers (n=4 unique participants). Interviews were conducted by the lead author (CM) within the prison setting. These were conducted on a one-to-one basis in a private room, out of earshot of other participants and module facilitators/organisers. With the prior informed and written consent of participants, interviews were audio-recorded for later transcription and detailed verbatim analysis. All interviewees were guaranteed anonymity and confidentiality, and they were informed that they may withdraw from the research process at any stage. To ensure anonymity participants have been assigned the designation P with a random number. The module organisers/facilitators have also been assigned the designation F alongside a random number. Computer Assisted Qualitative Data Analysis software (CAQDAS) NVivo 12 was used to code, organise, and analyse the interview data (Bazeley and Jackson, 2014).

The seven participants that took part in the Football and Society (PPD386) module completed three validated psychological instruments to assess resilience (Brief Resiliency Scale, Smith et al, 2008), mental well-being (Warwick-Edinburgh Mental Well-being Scale-7, Tennant et al., 2007) and general health (General Health Questionaire-28[GHQ-28], Goldberg and Hillier, 1979). Participants completed these measures at baseline (on the day module delivery commenced) and then at the end of the programme (on the day that the module delivery concluded). Mean average and standard deviation statistics are presented in Table 12.2.

TABLE 12.2 Mean and standard deviation scores for the psychological scales at baseline and end point

Psychological Well-being Scale	*Baseline (Mean/SD)*	*End Point (Mean/SD)*
Warwick Edinburgh Mental Wellbeing Scale (WEMWS)	60 (6.4)	61 (4.9)
Brief Resiliency Scale	3.7 (.33)	4.5 (.56)
General Health Questionnaire (GHQ-28) Total Score	11.2 (4.2)	8.0 (5)
Somatic	3.6 (3.3)	1.7 (2.1)
Anxiety	.71 (1.5)	.57 (.71)
Social	6.6 (.53)	5.3 (2.9)
Depression	0 (0)	0 (0)

Quantitative findings

The Warwick Edinburgh Mental Well-being Scale mean scores increased between baseline and follow up. An increase in score is indicative ofpsychological improvement. There was little change in scores in resilience between the start and end of the module. Mean values decreased for the total score for the GHQ-28 from baseline to follow-up. Higher scores on the GHQ-28 indicate a greater possibility of psychological distress. The GHQ-28 was further analysed by averaging four separate factors of the scale: anxiety/somatic, social dysfunction, somatic symptoms, and depression. Mean scores decreased for anxiety/somatic, social dysfunction, and somatic scales. There was no change in depression, this may be due to all participants scoring 0 at baseline and this remaining unchanged. The issue of a low sample size prevented the use of inferential statistical tests being calculated on the data. A larger sample size is needed to enhance statistical power to detect any changes that might be occurring. Further, the inability to connect key demographic data with these measures limits the type of analysis that can be undertaken. Overall, the trends in the data from baseline to module completion are encouraging, and in the direction expected of an effective intervention on improving general physical health, mental well-being, resilience and reducing distress.

Qualitative findings

There were several key findings in relation to being more knowledgeable about the academic content of the programme as well as improving their mental health and well-being, these are discussed below.

Development of academic and practical knowledge

The development of academic (theory-based) and practical knowledge can have a positive impact on mental health (Farrier et al., 2019). Research has found that individuals with higher educational experience are more likely to report feelings of eudaimonic and hedonic well-being, as they have an increased likelihood of perceiving their lives as meaningful, experiencing more positive emotions, and encountering fewer negative ones (Nikolaev, 2018). While the majority of interview participants had no experience of higher educational learning prior to the programme, participants frequently cited the sense of meaning that the module brought to their period of imprisonment, and the positive impact that the module had on their levels of knowledge on various facets of the sociology of football as important to them. Most interviewees were able to discuss, in impressive historical and academic detail, the key themes underpinning the taught sessions: from the impact of commercialisation on supporters of the game in the aftermath of the 1990 Taylor Report (a report on the inquiry after the Hillsborough, United Kingdom stadium disaster which claimed 96 lives and caused over 700 injuries); to current debates on the 'criminalisation' of working-class supporters for 'cultural singing'; to the role of women's football; and the impact of racism and intolerance on supporters and players. For many of the participants that took part in both modules, the development of their academic knowledge in the first module was one of the main reasons they enrolled on the second module and to continue learning:

> The first round [referring to module] I really enjoyed all the different people [guest lecturers] coming to talk to us, with the books that you get as well and the history of some parts of football, particularly the social aspects of football... That made me come back and do a little more again and see who else was going to come in and listen to what they have to say and stuff like that. That was a massive reason why I came back for the second round.
>
> *(P 4)*

Participants were often able and were encouraged to relate elements of the module content to their own experiences. In particular, one guest lecture on psychology and mental health in sport resonated with a number of participants. It allowed them to to reflect on their own mental health and well- being, how they coped with their initial transition when entering the prison, and ongoing challenges during their time in custody:

> I enjoyed that [mental health and well-being in sport session] from having to go to a psychologist myself.... It was interesting to hear him talking about some of the mindsets to certain things.
>
> *(P 1)*

For the first module, assessment in the form of oral presentation was received well. While many participants were initially apprehensive about speaking/ presenting in front of their peers, many believed that the learner-centred preparation and the delivery of oral presentations increased their self-confidence and communication skills (also see Brooks and Wilson, 2014). With a practical emphasis on principles and drills, the assessment of delivering a coaching session in the second module was unanimously praised by participants for its impact. In particular, the applied, reflective nature of the assessment encouraged participants to think differently about their practical input and what they could do differently in the future. While the participants found the assessments daunting initially, they found the process of public speaking and self-reflecting empowering, which contributes to hedonic and eudaimonic well-being (see Layous et al., 2022):

> I gained a bit more confidence speaking in groups, that would not be something I'm not used to so that was sort of a new experience for me... I think the more I did courses like this, the more engaged I would get in debates and stuff, and I'd get more confidence.
>
> *(P 6)*

Accreditation and future education and employment pathways

It became apparent that one of the main motivations to take part in the modules, alongside the physical element of playing football, was the opportunity to complete accredited university modules. Organisers/facilitators highlighted that the 'partnership' between the IFA and UU bestowed kudos and a quality standard upon the modules, and that the module's undergraduate credits could be used to assist any participants wishing to study with UU upon their release from prison. Most participants were keen to build their curricula vitae whilst in prison. The modules therefore dovetailed with other academic/

training qualifications that participants were working towards (for example, some were completing A-level Qualifications [a secondary level qualification in the UK] and others were reading undergraduate degrees with the Open University[14]). It was believed that the accredited status of modules on the Stay Onside: Applied Football Studies programme encouraged and further supported these educational pathways:

> With this giving us some credits towards a degree or a cert or a diploma, it would definitely encourage me to want to build on those points and take the next step or take a diploma or a degree and even go further. This would definitely encourage me to take that extra step.
>
> *(P 2)*

Building eudaimonic well-being through teamwork and social interactions

Module participants felt that the Stay Onside programme had helped improve their communication skills, teamwork, and self-confidence. Module activities were, in part, designed to facilitate a range of teamwork and team-building exercises that could help participants develop these 'soft skills', but also in-line with research, bolster their eudaimonic well-being (Peiró et al., 2021). It was observed that participation in both modules had helped improve relationships in three key areas: with the module facilitators/organisers, with other prisoners, and with family members. In terms of building trust and relationships with module facilitators/organisers, participants attributed this to the 'down to earth' nature of those delivering the module, which they found relatable. Interviewees were asked whether they had made friends on the programme, and several responded by saying that they had developed friendships with the course facilitators/organisers. Other participants felt that they had deepened their relationships with their peers because of their involvement in the modules:

> You have got to know [other prisoners]. When [name removed] was doing it and he was next door to me, and I think in five years we hardly spoke, but that there I found myself speaking to people a bit more on "What did you think about that today?" you know and the reflections of your sessions afterward.
>
> *(P 1)*

In terms of strengthening relationships with family members, many of the participants spoke at length about how their involvement had given them 'something to talk about' with family members (particularly partners or children), or increased their confidence to get involved in football coaching with their children upon their release:

> Whether it's your misses, or your mates, or my ma, or my sister, or whoever. I really hope that they have something to talk to me about other than asking about the kids. We don't have a huge amount to tell them. So, it was great to actually have something to talk to them about, and doing the course was an excuse to talk to them about something other than we had chips for dinner today. And obviously they were very helpful, they should get a lot of credit for it [help with the collating information for the presentations]... they were great for anything like that... they were getting these phones calls: "Who scored more goals – Ronaldo in comparison to Messi?... about different facts of the game, or random sports... You have to ask someone to Google that".
>
> *(P 7)*

There were examples of how the course could help improve well-being by building competence in coaching, where the person as had aspirations to give back to the community or complement leisure activity with their children:

> I would have a bit more confidence to take a coaching session, which I probably wouldn't have had 6–7 weeks ago... My wee lads play football and, you know it would give you a wee bit of confidence to maybe help out along the way... maybe helping out with sessions and stuff that I'd certainly look into it.
>
> *(P 8)*

Increase in physical fitness

Most participants referred to how their participation in the modules had assisted in improving their physical fitness. In addition to the weekly hour (or hour and a half) of playing football, participants started to train independently two-to-three times per week to improve their fitness in advance of the next session. This promotion of physical activity was also perceived to have improved mental health and overall well-being for some, increasing well-being from a hedonic perspective through the generation of immediate positive effects (see Jenkins et al., 2022).

The programme had a ripple effect in-terms of physical fitness. Due to the high security restrictions placed on prisoners on the separated regime, the participants had limited access to the main prison gymnasium. Therefore, improvements in their physical fitness were also aided by a strength and conditioning coach for an international football team contributing a sesson to the programme. After his classroom session, the coach spent time discussing how the prisoners could maximise the fitness equipment they had in the prison. Following his session, the coach developed a bespoke exercise plan for the participants based on the equipment available to them. The aim of the plan was to impove physical as well-being. This strength training programme included advised exercises along with set/rep advice as well as potential weights and rest periods[15]:

> He gave us three or four different training exercises like to do with core and legs and stuff like that... I train twice a day with weights and cardio and take a few programmes. So, we can take some of that and go and implement it ourselves, and try and sort of do it based on the internationals and the way their programmes are set and stuff like that there.
>
> *(P 1)*

Lessons learned through self-reflection

While there were clear positive impacts associated with participation in both Stay Onside: Applied Football Studies modules, there were also some key challenges and lessons to be learned from the delivery of the modules.

Information technology and Facilities

All the participants and module facilitators/organisers welcomed the opportunity to conduct the modules together within the prison environment. However, on several occasions, participants raised the issue of the poor quality of equipment provided to deliver the sessions. For module facilitators/organisers, this sometimes related to the antiquated nature of some of the equipment they had to use for delivering presentations. Another point to bear in mind is that, again for security considerations, prisoners could not use the internet to conduct their own research for their presentations. While this led to a related challenge with regards to an over-reliance on textbooks, it also meant that it was more difficult for module participants to conduct their own research and explore learning in a more independent, learner-driven, and interactive manner outside of class hours.

Accessibility of academic material

While most participants welcomed and enjoyed the academic elements of the modules, particularly studying the provided textbooks and assigned reading, several participants admitted to struggling with some academic elements of the modules. It was also suggested by several participants and module facilitators/organisers that a broader range of readings could be provided in future modules in the series including non-academic materials (e.g. newspaper sources), to make the process inclusive for those prisoners less used to academic study, and for those with lower levels of literacy. It was suggested that while prisoners were given whole textbooks, but only assigned a single chapter to read, the size of the book itself may be daunting. Participants proposed that it may be worthwhile exploring whether there is a more accessible way of furnishing individuals with reading material in a less intimidating form, including printing out chapters (copyright permitting).

Conveying Module Information

There was a consensus that the way information about registering for the modules was provided to prisoners could be improved, with participants referred to hearing about the modules through a variety of different means. More consistency was called for, whether this was through increased engagement with prison officials and prisoners designated to relaying information about education, or more widely advertising future modules in the prison setting via posters and information sheets.

Scheduling/Timing

The final challenge was the occasional scheduling conflicts between module delivery and alternative academic courses that individuals were also enrolled in, particularly by another provider. It was suggested by both participants and module facilitators/organisers that a summer delivery of the Stay Onside: Applied Football Studies modules may better suit those participants who were also Open University students.

Going forward

Participants spoke positively about the impact of the Stay Onside: Applied Football Studies modules across several key areas. These included the positive impact of the football element of the modules on their own mental and physical health; the significant impact of the taught/academic element of the modules on levels of knowledge, confidence, communication skills, attitudes towards exercise and each other; and the perceived impact on future education and employment pathways for participants upon their return to the community. Despite these positive outcomes it remains too early in the process of evaluating the first cohort of separated prisoners involved in the accredited modules to determine if their involvement and participation will assist in creating pathways into coaching, clubs, and community integration upon their release. The cultivation of such pathways, particularly links with the IFA grassroots coaches and local clubs, should be an active consideration in the iterative, sustainable development of the Stay Onside: Applied Football

Studies series. However, more longitudinal data is required in future to assess to what extent the outcomes of the modules meet the well-intentioned aspirations of participants with regards their future pathways at present.

Acknowledgements

The authors would like to thank John Bell, Philip McCready, and Colm Walsh for the support they provided as research associates on this project.

Notes

1 The term 'prisoner' is used more as a reflection on the temporary state of individuals, rather than the core of their identity.
2 A high-security (equivalent to Category A in England and Wales) prison in Northern Ireland.
3 Those prisoners who attribute their indictable charges to their political motivations, their acts are often committed in conjunction with their membership of paramilitary organisations (Scraton, 2015).
4 Paramilitaries are illegally formed militant-like organisations (Hayes and McAllister, 2005).
5 Internment refers to the indefinite confinement of those suspected of acting in a way that might disrupt peace (Spjut, 1986). Internment was used by the British government intermittingly across the island of Ireland throughout the 20th Century (Brück, 2015).
6 Under the Northern Ireland (Emergency Provisions) Act (1973) jury trials in NI were abolished in cases of political violence due to fears of witness intimidation. Instead, suspects are tried in controversial non-jury 'Diplock courts' by one judge (Jacobs, 2010).
7 This began with 'blanket protests' (refusal to wear prison clothing), followed by 'no-wash' or 'dirty' protests with prisoners smearing excrement around their cells, and culminated in hunger strikes.
8 The original 'Stay Onside' programme continues to be delivered to prisoners not on the separated regime across the prison estate. The bespoke 'Stay Onside: Applied Football Studies' series of modules is currently only available to prisoners on the separated regime, and therefore they are the only prisoners that receive credits towards a degree at UU.
9 UU's Academic Office is responsible for overseeing the approval of UU's award-bearing programmes of study. Evaluation procedures have been developed to ensure that courses and undergraduate Honours subjects are of a type and quality consistent with the University's overall objectives and that their aims, organisation, content, teaching, learning and assessment methods, and the resources available to support them are appropriate.
10 A third module, Critical Perspectives on Football (PPD407), was delivered and evaluated between November- December 2022, and a fourth module Football and the Community (PPD406), was delivered and evaluated between January-February 2024. However, the data is yet to be analysed.

11 The six sessions were originally scheduled to take place on a weekly basis in November and December 2021 but after the first three sessions took place there was a Covid-19 outbreak in the prison and the module had to break until March 2nd 2022.
12 John Hughson, Kevin Moore, Ramón Spaaij and Joseph Maguire's (2017) edited book: The Routledge Handbook of Football Studies. London: Routledge; and Jamie Clelland's (2015) book: A Sociology of Football in a Global Context. London: Routledge.
13 High-security prisons are those with the most secure levels of custody in the prison estate. Different houses or units within prisons can also have higher levels of security restrictions based upon perceived threat of prisoners escaping or from doing harm to themselves, other prisoners, or prison officers.
14 Although a challenge that was highlighted was that such formal educational provision was reserved for sentenced prisoners, and not those on remand.
15 Including flat barbell bench press, standing barbell shoulder press, incline barbell bench press, flat dumbbell bench press, seated dumbbell shoulder press. Advice also focused on a plethora of other exercises including, but not limited to, deadlifts, pull-ups, dumbbell/barbell rows, squats, leg presses, calf raises/presses.

References

Amtmann, J., & Kukay, J. (2016). Fitness changes after an 8-week fitness coaching program at a regional youth detention facility. *Journal of Correctional Health Care, 22*(1), 75–83.

Battaglia, C., di Cagno, A., Fiorilli, G., Giombini, A., Borrione, P., Baralla, F., … & Pigozzi, F. (2014). Participation in a 9-month selected physical exercise programme enhances psychological well-being in a prison population. *Criminal Behaviour and Mental Health, 25*(5), 343–354.

Bazeley, P., & Jackson, K. (2014) *Qualitative Data Analysis with NVIVO.* 2nd ed. First published, 2007. Los Angeles, London, New Delhi, Singapore and Washington: Sage.

Bell, C., Gormley-Heenan, C., & Morrow, D. (2019) The B9 Review Team: Report on Education and Training Opportunities for Prisoners in the Separated Regime in Northern Ireland. Available online at: www.justice-ni.gov.uk/sites/default/files/publications/justice/19-b9-review-prisons.pdf (accessed May 29, 2022)

Brooks, G., & Wilson, J. (2014). Using oral presentations to improve students' English language skills. *Kwansei Gakuin University Humanities Review, 19*(1), 199–212.

Brück, J. (2015). 'A good Irishman should blush every time he sees a penny': Gender, nationalism and memory in Irish internment camp craftwork, 1916–1923. *Journal of Material Culture, 20*(2), 149–172.

Bryson, A., McEvoy, K., & Albert, A. (2021). Political prisoners and the Irish conflict 100 years on. *The Howard Journal of Crime and Justice, 60*(S1), 79–91.

Criminal Justice Inspection Northern Ireland. (2018). *Resettlement: An Inspection of Resettlement in the NI Prison Service.* Belfast: Criminal Justice Inspection Northern Ireland.

Contreras-Osorio, F., Campos-Jara, C., Martínez-Salazar, C., Chirosa-Ríos L., & Martínez-García, D. (2021). Effects of sport-based interventions on children's

executive function: A systematic review and meta-analysis. *Brain Sciences, 11*(6), 755
Delle Fave, A. (2014). Eudaimonic and hedonic happiness. In A. C. Michalos (Ed.), *Encyclopedia of Quality of Life and Wellbeing Research* (pp. 1999–2004). Dordrecht, Netherlands: Springer.
Delle Fave, A., Massimini, F., & Bassi, M. (2011). *Psychological Selection and Optimal Experience across Cultures: Social Empowerment through Personal Growth* (Vol. 2). New York: Springer Science & Business Media.
Diener, E., Lucas, R. E., & Oishi, S. (2018). Advances and open questions in the science of subjective well-being. *Collabra: Psychology, 4*(1), 15. https://doi.org/10.1525/collabra.115
Dwyer, C., & McAlinden, A. M. (2015). Crime and criminal justice in Northern Ireland: Conflict, transition and the legacy of the past. In A-M McAlinden, C Dwyer (Eds.) *Criminal Justice in Transition: The Northern Ireland Context.* Oxford: Hart Publishing.
Ekholm, D. (2019) 'Sport as a means of governing social integration: Discourses on bridging and bonding social relations,' *Sociology of Sport Journal, 36,* 152–161.
Farrier, A., Baybutt, M., & Dooris, M. (2019). Mental health and wellbeing benefits from a prisons horticultural programme. *International Journal of Prisoner Health, 15*(1), 91–104.
Gallant, D., Sherry, E., & Nicholson, M. (2015). Recreation or rehabilitation? Managing sport for development programs with prison populations. *Sport Management Review, 18*(*1*), 45–56.
Goldberg, D. P., & Hillier, V. F. (1979). A scaled version of the General Health Questionnaire. *Psychological Medicine, 9*(1), 139–145.
Hayes, B. C., & McAllister, I. (2005). Public support for political violence and paramilitarism in Northern Ireland and the Republic of Ireland. *Terrorism and Political Violence, 17*(4), 599–617.
Jacobs, L. M. (2010). It's time to leave the troubles behind: Northern Ireland must try paramilitary suspects by Jury rather than in Diplock-type courts. *Texas International Law Journal, 45,* 655.
Jenkins, M., Lee, C., Houge Mackenzie, S., Hargreaves, E. A., Hodge, K., & Calverley, J. (2022). Nature-based physical activity and hedonic and eudaimonic wellbeing: The mediating roles of motivational quality and nature relatedness. *Frontiers in Psychology, 13,* 74.
Layous, K., Kurtz, J. L., Wildschut, T., & Sedikides, C. (2022). The effect of a multi-week nostalgia intervention on well-being: Mechanisms and moderation. *Emotion, 22*(8), 1952.
Luna, P., Rodriguez-Donaire, A., Rodrigo-Ruiz, & Cejudo, J. (2020). 'Subjective well-being and psychosocial adjustment: Examining the effects of an intervention based on the sport education model on children,' *Sustainability, 12*(4570), 1–15.
Martin, R. E., Adamson, S., Korchinski, M., Granger-Brown, A., Ramsden, V. R., Buxton, J. A., … Hislop, T. G. (2013). Incarcerated women develop a nutrition and fitness program: Participatory research. *International Journal of Prisoner Health, 9*(*3*), 142–150.
McKittrick, D., & McVea, D. (2002). *Making Sense of the Troubles: The Story of the Conflict in Northern Ireland.* Leiden: New Amsterdam Books.

Meek, R. (2018). *A Sporting Chance: An Independent Review of Sport in Youth and Adult Prisons*. London: Ministry of Justice.

Meek, R., & Lewis, G. E. (2014). The impact of a sports initiative for young men in prison: Staff and participant perspectives. *Journal of Sport & Social Issues, 38*(2), 95–123.

Mental Health Foundation of New Zealand. (2010). *Flourishing, Positive Mental Health and Wellbeing: How Can They Be Increased?*. Available at: www.mentalhealth.org.nz/assets/Flourishing/ Flourishing-and-Positive-Mental-Health-Dec2010.pdf (Last Accessed: September 12, 2019)

Murray, C., Bell, J., McCready, P., Walsh, C., Breslin, G., & Coyle, B. (2022a) *Piloting an Accredited Sport-Based Intervention with Prisoners. An Evaluation of the 'Introduction to the Sociology of Football' (PUP385) Module*. Belfast: Ulster University.

Murray, C., McCready, P., Bell, J., Walsh, C., Breslin, G., & Coyle, B. (2022b). *Examining Pedagogical and Design Elements of an Accredited Sport-Based Intervention with Prisoners. A Psychosocial Evaluation of the 'Football and Society' (PUP386) Module*. Belfast: Ulster University.

Murray, C., Coyle, C., Morgan, H., Marder, I., Woods, D., Haughey, T., Genovesi, F., Maycock, M., Meek, R., Parker, A., Smith, A., Kay, C., Brink, G., Rovers, H., Haudenhuyse, R., Roe, D., Contreras- Osorio, F., Donohue, B., Bohall, G., Martinez, N., Martos Garcia, D., Whitley, M., Norman, M., Demalija, R., Sherry, E., Chitsawang, N., Aderonmu, K., & Breslin, G. (2024). International consensus statement on the design, delivery and evaluation of sport-based interventions aimed at promoting social, psychological and physical wellbeing in prison. *BMJ Open*.

Nikolaev, B. (2018). Does higher education increase hedonic and eudaimonic happiness?. *Journal of Happiness Studies, 19*, 483–504.

Ozkara, A. B., Kalkavan, A., Alemdag, S., & Alemdag, C. (2016). The role of physical activity in psychological resilience. *Baltic Journal of Sport and Health Sciences, 3*(102), 24–29.

Parker, A., Meek, R., & Lewis, G. (2014). Sport in a youth prison: Male young offenders' experiences of a sporting intervention. *Journal of Youth Studies, 17*(3), 381–396.

Peiró, J. M., Montesa, D., Soriano, A., Kozusznik, M. W., Villajos, E., Magdaleno, J., ... & Ayala, Y. (2021). Revisiting the happy-productive worker thesis from a Eudaimonic perspective: A systematic review. *Sustainability, 13*(6), 3174.

Ryff, C. D. (2018). Well-being with soul: Science in pursuit of human potential. *Perspectives on Psychological Science, 13*, 242–248.

Schulenkorf, N., Sherry, E., & Rowe, K. (2016). 'Sport-for-development: An integrated literature review,' *Journal of Sport Management, 30*(1), 22–39.

Scraton, P. (2015). Prisons and imprisonment in Northern Ireland. In A-M McAlinden, C Dwyer (Eds.) *Criminal Justice in Transition: The Northern Ireland Context*. Oxford: Hart Publishing.

Smith, B. W., Dalen, J., Wiggins, K., Tooley, E., Christopher, P., & Bernard, J. (2008). 'The brief resilience scale: Assessing the ability to bounce back,' *International Journal of Behavioural Medicine, 15*(3): 194–200.

Spaaij, R. (2013). 'Changing people's lives for the better? Social mobility through sport-based intervention programmes: Opportunities and constraints,' *European Journal for Sport and Society, 10*(1): 53–73, DOI: 10.1080/16138171.2013.11687910

Spjut, R. J. (1986). Internment and detention without trial in Northern Ireland 1971–1975: Ministerial policy and practice. *The Modern Law Review*, *49*(6), 712–739.

Taliaferro L. A., Eisenberg M. E., Johnson K. E., Nelson T. F., Neumark-Sztainer D. (2011). 'Sport participation during adolescence and suicide ideation and attempts,' *International Journal of Adolescent Medicine Health*, *23*, 3–10.

Tennant, R., Hiller, L., Fishwick, R., Platt, S., Joseph, S., Weich, S., ... & Stewart-Brown, S. (2007) 'The Warwick-Edinburgh mental well-being scale (WEMWBS): Development and UK validation. *Health and Quality of life Outcomes*, *5*(1), 1–13.

Vella, S. A., Swann, C., Batterham, M., Boydell, K. M., Eckermann, S., Fogarty, A., Hurley, D., Liddle, S. K., Lonsdale, C., Miller, A., Noetel, M., Okely, A. D., Sanders, T., Telenta, J., & Deane. F. P. (2018). 'Ahead of the game protocol: a multicomponent, community sport-based program targeting prevention, promotion and early intervention for mental health among adolescent males,' *BMC Public Health*, *18*, 390, https://doi.org/10.1186/s12889-018-5319-7

Whitley, M. A., Massey, W. V., Camiré, M., Blom, L. C., Chawansky, M., Forde, S., Boutet, M., Borbee, A., & Darnell, S. C. (2019). A systematic review of sport for youth development interventions across six global cities. *Sport Management Review*, *22*(2), 181–193. https://doi.org/10.1016/j.smr.2018.06.013

Woods, D., & Breslin, G. (2019). Reflections on implementing the Active Choices Rugby Programme to enhance mental health and well-being of young men in prison. In *Mental Health and Well-being Interventions in Sport* (pp. 128–143). London: Routledge.

Woods, D., Breslin, G., & Hassan, D. (2017). A systematic review of the impact of sport-based interventions on the psychological well-being of people in prison. *Mental Health and Physical Activity*, *12*, 50–61.

Further reading

Meek, R. (2018). *A Sporting Chance: An Independent Review of Sport in Youth and Adult Prisons.* Ministry of Justice: London.

This report gives a list of recommendations for the inclusion of sport-based interventions in prisons and demonstrates what is required in the UK.

Murray, C. (2023). *Young Men, Masculinities and Imprisonment: An Ethnographic Study in Northern Ireland.* London: Palgrave Macmillan.

As the research we report took place in a prison in Northern Ireland, this is an interesting read for anyone conducting research in prisons in Northern Ireland or other post conflict societies.

Murray, C., Coyle, C., Morgan, H., Marder, I., Woods, D., Haughey, T., Genovesi, F., Maycock, M., Meek, R., Parker, A., Smith, A., Kay, C., Brink, G., Rovers, H., Haudenhuyse, R., Roe, D., Contreras- Osorio, F., Donohue, B., Bohall, G., Martinez, N., Martos Garcia, D., Whitley, M., Norman, M., Demalija, R., Sherry, E., Chitsawang, N., Aderonmu, K., & Breslin, G. (2024). International consensus statement on the design, delivery and evaluation of sport-based interventions aimed at promoting social, psychological and physical wellbeing in prison. *BMJ Open*

This international consensus statement advises on designing, delivering, and evaluating sport-based interventions (SBIs) aimed at promoting social, psychological and physical wellbeing in prison. It provides guidance on: i) minimum levels of competence for those designing and delivering SBIs; ii) the design and delivery of inclusive programmes prioritising disadvantaged groups; and iii) evaluation measures which are carefully calibrated both to capture proposed programme outcomes and to advance an understanding of the systems, processes, and experiences of sport engagement in prison.

Woods, D., & Breslin, G. (2021). *Evaluation and Reflections from the Use of Implementation Science to Accommodate a Community Mental Health Awareness Programme to a Prison. Issues and Innovations in Prison Health Research: Methods, Issues and Innovations*, 187–210.

This chapter highlights some of the challenges and solutions to integrating a community menta health programme into a young men's prison and highlights the benefits of including theory based interventions.

13

ANOTHER CALL TO ACTION

Critical reflections and the way forward for mental health in sport

Gavin Breslin and Gerard Leavey

A call to action

There have been many 'Calls to Action' in public health to prevent the onset of physical illness (see www.who.int/). We argue here for another call to action in supporting elite and non-elite athlete's mental health. Although sport has many protective factors for health and wellbeing, the sport environment or non-supportive climate where a *winning at all costs* ethos is adopted can prove catastrophic. In each chapter we have highlighted how evidence and theory informed intervention programmes can be helpful in supporting the mental health of those involved in sport. We now reflect on the chapters and present a way forward for mental health in sport and propose a call to action by associations of sport. Since the first edition of this book (Breslin and Leavey, 2019) progress has been made in supporting mental health in sport, but put simply, not enough has been achieved, and we still have a long road to go in supporting our athletes, coaches, and referees.

Critical reflections: Mental health interventions in sport

Public health has much to gain from well-designed and implemented sports-based interventions to improve mental health and wellbeing. However, such interventions may be among the most complex to deliver and evaluate, grappling with highly varied contextual challenges of permissions and access, and ensuring fidelity in the training and delivery of the intervention programme and the expectations and acceptability of those participating, whether they be young people or adults, coaches, referees, people who are disabled, people with addictions, those with physical or mental disorders or people in prison.

DOI: 10.4324/9781003291695-15

Our purpose in bringing together some of the key researchers in the field of sports and mental health was to create a rich informational resource, based on insights gained from practice and experience upon which fellow academics and practitioners could draw. Importantly, we wanted to extend and update the first edition of Mental Health and Wellbeing Interventions in Sport (Breslin and Leavey, 2019) to offer useful exemplars of contemporary research, theory and practice in order to better prepare practitioners to intervene and support the mental health and wellbeing of those involved in sport. The goal was particularly important as our recent updated systematic review of mental health interventions in sport concluded that despite sport-based interventions' potential for significant public health gains, they remain underdeveloped and poorly theorised (Breslin, et al, 2022). In achieving our goal, we hope to further stimulate critical enquiry of the evidence-based reflection on current practice and force precision in future development of programmes to improve mental health and wellbeing of those involved sport.

The first edition of this book was the first of its kind to explore the detailed plans and approaches of those expert practitioners and researchers in this emerging field, our second edition adds to these plans and approaches and includes new chapters exploring referees mental health as a result of verbal and physical abuse, interventions in sport psychiatry adopting a biopsychosocial model and further chapters describing sport based interventions in prisons The authors of each chapter have provided detailed accounts of how they conducted a needs assessment, determined a suitable framework for programme delivery (or, as in some cases, not!), how they evaluated their programmes, and finally, how they could have improved some steps of programme design having had time to reflect on the programme implementation process. The authors' reflections illustrate how intervening to raise awareness or improve mental health presents considerable and complex challenges, and even though we should be cautious in programme design and delivery, the demand for innovative prevention and treatment interventions is high amongst the sporting community.

As highlighted in the chapters, there is considerable heterogeneity in sports settings, populations covered, and health and well-being problems targeted. Each of the chapters offers insights into the challenges faced by practitioners and researchers in context-specific settings and provides useful critical first-hand experience about how these should be addressed during the development and implementation of sport-based interventions. Key among these is the need for sound theoretical underpinning for the programmes (Hammond and Meek, Chapter 10: Breslin, et al Chapter 5), i.e. what are the outcomes to be achieved and what is the logic model or theory of change that will optimally facilitate these? Others point to the need for building community-based participatory approaches or co-production with those with lived experience ensuring that all the key stakeholders (including end users) views and attitudes are understood and accommodated within the programme, minimising the later emergence of problematic assumptions and resistance to various aspects of the intervention. For example, Vella et al. (Chapter 6) in their Ahead of the Game programme, demonstrated that successful implementation depended on a deep engagement and embedding within the participating clubs' cultures and organisational structures. They also consider a systems approach to design and implementation, an approach that is showing some promise in other areas of public health and well-being improvement (i.e, obesity (see Bagnall et al., 2019; Breslin et al, 2023). Importantly too, they highlight the need for careful consideration of selecting partners in other countries to upscale their programme whilst also having pragmatic flexibility in the roll-out of the programme while still retaining fidelity to the model. Similarly, Smith et al. (Chapter 9) adopt a realist evaluation (Pawson & Tilley, 1997; Pawson, 2006) to understand programme contexts and uncover the often 'hidden' mechanisms that undermine successful implementation. Again, central to achieving the goals of any programme is engagement with diverse stakeholders, understanding relationships, and gaining the confidence and involvement of champions within the target setting.

Donohue and Brooks (Chapter 2) adopt a thoughtful and helpful reflective stance within their review of The Optimising Performance Programme in Sport (TOPPS) where Family Based Therapy is used with college athletes to prevent and treat mental illness. The authors describe the programme content and provide a rationale for the use of suitable mental disorder screening tools and guided use of psychometric testing. TOPPS has considerable promise in dealing with mental disorder in a non-stigmatising way, but given the stigma associated with such problems, the authors underscore the value of sensitive adaptation of programmes in all settings. TOPPS has been implemented in a randomised controlled trial as well as evidenced effectiveness in numerous athlete case studies. From our review of the studies associated with TOPPS it demonstrates a programme that has undergone the most rigorous of research evaluations, has been adjusted to different populations (adolescents, college students, athletes, stage artists, various ethnic groups etc) and settings (schools, universities, community groups and businesses) and shows the most promise. It remains to be seen however whether TOPPS could be effective outside North America where the student athlete support services and culture around college sport varies, and whether the programme could be adjusted in parts to online delivery to reach more athletes. TOPPS is currently being extended internationally, and online modules are being created, evaluations are being considered. Also, with a focus on student/college athletes, the State of Mind Ireland programme (Chapter 5) shows it can destigmatise mental health through a short psychoeducation programme. The SOMI programme continues to be adjusted by the authors, to include self-determination theory in its design and evaluation (see Shannon, Breslin et al., 2019; Shannon,

Hanna et al., 2020). The programme has also been revised to include mindfulness-based exercises to improve well-being and has showed some success. The authors have also adjusted the programme for inclusion in prison settings where it was accepted by this population and where positive changes in mental health awareness outcomes have been shown (See Chapter 11). Nixdorf et al. (Chapter 3) in their comprehensive and detailed exposition of a CBT programme to reduce burnout and depression among junior elite swimmers indicate the need for simply understanding the competing demands and structures of their participants' lives. If this understanding is not apparent by the practitioner the intervention itself may become a source of anxiety and stress. Turner et al in Chapter 4 showed how mental health could be bolstered using Rationale Emotive Behaviour Therapy with Sarah a paralympic athlete. Working on Sarah's anger and resentment to significant others in her personal life the authors presented a step-by-step procedural approach to supporting Sarah. Of particular interest in this case study was the views of the practitioners and their reflections on professional practice and training, so crucial to enhancing the practitioner's professional development.

Brick and colleagues in Chapter 8 describe the much neglected issue of match officials and the link to mental health and drop out of officiating. What was apparent was the limited number of studies, those that were available being mainly cross-sectional, and the need to develop evidenced based interventions. An emerging area of research study that requires careful consideration in how to tackle an established culture wherein athletes, coaches and spectators feel it is okay to verbally abuse referees is required.

Sport psychiatry and a case study in rugby of managing a brain injury was described in chapter 7. The support provided by the psychiatrist and the biopsychosocial approach demonstrated the move in athlete support beyond a medical model only. It was apparent that many psychosocial considerations were considered in the treatment model for the player. In this case study it was apparent that we can gain a lot from interdisciplinary working and sharing of approaches to supporting athlete mental health.

Lastly, Woods and Breslin (Chapter 11) and Murray and collaborators (Chapter 12) bring attention to the benefits of the researcher engaging in reflections on their role in evaluating mental health in sport programmes in prison settings, and the challenges that extreme or unconventional research environments present when conducting research. What was apparent in their reflections was that despite extreme conditions and a population who regularly challenge authority, sport was perceived as acceptable for them to take part in. Once involved in the programme, improvements where shown in participants physical and mental health outcomes. Perhaps sport can be used to regulate before we try and educate or apply therapeutic techniques! Given the challenges in these environments and the limited amount of research evidence to guide practice, Murray et al make the case for the establishment of an expert panel to develop a mental health and well-being in sport consensus statement to guide researchers on what to expect when conducting sport based mental health interventions in prison settings. The consensus statement will also help policy makers and practitioners when developing content for interventions that use sport to target mental illness in prison.

With the detail provided in each chapter and across various populations, we hope you too are aided in how to plan, take cognisance of the environment/ setting and select appropriate programme content, then how to implement and evaluate such interventions. To support you further, we make some suggestions for the way forward in mental health in sport, and we strongly recommend that you access the additional readings highlighted in each of the chapters to further support your learning in advancing this field of research, theory and practice.

The way forward for mental health in sport

There has been a recent flourishing of mental health awareness programmes in sport, as evidenced by the Chapters in this book. Although these highlight the wide variation in programme conception, design, measurement, delivery methods, use of theory and evaluation, there appears to be little consensus on the ability to compare practice (see also Rice et al., 2016; Breslin et al., 2017; 2022). Based on this variation, we have launched the *Psychosocial and Policy-Related Approaches to Mental Health Awareness in Sport-Consensus Statement* (Breslin et al, 2019). The consensus statement aims to assist programme designers, deliverers and policy makers on: (a) definitions of mental health awareness outcomes, and (b) methods for conducting and reporting interventions with sporting population groups (i.e. coaches, athletes and officials). Since 2017, several consensus statements in sport have been published that have focused on elite athletes or elite athlete clinical service provision (Schinke, Stambulova, Si, & Moore, 2017; Moesch et al., 2018), overtraining (Meeusen et al., 2013), or that have been specific to a mental disorder (Mountjoy et al., 2014). A recent systematic review was conducted by Vella et al. (2021) to provide an overview of existing statements. From the thirteen statements reviewed they were categorised into themes: 1. writing a mental health plan; 2. provision of mental health care; 3. athlete support system; 4. high risk events; 5. athlete mental health; and 6. future directions. Despite being considered by each author to be a foundation for policy makers to start planning, the quality of the statements were considered low, particularly in the areas of stakeholder engagement and rigor of development. More robust development methods were advised and caution over their use.

Similarly, a scoping review of peer reviewed articles and grey literature of athlete mental health within competitive sport interventions, position/

consensus statements and policy showed that interventions mainly resulted in moderate or non-significant findings. Position/consensus statements provided recommendations for organisational strategy, but were viewed to lack detail to guide applied practice (Prior, Papathomas & Rhind, 2022). However, an evidenced-based *Wellbeing in Sport Policy Action Plan for Northern Ireland* demonstrates how sport environments can be used to improve mental health for all involved in sport and the surrounding community (Sport Northern Ireland, 2019). Indeed, in the development of the Action Plan the *Working Group in Mental Health and Wellbeing in and Through Sport* highlighted the absence of available research in the form of systematic reviews to guide policy creation. This led to the group commissioning their own research, resulting in a substantial review (Breslin et al., 2017) which revealed inconsistencies between study methods and measures resulting in the ability to draw conclusions highly problematic. This is the time to encourage consensus in how we go about promoting mental health and supporting those involved in sport. Some reasons for the development of a consensus statement were shared at a symposium in Dublin Ireland, these are represented in Box 13.1 below:

BOX 13.1 SEVEN REASONS WHY A CONSENSUS STATEMENT ON MENTAL HEALTH IN SPORT IS REQUIRED?

1 There has been *increasing recognition* of mental health issues in sport
2 Growth of *sport-based* mental health awareness programmes
3 Variation in programme content, design, theory and evaluation
4 Uncertain what *outcomes* or *impact* programmes are having
5 Variations in *measurement tools* selected- and variation in *validation and reliability* of these tools
6 What is the *minimal training* for sport and exercise psychologists or *club officers* in supporting or guiding programme content development?
7 What recommendations can we provide *policy makers?*

In response to the gap in recommendations to aid policy makers, the consensus statement builds on previous statements, with a specific focus on determining effective reporting of mental health awareness programmes for effective policy design (Breslin et al., 2019; Sport Northern Ireland, 2019). The key objectives of the consensus statement are: (1) To define mental health awareness constructs for inclusion in programmes in sport; (2) To identify valid measures for use in intervention studies with the sporting population, and establish standards for data collection, analysis and reporting procedures and; (3) To provide policy makers with guidance for implementing awareness programmes in sport.

In the development of the consensus statement, a two-day meeting of experts was facilitated, comprising international stakeholders representing various groups (e.g. research, policy, sporting organisations, mental health charities, safeguarding, etc). The first was at a satellite symposium at the European College of Sports Science (ECSS) Congress in Dublin, Ireland (July 2018), and the second was at the British Psychological Society's Division of Sport and Exercise Psychology, Annual Conference in Belfast (December 2018). Representatives were from the following groups: (1) Professionals with experience in sports teams; (2) Sports federations and organisations; (3) Researchers in the field of sports; (4) Editorial members of scientific journals, and; (5) Policy makers in sport.

Prior to the first meeting, a series of statements were produced in a draft version of a statement and distributed online to all attendees and other recommended persons who could not attend. The Delphi method was used to determine the adequacy of the statements for inclusion in the final document. A revision was then prepared, and a summary was shared requesting further views from a wider audience during a six-week period. All remarks received were reviewed by two lead authors and, if applicable, were incorporated into revisions of the manuscript, where a suggested change was not incorporated, a written explanation was prepared and distributed to group members. After the final iteration, all members of the group were asked to confirm their agreement with the final consensus statement that was then published. The consensus statement provides evidence and theory-based guidance on awareness definitions, programme content, and methodological approaches for the design, implementation and evaluation of mental health awareness programmes in sport. Given the time (four years from time of writing) since the launch of the statement, initial uptake was positive, but that since waned, this maybe in part due to the COVID-19 pandemic and the shift of human and financial resources to other areas of public health priority. Furthermore, the list of actions from the Wellbeing in Sport Action Plan (Sport Northern Ireland, 2019) require further strategic focus, follow-up and integration across sport. What is required is another 'Call to Action' and an injection of motivation and momentum to promote mental health in sport.

We would like to thank each of the authors for contributing to the book. We also want to highlight an appreciation for the endeavours made by the authors in bringing about positive changes to many people's lives. Finally, we hope that this book will aid you in applying what you have learned into your own practice, and with an open mind reflect on your practice for the improvement of mental health of those involved in sport for the action plan to be fully implemented.

References

Bagnall, A. M., Radley, D., Jones, R., Gately, P., Nobles, J., Van Dijk, M., … & Sahota, P. (2019). Whole systems approaches to obesity and other complex public health challenges: A systematic review. *BMC Public Health, 19*, 1–14.

Breslin, G., Shannon, S., Haughey, T., Donnelly, P., & Leavey, G. (2017). A systematic review of interventions to increase awareness of mental health and well-being in athletes, coaches and officials. *Systematic Reviews 31, 6*(1), 177. doi: 10.1186/s13643-017-0568-6

Breslin, G., Smith, A., Donohue, B., Donnelly, P., Shannon, S., Haughey, T. J., … & Leavey, G. (2019). International consensus statement on the psychosocial and policy-related approaches to mental health awareness programmes in sport. *BMJ Open Sport & Exercise Medicine, 5*(1), e000585.

Breslin, G., Shannon, S., Cummings, M., & Leavey, G. (2022). An updated systematic review of interventions to increase awareness of mental health and well-being in athletes, coaches, officials and parents. *Systematic Reviews, 11*(1), 1–29.

Breslin, G., Wills, W., McGowan, L., Mack, J. B., Reynolds, C. M. E., & McAvoy, H. (2023). *A Whole Systems Approach to Obesity Prevention: A Rapid Synthesis of Evidence to Inform the Northern Ireland Obesity Prevention Strategy Project Board.* Institute of Public Health, Belfast.

Meeusen, R., Duclos, M., Foster, C., Fry, A., Gleeson, M., Nieman, D., Raglin, J., Rietjens, G., Steinacker, J., & Urhausen, A. (2013). Prevention, diagnosis and treatment of the overtraining syndrome: Joint consensus statement of the European College of Sport Science (ECSS) and the American College of Sports Medicine (ACSM). *European Journal of Sport Science, 13*(1), 1–24. doi: 10.1080/17461391.2012.730061

Moesch, K., Kenttä, G., Kleinert, J., Quignon-Fleuret, C., Cecil, S., & Bertollo, M. (2018). FEPSAC position statement: Mental health disorders in elite athletes and models of service provision. *Psychology of Sport and Exercise, 38*, 61–71.

Mountjoy, M., Sundgot-Borgen, J., Burke, L., et al. (2014). The IOC consensus statement: Beyond the female athlete triad – Relative Energy Deficiency in Sport (RED-S). *British Journal Sports Med, 48*, 491–497.

Pawson, R. (2006). *Evidence-Based Policy: A Realist Perspective.* London: Sage Publications.

Pawson, R., & Tilley, N. (1997). *Realistic Evaluation.* London: Sage Publications.

Prior, E., Papathomas, A., & Rhind, D. (2022). A systematic scoping review of athlete mental health within competitive sport: Interventions, recommendations, and policy. *International Review of Sport and Exercise Psychology*, 1–23. doi: 10.1080/1750984X.2022.2095659

Rice, S, M., Purcell, R., De Silva, S., et al. (2016). The mental health of elite athletes: A narrative systematic review. *Sports Medicine, 46*, 1333–1353.

Schinke, R. J., Stambulova, N. B., Si, G., & Moore, Z. (2017). International society of sport psychology position stand: Athletes' mental health, performance, and development. *International Journal of Sport and Exercise Psychology.* doi:10.1080/1612197X.2017.1295557

Shannon, S., Breslin, G., Haughey, T., Sarju, N., Neill, D., Lawlor, M., & Leavey, G. (2019). Predicting student-athlete and non-athletes' intentions to self-manage mental health: Testing an integrated behaviour change model. *Mental Health & Prevention, 13*, 92–99.

Shannon, S., Hanna, D., Leavey, G., Haughey, T., Neill, D., & Breslin, G. (2020). The association between mindfulness and mental health outcomes in athletes: Ttesting the mediating role of autonomy satisfaction as a core psychological need. *International Journal of Sport and Exercise Psychology*, 1–16.

Sport Northern Ireland. (2019). *Wellbeing in Sport Action Plan 2019–2025.* Retrieved September 29, 2023, from www.sportni.net/wp-content/uploads/2020/02/NI-Wellbeing-in-Sport-Actoin-Plan-2019-2015_Final.pdf

Vella, S. A., Schweickle, M. J., Sutcliffe, J. T., & Swann, C. (2021). A systematic review and meta-synthesis of mental health position statements in sport: Scope, quality and future directions. *Psychology of Sport and Exercise*, *55*, 101946.

INDEX

Note: Figures are indicated by *italics*. Tables are indicated by **bold**.